The Microanalysis of Political Communication

How do politicians cope with questions and interruptions? How do they invite applause and audience appreciation? How often do they avoid replying to questions, how and why do they do this and what are the consequences of their evasions?

Such questions are posed and answered by this series of original studies of political speeches and televised political interviews conducted by the author and his colleagues. They were based on the Annual Party Political Conferences (1996–2000) and the last five General Elections (1983–2001) in the UK. Both verbal and non-verbal features of communication are examined, including hand gestures, applause, interruptions, questions, replies and non-replies to questions.

As a result of applying the techniques of microanalysis, we have a greater awareness of how applause can occur both invited and uninvited in political speeches. We can evaluate more effectively the interview skills of both politicians and political interviewers. We have a better understanding of how and why politicians equivocate, handle interruptions and seek to present themselves in the best possible light. It is often the case that political speeches are dismissed as mere 'claptrap', while politicians are castigated for their evasiveness in interviews. But the detailed microanalytic research presented here brings fresh insights into the role played by this apparent 'claptrap and ambiguity' in the underlying political process.

This unique and highly contemporary study provides a rare interdisciplinary view of politics, communication and microanalysis. It will be valuable reading for advanced students and academics within the fields of social psychology, linguistics, political science, communication studies and sociology.

Peter Bull is a Senior Lecturer in the Department of Psychology at the University of York. He is the author of fifty academic publications, principally concerned with the microanalysis of interpersonal communication. These include several books, the most recent of which is *Communication under the Microscope: The Theory and Practice of Microanalysis* (Psychology Press, 2002).

Routledge research international series in social psychology
Edited by W. Peter Robinson
University of Bristol, UK

This series represents a showcase for both the latest cutting-edge research in the field, and important critiques of existing theory. International in scope, and directed at an international audience, applied topics are well represented. Social psychology is defined broadly to include related areas from social development to the social psychology of abnormal behaviour. The series is a rich source of information for advanced students and researchers alike.

Routledge is pleased to invite proposals for new books in the series. In the first instance, any interested authors should contact:

Professor W. Peter Robinson
Department of Experimental Psychology
University of Bristol
8 Woodland Road
Bristol BS8 1TN
E-mail: P.Robinson@bristol.ac.uk

1 Cooperation in Modern Society
Promoting the welfare of communities, states and organizations
Edited by Mark van Vugt, Mark Snyder, Tom R. Tyler and Anders Biel

2 Youth and Coping in Twelve Nations
Surveys of 18–20 year-old young people
Edited by Janice Gibson-Cline

3 Responsibility
The many faces of a social phenomenon
Hans-Werner Bierhoff and Ann Elisabeth Auhagen

4 The Psychological Origins of Institutionalized Torture
Mika Haritos-Fatouros

5 A Sociocognitive Approach to Social Norms
Nicole Dubois

The Microanalysis of Political Communication

Claptrap and ambiguity

Peter Bull

LONDON AND NEW YORK

First published 2003 by Routledge
11 New Fetter Lane, London EC4P 4EE

Simultaneously published in the USA and Canada
by Routledge
29 West 35th Street, New York, NY 10001

Routledge is an imprint of the Taylor & Francis Group

Typeset in Garamond by Wearset Ltd, Boldon, Tyne and Wear
Printed and bound in Great Britain by Antony Rowe Ltd, Chippenham,
Wiltshire

British Library Cataloguing in Publication Data
A catalogue record for this book is available from the British Library

Library of Congress Cataloging in Publication Data
Bull, Peter.
   The microanalysis of political communication : claptrap and ambiguity /
Peter Bull.
      p. cm.
Includes bibliographical references and index.
   1. Political oratory–Great Britain. 2. Campaign speeches–Great Britain.
3. Interviewing on television–Great Britain. I. Title.

PN4193.P6 B85 2003
808.5′1′08835–dc21
                                                              2002012734

ISBN 0–415–27382–X

Contents

Illustrations

Figure

Tables

Preface

In *Communication under the Microscope: The Theory and Practice of Micro-analysis* (Bull, 2002), the author set out to trace the development of micro-analysis, a distinctive and novel approach to the analysis of interpersonal communication. Its key feature is a belief in the value of studying social interaction through the detailed analysis of film, audiotape and videotape recordings. In this book, the focus is on the microanalysis of political communication. A series of original empirical studies by the author and his colleagues are presented, based on the detailed analysis of speeches and interviews.

Often political speeches are regarded as no more than 'claptrap', while politicians in interviews are typically castigated for their evasiveness in reply-ing to questions. But microanalytic research shows that there is much more to political discourse than this apparent 'claptrap and ambiguity'. In this book, detailed attention is given to how politicians seek to present them-selves in the best possible light, to how and why they equivocate, to how the analysis of equivocation and interruptions can give valuable insights into a politician's communicative style. Consideration is also given to how best to evaluate the interview skills of both interviewers and politicians. In addi-tion, a series of studies are presented on how and why applause occurs in political speeches.

The research programme was based principally on speeches and inter-views by the leaders of the three principal British political parties over the past few decades. These leaders are listed below:

Paddy Ashdown	(Leader of the Liberal Democrats, 1988–1999)
Tony Blair	(Leader of the Labour Opposition, 1994–1997; Labour Prime Minister from 1997)
William Hague	(Leader of the Conservative Opposition, 1997–2001)
Charles Kennedy	(Leader of the Liberal Democrats, from 1999)
Neil Kinnock	(Leader of the Labour Opposition, 1983–1992)
John Major	(Conservative Prime Minister, 1990–1997)
Margaret Thatcher	(Conservative Prime Minister, 1979–1990)

The speeches were video-recorded principally from the annual autumn Party Political Conferences (1996–2000), the interviews from General Elections (1987–2001). All these speeches and interviews were recorded off-air on a VHS videocassette recorder with slow-motion replay facilities. To avoid repetition, this detail is not mentioned in the Apparatus sections in Chapters 3–10.

The one study not based on party political leaders is that of hand gesture in political speeches, reported in Chapter 2. This was based on a Labour Party rally in St George's Hall, Bradford, West Yorkshire, and recorded on a portable video camera. Full details of the three speakers are given in that chapter.

Acknowledgements

There are many people who have contributed to the programme of research reported in this book. The author would particularly like to thank the following (in alphabetical order): Jude Brereton, Judy Elliott, Ann Gore, Leon Gore, John Kelly, John Local, Kate Mayer, Merel Noordhuizen, Derrol Palmer, Phil Rees, Michael Smis, Terry Squires, Matthew Thomas, Libby Walker, Bill Wells and Pam Wells.

The author would also like to thank the Leverhulme Trust and the Institute for Research in the Social Sciences (University of York) for financial assistance, and the Labour Party for permission to video-record a political rally at St George's Hall, Bradford.

Most of the research on which this book is based was first published in a series of academic journal articles. Permission to reproduce this material has been granted by the following publishers.

Reprinted by permission of Blackwells

Bull, P.E. and Mayer, K. (1993) How not to answer questions in political interviews. *Political Psychology*, 14, 651–666.

Reprinted by permission from the British Psychological Society

Bull, P.E. (2000) Do audiences only applaud 'claptrap' in political speeches? An analysis of invited and uninvited applause. *Social Psychological Review*, 2, 32–41.

Bull, P. (2001) Massaging the message: political discourse used in the recent election campaigns. *The Psychologist*, 14(7), 142–143.

Bull, P.E. and Elliott, J. (1995) Is John Major a major face-saver? An assessment of televised interviews with the party leaders during the 1992 British General Election. *Proceedings of the British Psychological Society*, 3, 65.

Bull, P.E., Elliott, J., Palmer, D. and Walker, L. (1996) Why politicians are three-faced: the face model of political interviews. *British Journal of Social Psychology*, 35, 267–284.

Reprinted by permission of Sage Publications

Bull, P.E. (1986) The use of hand gesture in political speeches: some case studies. *Journal of Language and Social Psychology*, 5, 103–118.

Bull, P.E. (1994) On identifying questions, replies and non-replies in political interviews. *Journal of Language and Social Psychology*, 13, 115–131.

Bull, P.E. (2000) Equivocation and the rhetoric of modernisation: an analysis of televised interviews with Tony Blair in the 1997 British General Election. *Journal of Language and Social Psychology*, 19, 222–247.

Bull, P.E. and Elliott, J. (1998) Level of threat: means of assessing interviewer toughness and neutrality. *Journal of Language and Social Psychology*, 17, 220–244.

Bull, P.E. and Mayer, K. (1988) Interruptions in political interviews: a study of Margaret Thatcher and Neil Kinnock. *Journal of Language and Social Psychology*, 7, 35–45.

Bull, P.E. and Mayer, K. (1989) Interruptions in political interviews: a reply to Beattie. *Journal of Language of Social Psychology*, 8, 341–344.

Bull, P.E. and Noordhuizen, M. (2000) The mistiming of applause in political speeches. *Journal of Language and Social Psychology*, 19, 275–294.

Bull, P.E. and Wells, P. (2002) By invitation only? An analysis of invited and uninvited applause. *Journal of Language and Social Psychology*, 21, 230–244.

Roger, D.B., Bull, P.E. and Smith, S. (1988) The development of a comprehensive system for classifying interruptions. *Journal of Language and Social Psychology*, 7, 27–34.

Reprinted by permission of John Wiley & Sons Ltd

Elliott, J. and Bull, P.E. (1996) A question of threat: face threats in questions posed during televised political interviews. *Journal of Community and Applied Social Psychology*, 6, 49–72.

1   The microanalysis of political communication

Introduction

During the twentieth century, research on communication underwent a revolution. Central to this new approach was the belief in the value of studying social interaction through the analysis of film, audiotape and videotape recordings of behaviour. Because such research is based on the detailed ('micro') analysis of both speech and nonverbal behaviour, the author has referred to it elsewhere as the microanalytic approach (Bull, 2002). In *Communication under the Microscope* (Bull, 2002), the author set out to trace the development of microanalysis. In this book, the author presents a series of original empirical studies conducted by himself and his colleagues on the microanalysis of political communication.

Microanalysis represents not only a distinctive methodology but also a distinctive way of thinking about communication (Bull, 2002). Undoubtedly, the analysis of film, audiotape and videotape recordings has facilitated discoveries which otherwise simply would not be possible. Indeed, the effect of the videotape recorder has been likened to that of the microscope in the biological sciences. Without recorded data which can repeatedly be examined, it is simply not possible to perform highly detailed analyses of both speech and nonverbal communication. But microanalysis did not develop simply as a consequence of innovations in technology. Film technology had been available since the beginning of the twentieth century; two of the earliest pioneers of cinematography, Muybridge and Marey, had a particular interest in analysing and recording movement patterns in animals and humans (Muybridge, 1899, 1901; Marey, 1895). The extensive use of this technology in the study of human social interaction has only really developed in the past few decades; its use reflects fundamental changes in the way in which we think about human communication (Kendon, 1982).

The introductory chapter to *Communication under the Microscope* (Bull, 2002, pp. 1–23) traces the intellectual influences that contributed to the development of microanalysis as a distinctive mode of thought. It also seeks to specify the key features of the microanalytic approach. The introductory chapter to this book is divided into three parts, the first two of which are based to a substantial extent on *Communication under the Microscope*. Part I outlines different approaches to the analysis of communication, which have contributed to microanalysis. Part II specifies the key features of micro-analysis, and then seeks to show their relevance to research on political communication. Part III summarises the programme of empirical studies to be presented in this book.

I. Approaches to the analysis of communication

The structural approach

Two early pioneers of communication research were Ray Birdwhistell (a linguist) and Albert Scheflen (a psychiatrist). Their collaboration was based on a number of shared assumptions, which made their approach highly distinctive. Thus, Birdwhistell and Scheflen regarded communication as a tightly organised and self-contained social system like language, which operates according to a definite set of rules. They saw the task of the investigator as to identify and articulate those rules. As such, their research has been referred to as the 'structural approach' (Duncan, 1969).

For example, Scheflen (e.g. 1964, 1973) studied psychotherapy sessions in great detail using a technique which he called Context Analysis. The method he recommended was a natural history one: through repeated viewing of videotape, the researcher can identify which of the nonverbal cues are ordered in sequential arrangements (Scheflen, 1966). One of his most important insights concerned the significance of what was termed 'postural congruence' – the way in which people imitate each other's postures. He observed that when people share similar views or social roles in a group, they often tend to express this by adopting similar postures (Scheflen, 1964). Conversely, dissimilar postures can indicate a marked divergence in attitude or status. Posture mirroring may also be used as a means of establishing rapport; a person may imitate another's postures to indicate friendliness and togetherness. Thus, posture mirroring may be indicative of the relationship between people.

Birdwhistell's principal concern was also with the study of nonverbal communication. He coined the term 'kinesics' to refer to the study of body movement, arguing that it could be analysed in a way that paralleled structural linguistics. In particular, he proposed that body motion is a learned form of communication, that it is patterned within a culture, and that it is structured according to rules comparable to those of spoken language. Those elements of body movement which are significant in communication he termed 'kinemes'. Of course, kinemes do not occur in isolation, they occur in patterns or combinations, referred to as 'kinemorphs' (by analogy with the linguistic term 'morpheme'). By the same token, kinemorphs can be organised into more complex patterns, referred to as 'kinemorphic constructions'.

Birdwhistell also devised a highly detailed system for categorising body movement (Birdwhistell, 1971), although it has never been clear how successfully this system could be applied in practice. In a very real sense, his work was programmatic: he was putting forward a plan for research, rather than actually carrying it out. Nevertheless, Birdwhistell was a highly influential figure. In particular, he focussed attention on the culturally shared meaning of certain forms of body movement. This meant that the significance of body movement could not be understood purely in terms of a narrow psychological approach concerned exclusively with its role as a means of individual expression (Kendon, 1982).

The significance of the structural approach can be usefully appreciated when set against the so-called 'external variable' approach (Duncan, 1969). This referred to an alternative strategy of attempting to relate communication to features external to the social context. Thus, a researcher might seek to investigate whether particular nonverbal behaviours are associated with particular personality traits: for example, by correlating scores on a questionnaire measure of extraversion with duration or frequency of gaze. This approach at one time typified much psychological research on communication, and was rightly criticised for its failure to take account of the structural organisation of social interaction (Duncan, 1969). Almost all contemporary communication researchers would now regard an awareness of the importance of structure and context as axiomatic.

Sociological approaches

Closely related to the structural approach is that taken within sociology. In fact, there are two distinctive sociological strands of research of particular importance: conversation analysis and the work of Erving Goffman.

Goffman

Goffman's principal concern was the study of social interaction. Of course, in this he was not alone, but there are a number of features which make his particular approach distinctive. One important innovation was that he regarded everyday social interaction as something worthy of study in its own right, rather as a means of studying more traditional sociological concerns, such as a primitive or sophisticated mentality, or the structure of kinship or power relationships (Burns, 1992). Another was his ability to take what might be regarded as commonplace observations, and to recast them in terms of a novel conceptual framework. Although he has had a profound influence, in no sense was his work based on the detailed analysis of either video or audio recordings. Rather, he worked from his own participant observations of social interaction, and from material such as etiquette books and advertisements. His significance was much more as a theorist, as someone who put forward a conceptual framework within which social interaction could be studied.

Thus, Goffman developed a theory to explain the ways in which people present themselves in daily life, support or challenge the claims of others and deal with challenges to their own identity (Goffman, 1959, 1961, 1971). A particularly good example of Goffman's influence can be seen in the impact of his first published article, 'On face-work: an analysis of ritual elements in social interaction' (1955). In this paper, he formulated a number of ideas concerning the importance of what he called 'face-work': strategies both for avoiding threats to face and repairing damage to face when it has occurred. Goffman's ideas have proved remarkably enduring. According to one review, the intellectual roots of virtually all contemporary research on face can be traced to this 'seminal' essay (Tracy, 1990).

Most significant of these is the contribution of two linguists, Penelope Brown and Steve Levinson (1978; 1987), who were the proponents of what has come to be known as 'politeness theory'. Following Goffman, they defined 'face' as the public image which every person wishes to claim. Face claims, they proposed, can be positive or negative. Positive face concerns the desire to be appreciated by others, negative face the desire for freedom of action. Brown and Levinson also attempted to show how strategies in conversation can be seen to reflect these two principal aspects of face. This concept of face has had an important influence on the studies of political interviews reported in this book (see especially Chapters 8–10).

Conversation analysis

The other major sociological contribution is what has become known as 'conversation analysis'. This emerged out of a sociological approach known as 'ethnomethodology'. Ethnomethodologists were highly critical of the way in which quantitative sociologists imposed what they perceived as arbitrary categories in their classification of sociological phenomena. Instead, ethnomethodologists believed in the importance of the participants' own formulations of their everyday interactions, and advocated that these should be a principal focus of study. It was to these formulations that the prefix 'ethno' referred.

Many of the basic assumptions of conversation analysis stem from a series of lectures given by Harvey Sacks in 1964 and 1965 (Sacks, 1992). The innovative and striking feature of these lectures was the recognition that talk can be studied as an activity in its own right, rather than as a means of studying other processes. Other important features were the proposals that ordinary talk is systematically, sequentially and socially organised, and that no detail of interaction (however trivial it may seem) can be dismissed as disorderly, accidental or irrelevant (Heritage, 1989).

The idea that ordinary talk is orderly contrasted sharply with prevailing models of language at that time (Lalljee and Widdicombe, 1989). In seeking to analyse people's capacity for language, Chomsky had argued for an important distinction between competence and performance. Competence represented an idealised model of people's linguistic ability, whereas performance (what people actually do in their talk) was assumed to be a degenerate version of competence (Lalljee and Widdicombe, 1989). In contrast, Sacks argued that ordinary talk could be formally described in terms of socially organised, culturally available rules and procedures. It should be studied not as a deviant version of people's competence, but as orderly in its own right.

Although Sacks' lectures were delivered in the mid-1960s, conversation analysis only began to have a wider impact in 1974, following the publication of a paper on how people take turns in conversation (see Kendon, 1988). This paper (Sacks *et al.*, 1974) identified a number of distinctive features considered to characterise turn-taking, and proposed a system of rules to account for the way in which it is organised.

In the paper by Sacks *et al.*, details were also given concerning a novel procedure for transcribing conversation. The aim was to reproduce as far as possible both the sound and structure of conversation. In order to do this, standard spelling was frequently ignored. For example, 'back in a minute' becomes 'back inna minnit', while 'lighting a fire in Perry's cellar' becomes 'lightin' a fiyuh in Perry's celluh'. A number of conventions were also devised to indicate the sequential structure of utterances in conversation. A double oblique sign (//) indicates the point at which a current speaker's talk is overlapped by the talk of another, while an equals sign (=) refers to what was called 'latching', where there is no interval between the end of one person's utterance and the start of another. Subsequently, one researcher has even been concerned to devise highly detailed ways of representing different kinds of laughter (Jefferson, 1984). In one excerpt, a laugh is transcribed as 'ihh hh heh heh huh', while in another a different form of laughter is transcribed as 'hhhh HA HA HA HA'. Thus, in conversation analysis, the transcription becomes an important part of the research. Through such faithful attention to detail, it was claimed that other analysts are given the opportunity to identify systematic regularities which might have eluded the initial investigators.

This method of transcription is highly distinctive, and constitutes one of the most characteristic features of the conversation analytic approach. It is also the point at which Schegloff's work diverged most clearly from Goffman's. Although Sacks was a student of Goffman and clearly learned a great deal from him (Schegloff, 1989), their approaches were fundamentally different. Whereas Sacks analysed social interaction in the finest of detail, Goffman painted with a broad brush. Whereas Goffman's influence was essentially that of a theorist, Sacks pioneered a methodology whereby it was possible to test empirically his own theoretical presuppositions concerning the structure and organisation of conversation.

Both Goffman and Sacks have had an enormous influence on communication research. If Goffman is open to criticism, it is because he failed to back up his observations through the analysis of either video or audio recordings. His contribution was to supply the theoretical scaffolding; the nitty gritty of detailed microanalysis he left to others. With Sacks, it is entirely the reverse. Sacks *et al.* (1974) wrote that the aim of a conversation analysis transcript was 'to get as much of the actual sound as possible into our transcripts, while still making them accessible to linguistically unsophisticated readers'. The success of this procedure is seriously open to question. There are plenty of features of speech which such transcriptions omit, for example, tempo, pitch, loudness, vowel quality and voice quality. At the same time, there is also a problem that the attempt to reproduce the sound of speech can make the text quite impenetrable. So, for example, one of Sacks *et al.*'s (1974) extracts reads, 'I'd a' cracked up 'f duh friggin (gla-i(h)f y'kno(h)w it) sm(h)a(h) heh heh.' How accessible this is to a linguistically sophisticated reader is seriously open to question – let alone to an unsophisticated one.

In this author's view, a transcript is best used not as a substitute for the recording, rather as a form of assistance. If researchers work from the transcript alone, they may miss important points of detail which were not annotated on the original transcript. Indeed, Sacks *et al.*'s analysis of turn-taking has been criticised for precisely this point (e.g. Power and dal Martello, 1986; Cowley, 1998). The best technique is to view or listen to the tape in conjunction with a transcript, ideally in the form of a video-recording, so that researchers can not only hear what is said and how it is said, but can also see any associated nonverbal behaviour for themselves. This is the approach taken in all the empirical studies reported in this monograph.

Speech Act Theory

A parallel development in linguistic philosophy was the development of Speech Act Theory. Initially, these ideas were elaborated by John Austin in 1955 in the William James lectures at Harvard University, subsequently to be published posthumously in 1962 under the title, *How to do Things with Words*. In order to acquire a fuller understanding of Austin's ideas, they need to be set in the context of academic philosophy at that time (Potter and Wetherell, 1987). In particular, Austin was attacking the view of logical positivism, that if a sentence cannot be verified as either true or false, it should simply be regarded as meaningless. More broadly, Austin was attacking a whole spectrum of views which regarded the central function of language as describing a state of affairs, or stating some facts. In contrast, the main proposition of Speech Act Theory was that language can be regarded as a form of action.

So, for example, to say 'I'm sorry' is not to convey information about an apology, nor to describe an apology; it does in itself constitute the act of apologising. But Speech Act Theory is not based on a distinction between some sentences which do things and other sentences which describe things.

Instead, Speech Act Theory presents this distinction in a different way. Its fundamental tenet is that all utterances both state things and do things, that is to say, they have both a meaning and a force. Indeed, there is also a third dimension: utterances can have an effect, consequent upon meaning and force.

Speech Act Theory represented a radical departure from views which were then current in the philosophy of language. Previous work had been concerned with the formal, abstract properties of language, to be dealt with in the same way as logic and mathematics. In contrast, Speech Act Theory focussed on language as a tool, as a means of doing things. In spite of this, Speech Act Theory is still essentially a branch of philosophy. It was developed primarily in the context of debates within philosophy, and little consideration was paid to the practical problems of applying the theory to everyday talk occurring in natural situations. Its enduring influence has come from other intellectual traditions such as conversation analysis and discourse analysis, which have sought to investigate empirically how social actions (such as ordering and requesting, persuading and accusing) are accomplished in language.

Discourse analysis

Discourse analysis is an approach which has a number of features in common with conversation analysis and Speech Act Theory. The term 'discourse' is used in a broad sense to cover all forms of spoken interaction, formal and informal, as well as written texts of all kinds. So discourse analysis can refer to any of these forms of communication (Potter and Wetherell, 1987).

There are many forms of discourse analysis, associated with several different academic disciplines; indeed, discourse *analyses* might be a more appropriate term. Discourse analysis originated in branches of philosophy, sociology, linguistics and literary theory. It is currently being developed in a variety of other disciplines as well, including anthropology, communication, education and psychology (Wood and Kroger, 2000).

At least three main approaches can be distinguished (van Dijk, 1997). There are those that focus on discourse 'itself'; that is, on structures of text or talk. Such analyses are concerned with abstract properties such as the narrative structure of a story, the use of rhetorical devices in speeches, or the placing of headlines in news reports. Second, discourse may be analysed in terms of the social actions accomplished by language users. One of the themes strongly stressed in both Speech Act Theory and conversation analysis is that people use language to do things. This focus on language function or action is a major component of discourse analysis. Finally, analyses of discourse presuppose that language users have knowledge. To understand a sentence or to interpret the topic of a text presupposes that language users share a vast repertoire of sociocultural beliefs on which their interpretations are based. Hence, the analysis of cognition has been a third substantive area of research.

One well-known example of discourse analysis is the work of Jonathan Potter, Margaret Wetherell and Derek Edwards. Their principal concern has been with language as a form of action, a means of accomplishing a variety of social functions. According to Potter and Wetherell (1987), a person's use of language will vary according to its function; that is to say, it will vary according to the purpose of the talk. For example, in describing a person to a close friend on one occasion and to a parent on another, a narrator may emphasise very different personal characteristics. Neither of these accounts is seen as the 'true' or 'correct' one, they simply serve different functions.

In cases such as these, it is proposed that people are using language to construct versions of the social world. 'The principal tenet of discourse analysis is that function involves construction of versions, and is demonstrated by language variation' (Potter and Wetherell, 1987, p. 33). The proposal is not that some forms of talk are merely descriptive, while others are deliberately constructed: all language, even language which passes as simple description, is regarded as constructive. However, the term 'construction' is not meant to imply that the process is necessarily deliberate or intentional. The person who produces the account does not necessarily do this in a calculating or conscious way. Nevertheless, a version emerges as people try to make sense of something that has happened to them, or engage in such activities as justifying their own actions or blaming others.

Two further features are stressed in what has been called the Discursive Action Model (Edwards and Potter, 1993). One of these is the problem of 'stake' or 'interest'. An interested or motivated account runs the risk of being discounted on precisely that basis (for example, with the remark, 'Well, he would say that, wouldn't he?'). Thus, speakers endeavour to construct their account in such a way that it will be understood as factual, and not dismissed as partisan or simply biased. Discourse analysis seeks to understand how such an account is constructed to achieve that particular effect.

The other feature is 'accountability' (Edwards and Potter, 1993). In reporting events, speakers routinely deal with the accountability of the people they are describing for their actions. At the same time, speakers are also accountable for their own actions, including the accuracy and interactional consequences of the narratives which they produce. Thus, speakers may seek either to claim credit or to distance themselves from the events which they report, depending upon the function of the talk. The ways in which both these aspects of accountability are constructed in narratives is the focus of an approach from the perspective of discursive psychology.

However, it should be noted that the discursive psychology of Potter, Wetherell and Edwards is only one formulation of discourse analysis; there are many others. Furthermore, there are also significant differences of opinion between different analysts. For example, van Dijk (1997) regards the analysis of cognition as one of three substantive areas of research in discourse analysis. Conversely, discursive psychology is presented as a radical alternative to cognitive social psychology, a means whereby cognitive concepts such as memory, attitudes and attributions can be re-conceptualised in terms of discursive actions (Edwards and Potter, 1992). Thus, Potter and Wetherell (1987) regard language not as a means of representing inner thoughts, ideas or attitudes, rather as a means of accomplishing a variety of social functions.

Another controversial feature of discursive psychology is that it seems to embody a position of philosophical relativism. According to Potter and Wetherell (1987), a person's use of language varies according to its function: it is not possible to say whether an account is a 'true' or 'false' one, accounts simply serve different functions. But if this is the case, it would appear as if all accounts are as good as one another, and there would appear to be no way to choose between them. Again, if neither thoughts, nor ideas nor attitudes can be inferred from discourse, then it might appear that there is nothing beyond discourse, and discourse analysis can only be used to make inferences about discourse. Taken to this extreme, discursive psychology seems to lead to a dead-end. However, relativism is not intrinsic to all discourse analysis; indeed, discursive psychology has been criticised by other discourse analysts precisely because of its relativist stance (e.g. Parker, 1992).

Ethology

A characteristic feature of both conversation analysis and discourse analysis is that they are based on the analysis of naturally occurring situations. This is also true of another approach which stems from an entirely different intellectual tradition. Ethology developed initially as a branch of zoology, concerned with the study of animal behaviour in its natural habitat, but its techniques have subsequently been extended to the analysis of human behaviour. In ethology, special emphasis is laid on observing behaviour in its natural environment. The typical research methods are naturalistic observation and field experiment. Where films or tapes are made, ethologists have developed a number of techniques for concealed filming in order to not upset the natural flow of behaviour. Thus, a movie camera with an angle lens was used by the ethologist Iraneus Eibl-Eibesfeldt (1972) to make his recordings. This enabled him to make recordings in a different direction from where the camera was pointed, and was intended to minimise self-consciousness in the people he observed.

Ethologists work on the assumption that behaviour is, to a considerable extent, inherited and they seek to interpret behaviour in terms of its evolutionary functions. One of the forerunners of ethology was Charles Darwin. He realised that if his theory of natural selection was to explain the evolution of animal species, then it also had to be able to account for behaviour. In fact, Darwin's work contains much material that would now be described as ethological, although it would be anachronistic to describe Darwin either as an ethologist or as the founder of ethology. The first person to use the term 'ethology' in its modern sense was Oscar Heinroth, in a paper published in 1911 (Thorpe, 1979). The title of 'The father of modern ethology' was also applied to Konrad Lorenz (Huxley, 1963), who became most famous for his writings on aggression. However, Lorenz acknowledged Heinroth as the source of his inspiration, and in one place defined ethology as 'the subject which Heinroth invented' (Thorpe, 1979).

Heinroth studied ducks and geese. He found that greylag geese would vocalise in one way when they were about to walk or fly as a family, in another way just before merely walking rapidly. These distinctive vocalisations he called 'intention movements', because they typically occurred just prior to performing the actual behaviour. Julian Huxley (1914) studied the diving bird known as the great crested grebe. He used the term 'display' to describe the complex postures and water 'dances' which he observed. Subsequently, Tinbergen proposed that behaviour itself could evolve specifically for its signalling value, and that it did so by exhibiting the twin qualities of conspicuousness and simplicity (Tinbergen, 1953).

Lorenz and Tinbergen referred to these signalling behaviours as 'fixed action patterns', pre-programmed innate responses which would occur in response to appropriate 'releasers' in the environment. However, modern ethologists regard this analysis as mechanistic and outdated (Fridlund, 1994). They now regard culture as formative in its own right, and view both non-humans and humans as more than reflexive automata. Thus, non-human postures, squawks and grunts have been observed to be dependent upon context in both their perception and production (e.g. Smith, 1969, 1977). Furthermore, if signalling evolves through natural selection, it may also evolve through learning: there appear, for example, to be regional dialects in birdsong (Smith, 1977).

A good example of ethological research comes from the study of social hierarchy in both humans and animals. Ethologists have observed that conflicts between members of the same species often take place within specific rules; this has the advantage of reducing the risk of serious injury or death. Such conflicts may take the form of what are called 'threat displays', which signal one individual's likelihood of attacking another. The conflict may be resolved when one contestant performs 'appeasement gestures' as a sign of submission (Eibl-Eibesfeldt, 1973).

In ethological terms, threat displays and appeasement gestures are seen as ways of resolving conflict; they can also lead to the establishment of social hierarchies through which future conflict may be regulated. An important clue to the nature of a social hierarchy is who looks at whom, known as the 'structure of attention' (Chance, 1967). According to this view, the most important animal or the most important person in the group is the focus of the subordinates' attention. In fact, not only does the pattern of gaze provide clues to the social structure of the group, it also constitutes a means whereby influence is exerted: as the recipient of gaze, the dominant individual is more easily able to exert influence over others.

Ethological concepts have been highly influential on the microanalytic approach. Indeed, the parallels between ethology and other microanalytic approaches have been noted by a number of investigators. For example, Goffman, when he came to write *Relations in Public* (1971), adopted the title of 'human ethologist'.

Communication as skill: a social psychological approach

One of the most significant influences on microanalysis has been the proposal that communication can be regarded as a form of skill. In 1967, an important paper appeared entitled 'The experimental analysis of social performance'. In this article, Michael Argyle and Adam Kendon argued that social behaviour involves processes comparable to those involved in motor skills, such as driving a car or playing a game of tennis. Given that we already know a great deal about motor skill processes, they proposed that this knowledge could be applied to advance our understanding of social interaction.

The social skills model – as it has become known – was subsequently elaborated in Argyle's books on social interaction (for example, Argyle, 1969, 1978). In the original social skills model, six processes were considered to be common to motor skills and social performance: distinctive goals, selective perception of cues, central translation processes, motor responses, feedback and corrective action, and the timing of responses. Each of these processes is discussed in turn below.

1 *Distinctive goals* can be seen, for example, in the process of driving a car. The superordinate goal of reaching one's destination may also involve subordinate goals, such as overtaking a slow-moving vehicle, crossing a difficult junction, or joining a main road in heavy traffic. So too social performance can be seen as having distinctive goals. In a job interview, the superordinate goal of the interviewer – to select the right person for the job – necessitates a number of subordinate goals, such as obtaining information from the interviewee, and establishing satisfactory rapport in order to achieve those ends.
2 *The selective perception of cues* is a key process in the performance of any skill. Not all information is of equal value: that is to say, the skilled performer may pay particular attention to certain types of information relevant to achieving their objective, while ignoring irrelevant information. Indeed, one mark of skilled performance may be to learn what input can be ignored. A skilled public speaker learns to sense the interest and attention of the audience, and to adjust the performance appropriately, whereas the conversational bore completely fails to read the response of his or her listeners.

3 *Central translation processes* prescribe what to do about any particular piece of information. The term 'translation' refers to the rule by which a particular signal is interpreted as regarding a particular action. An important feature of skills acquisition consists in the development of such translations which, once learned, can be readily and immediately acted upon. It is in the development of new translations that a great deal of hesitancy and halting can often be observed.

4 *Motor responses* refer to behaviours which are performed as a consequence of central translation processes. The learner driver may initially find it extremely difficult to change gear, but with practice the movements become quite automatic. So, too, with social behaviour. Initial learning may be quite awkward, but with extensive practice large chunks of behaviour can become fluent and habitual. Indeed, social behaviour can become too automatic. The monotone of museum guides who have repeated their guided tour too often is one well-known example of automatised behaviour. Similarly, there was the unfortunate case of a lecturer who reported that 'he had reached a stage where he could arise before his audience, turn his mouth loose, and go to sleep' (Lashley, 1951; cited in Argyle, 1969).

5 *Feedback and corrective action* refer to the ways in which individuals may modify their behaviour in the light of feedback from others. Just as in a central heating system, where the information from a thermostat regulates the heating output, so too feedback is important in the context of social interaction. For example, a teacher who sees that pupils have not understood a point may repeat it slowly in another way; again, a salesman who realises that he is failing to make an impact may change his style of behaviour. Argyle proposed that feedback is obtained principally from nonverbal cues. So in conversation a speaker will typically scan the other's face intermittently to check whether the listener understands, agrees or disagrees, and whether he or she is willing for the speaker to continue talking.

6 *Good timing and rhythm* are also important features of social skills. Without correct anticipation as to when a response will be required, interaction can be jerky and ineffective. Taking turns is the characteristic way in which conversation is structured. In larger groups, turn-taking can sometimes be problematic, because opportunities to speak can be quite restricted. Choosing the right moment to make a point in a group discussion is a useful example of the social skill of good timing.

The concept of social skill has not been without its critics. Although there are significant similarities between motor and social skills, there are also important differences (Hargie and Marshall, 1986). For example, since social interaction by definition involves other people, it is necessary to consider the goals not only of one individual but of all those involved, as well as their actions and reactions towards one another. In this sense, social behaviour is often much more complex than motor performance.

The role of feelings and emotions is another feature neglected by the original social skills model. The importance of mood and emotional state in communication is widely recognised (e.g. Parkinson, 1995), and can have an important bearing on responses, goals and perceptions in social interaction. Furthermore, whereas we often take into account the feelings of other people with whom we interact, this is clearly not the case in learning to perform a motor skill.

The perception of persons differs in a number of ways from the perception of objects. We perceive the responses of the other person with whom we communicate. We may also perceive our own responses, in that we hear what we say, and can be aware of our own nonverbal behaviour. Furthermore, we can be aware of the process of perception itself, referred to as 'metaperception'. We make judgements about how other people are perceiving us, and we may also attempt to ascertain how they think we are perceiving them. Such judgements may influence our own behaviour during social interaction (Hargie and Marshall, 1986).

The social situation in which interaction occurs is important for an understanding of social skills. Significant features which may affect social interaction are the roles which people play, the rules governing the situation, the nature of the task and the physical environment. In addition, personal factors, such as age, gender and physical appearance, will be important in the way in which people behave towards one another (Hargie and Marshall, 1986).

In the light of these criticisms, a revised version of the social skills model was proposed (Hargie and Marshall, 1986). The original model was extended to take account of two people interacting with one another: thus, feedback comes from our own as well as from other people's responses. The term 'central translation processes' was replaced with the term 'mediating factors' to allow for the influence of emotions as well as cognitions on behaviour. The original model was also further revised to take account of what was termed the 'person–situation context' (Hargie, 1997). Person factors can include personality, gender, age and appearance, while situation factors refer to features such as social roles, social rules and the cultural context within which interaction takes place.

Despite these criticisms, the social skills model continues to be highly influential. One of the most important proposals of the original model was that, if communication can be regarded as a skill, then it should be possible for people to learn to communicate more effectively, just as it is possible to improve performance on any other skill (Argyle and Kendon, 1967). This proposal was formalised in what was termed 'social skills training'. More recently, it has become known as 'communication skills training', and has been used extensively in a wide variety of social contexts (see Bull, 2002, pp. 130–144).

II. Key features of the microanalytic approach

Despite important differences of opinion and emphasis between these communications scholars, they do share a number of common assumptions. These can be seen to embody a distinctive way of thinking about communication, which the author has referred to as 'microanalysis' (Bull, 2002). Its principal themes are presented below, together with a consideration of their implications for the research reported in this book.

Communication is studied as it actually occurs

A key feature is a concern with the analysis of communication as it actually occurs through the detailed analysis of film, videotape or audiotape. This marked a radical shift from the traditional concern with the study of communication in terms of what it should be – in terms of, for example, its efficiency, clarity or persuasiveness. The focus on communication as it actually occurs can be seen to characterise all the different approaches to communication analysis described above (pp. 2–12), and can be regarded as one principal underlying theme of microanalytic research. In the studies presented here, communication as it actually occurs is studied through the detailed analysis of video-recordings of political speeches and political interviews.

Communication can be studied as an activity in its own right

Another important theme is the proposal that communication can be studied as an activity in its own right. Just as Goffman made social interaction itself the focus of his investigations, so too an important and innovative feature of conversation analysis was the recognition that talk can be studied as talk, rather than as a means of studying other social processes. Similarly, the focus of discourse analysis is exclusively on discourse itself: how it is constructed, its functions and on the consequences which arise from different ways in which discourse is organised. In the research reported here, it is political interviews and political speeches themselves which are the focus of investigation.

All features of interaction are potentially significant

A further distinguishing feature of the microanalytic approach has been the expansion of what behaviour can be regarded as communicative. In recent decades, the remarkable development of interest in nonverbal communication can be regarded as one such manifestation. So, too, is the extraordinary detail in which conversation analysts seek in their transcripts to represent as exactly as possible the way in which conversation sounds. The underlying assumption is that all features of interaction are potentially significant, and therefore should not be dismissed out of hand as unworthy of investigation.

In the research to be presented here, considerable attention is given to fine details of communication, which anyone not familiar with the micro-analytic approach might regard as trivial or unimportant. The initial study reports an analysis of the use of hand gestures in political speeches. Later studies of political speeches focus on the synchronisation of applause, and on the subtle differences between invited and uninvited applause. The studies of political interviews also focus on a number of fine details of inter-action: on interruptions, on different ways in which politicians may equi-vocate and on different ways in which questions may threaten the face of a politician.

Communication has a structure

A related proposal is that communication has a structure. Although inter-action may seem at first sight to be disorderly or even random, it cannot be assumed to be so, and one of the tasks of the investigator is to analyse whether an underlying structure can be discerned. Structure can take a variety of forms. Interaction may be sequentially organised, that is to say, certain behaviours or features of conversation may occur in a regular order. It may be hierarchically organised, that is to say, behaviour or conversation may be organised into higher-order units. It may also be organised in terms of social rules.

The research reported here is guided by the underlying assumption that communication has a structure. Thus, applause in political speeches does not occur in response to just anything a politician says. It has been shown that applause can be invited by the speaker through a range of rhe-torical devices embedded in the structure of speech specifically for this purpose (Atkinson, 1983, 1984a, 1984b). It will also be shown that applause can occur uninvited, either directly in response to the content of speech (Chapter 3) or through a misreading of rhetorical devices (Chapter 5).

Similarly, the discourse of political interviews has its own particular structures. For example, although politicians are notorious for not replying to questions, equivocation does not occur all the time. It will be shown that politicians are much more likely to equivocate in response to certain ques-tions which create what is termed an *avoidance–avoidance conflict* (Bavelas *et al.*, 1990), where all the principal responses to a question may make the politician look bad, but equivocation seems to be the least face-damaging alternative (see Chapter 8).

Conversation can be regarded as a form of action

According to Speech Act Theory, language does not simply describe some state of affairs or state some facts: it is in itself a form of action. This pro-posal has been profoundly influential and underlies a great deal of research on the analysis of conversation. A principal concern has been the study of function. To a substantial extent, this represents the influence of Speech Act Theory: once it is accepted that speech is not only concerned with the transmission of information, but constitutes a form of activity in its own right, it is logical to conduct analyses on the nature of that activity.

Nowhere can this be more true than in the sphere of political communication. Political discourse is in itself a form of political action. Often dismissed as 'just' rhetoric, political discourse plays a vital role in the self-presentation of politicians and political parties, in the presentation of policies, in currying the widest popular support from the electorate. One important aspect of political discourse is self-presentation and face management, to which considerable attention is given in Chapters 8–10.

Communication is best studied in naturally occurring contexts

Common to almost all the approaches discussed so far is the proposal that communication is best studied in naturally occurring contexts. The one exception to this has been experimental social psychology; its proponents have traditionally made extensive use of laboratory-based experimentation as a means of studying communication. However, the trend in social psychology in recent years has also been towards naturalistic analysis.

In this context, the term 'naturalistic' is used very broadly to refer to almost any situation which has not been specifically set up as an experiment for the specific purpose of observing communication. Thus, televised broadcasts of political speeches and interviews might be seen as 'naturalistic', because these events have not been set up for the purposes of political communication research, they are simply part of the ongoing political process.

Communication can be regarded as a form of skill

The proposal that communication can be regarded as a form of skill represents one of the main contributions of the social psychological approach to communication. Indeed, it has been so influential that the term 'communication skills' has passed into the wider culture. In the studies to be reported here, considerable attention is given to the communication skills of both politicians and political interviewers. Thus, the analyses of political speeches reported in Part I have a number of implications for what can be regarded as skill in oratory. Similarly, in Part II the analyses of political interviews might be used to evaluate the communicative skills of both interviewers and politicians. It will be argued that, in political interviews, skill in face management and self-presentation is of central importance for the politician, especially given that tough interviewers will ask a high proportion of 'no-win' questions to which the politician cannot respond without incurring some damage to face.

Communication can be taught like any other skill

A related proposal is that communication can be taught like any other skill. This again has been highly influential in the wider culture; social or communication skills training has been widely used in a variety of personal and occupational contexts (see Bull, 2002, pp. 130–144). No studies of communication skills training were conducted in this research, although the results of the studies to be presented here could easily be used to improve the communication skills of both politicians and political interviewers, or indeed to improve the political perceptiveness of the electorate.

Macro issues can be studied through microanalysis

Also of particular importance for the wider culture is the assumption that major 'macro' social issues such as racism, politics or feminism can be analysed through microanalysis. In a sense, all the research studies to be reported here are concerned with the macro issue of political communication, which they seek to show can be illuminated through detailed microanalytic research.

Methodological issues

Although communication scholars arguably share a number of common assumptions, they do (unsurprisingly!) also have significant disagreements. Some of the most important arguments have been concerned with methodology: on how to actually conduct research. Such disagreements need to be considered, before outlining the programme of research to be presented in this book.

Traditionally, one of the main planks of academic psychology has been a belief in the value of the experimental method, and for many years this approach typified social psychological research on interpersonal communication. Intrinsic to the experimental method is a belief in the importance of quantification and the use of inferential statistics. A significant consequence of a quantitative approach is the need for categorisation. The advantage of this procedure is that it allows the researcher to reduce observed behaviour to frequencies or rates of occurrence, rather than attempting a detailed description of each event. These data can then be subjected to some sort of analysis using inferential statistics. Hence, a salient feature of communication research in experimental social psychology has been a preoccupation with the development of coding systems (Bull and Roger, 1989).

This approach has been subject to intensive criticism by those who favour naturalistic observation and a qualitative approach. One target of criticism has been the artificiality of the data obtained in laboratories, where the participants either knew or suspected that they were being recorded for the purpose of an experiment. Although these problems are not insurmountable, the use of naturalistic observation has increasingly become the preferred method of making observations in communication research.

The use of coding systems has also been criticised, on the grounds that such procedures are typically arbitrary, reductionist and distort the data to fit it into preconceived categories (Psathas, 1995). Furthermore, it is claimed that context and meaning are only dealt with in so far as they are specified in the category system (Psathas, 1995). Researchers in both conversation analysis and discourse analysis have also become increasingly concerned not to 'impose' preconceived categories on the data, but to make use of the ways in which people categorise themselves, as manifested in their own discourse (van Dijk, 1997).

However, there are a number of features which this critique of categorisation ignores. While it is certainly interesting to examine the ways in which people categorise themselves, this is not the only way of analysing interpersonal communication. Coding systems devised by outside observers can be highly informative. Coding systems can also change over time. That is to say, they can be improved to make a better representation of the phenomena. A good coding system can act as a valuable aid to perception, not necessarily as a hindrance. It may enable the researcher to identify phenomena which might not be immediately obvious to the untrained observer.

Research on nonverbal communication can be used to illustrate the value of coding systems. Because of the anatomical complexity of bodily movement, it can be very difficult to give precise descriptions of its physical appearance. Nowhere is this more true than in the facial musculature, which is capable of producing an extensive array of different expressions. These are highly varied, often subtle and intricate and hence can be very difficult to describe. The Facial Action Coding System (FACS) is a procedure for categorising facial movements, developed by Paul Ekman and Wallace Friesen (1978). By concentrating on the anatomical basis of facial movement, FACS can provide a detailed description of all the movements possible with the facial musculature. Thus, the system is not only comprehensive, it can also serve as an invaluable guide to perception, by helping the observer to identify complex facial movements and providing a language with which to describe them. Indeed, FACS has become widely accepted as the main technique available for analysing facial expressions, and there is now an extensive body of research using this procedure (see Ekman and Rosenberg, 1997).

The research studies to be presented in this book make extensive use of coding systems. The Body Movement Scoring System (Bull, 1987) was used to analyse hand gestures in political speeches in the study reported in Chapter 2. The studies of political interviews also make extensive use of coding systems. The Interruption Coding System (ICS) was devised by Roger *et al.* (1988) to provide a fine-grained analysis of interruptions; this system is described in Chapter 6. Another procedure was developed for identifying questions, replies and non-replies to questions in political interviews (Bull, 1994). This system is described in Chapter 7, where it was used in a series of studies on equivocation. It was also used in all the subsequent studies of political interviews (Chapters 8–10). A further coding system was devised for the analysis of face-threats in questions in political interviews (Bull *et al.*, 1996); this is reported in Chapter 8, and forms the basis for the studies of face reported in Chapters 8–10.

However, the research to be presented here was not based exclusively on coding systems. Qualitative as well as quantitative techniques were used wherever it was considered appropriate, and illustrative examples of political discourse are discussed throughout the book as a whole. Furthermore, in Chapter 3, an extensive qualitative analysis is presented of the kind of content which receives applause in political speeches. Thus, the methodological approach taken here is essentially pragmatic rather than ideological. In this author's view, neither quantitative and qualitative techniques – nor categorical and non-categorical approaches – need be regarded as mutually exclusive; they can be employed together to bring different insights on particular problems. This is the approach taken in this book.

III. Outline of research

The focus of the book is on two particular aspects of political communication – namely, interviews and speeches.

Political speeches

Collective applause is a phenomenon of considerable potential interest to the social psychologist. In the context of political speeches, applause can be seen as a highly manifest expression of group identity, a means whereby audiences not only praise the ingroup (their own party), but also derogate outgroups (their political opponents). As a group activity, applause also requires group co-ordination; hence, it raises interesting interactional questions as to how audiences are able effectively to synchronise their behaviour to applaud in concert rather than in isolation. Furthermore, applause is closely associated with rhetoric, a topic of direct interest to analysts of discourse.

The author's research on political speeches arose out of a long-standing interest in nonverbal communication, and a dissatisfaction with the rather contrived and constricted laboratory settings in which many such studies at that time were conducted. A particular concern was to look at the use of hand gestures in a natural setting where it occurred with a high degree of visibility, and for this purpose political oratory seemed ideal. The results of this study are reported in Chapter 2.

The purpose of this study was to investigate the functions of gesture in political speeches. Two speeches were used to analyse the relationship of hand gestures to vocal stress, a third speech to investigate the role of hand gestures in inviting and controlling audience applause. This latter analysis was conducted in the context of a theory of rhetoric developed by the sociologist, Max Atkinson (1983, 1984a, 1984b). This theory is concerned with the way in which rhetorical devices are used to invite applause, and is described in some detail in Chapter 2. It proved invaluable in understanding how hand gestures are used both to articulate the structure of applause invitations, as well as to refuse applause when it occurs at inappropriate points during a speech.

Atkinson's theory has, in fact, proved remarkably influential and provides some compelling insights into the stage management of political speeches. As such, it has become widely accepted, although it has always been open to criticism on a number of counts. Nevertheless, since the time when the original research was conducted in the 1980s, the theory has never been subjected to any systematic re-evaluation. In the remaining chapters of Part I, a series of studies are presented which were intended to do precisely this – to test the validity of Atkinson's theory of rhetoric.

According to Atkinson, collective applause is highly synchronised with speech, invited through rhetorical devices employed by the speaker for this purpose. The problem is that the theory as it stands does not account for negative instances which might be inconsistent with it; for example, collective applause which does *not* occur in response to rhetorical devices, and incidences of applause which are *not* synchronised with speech. Two studies which focussed on these concerns are presented in Chapters 3 and 4.

On the basis of these analyses, a revised version of Atkinson's theory of rhetoric was proposed. This was based on the proposition that not all applause in political speeches is invited through rhetorical devices; it can also occur uninvited in the absence of such devices. Furthermore, it does not have to be synchronous with speech, it can also be asynchronous. A study to test this model is reported in Chapter 5, intended to investigate the relationship between these different dimensions of applause: invited/ uninvited, synchronous/asynchronous, rhetorically formatted/non-rhetorically formatted.

Political interviews

The other major strand of the author's research on political communication has been concerned with the analysis of televised interviews. This arose initially out of an interest in the role of interruptions in conversation. To analyse interruptions, the Interruption Coding System (Roger *et al.*, 1988) was devised, based on two experiments conducted in a social psychology laboratory. However, the author wanted to test out this system in a non-experimental setting where interruptions occur with a high degree of frequency; for this purpose, the televised political interview seemed ideal. Thus, a study was conducted of interruptions in interviews with Margaret

Thatcher and Neil Kinnock broadcast during the 1987 General Election. This is reported in Chapter 6, together with a description of the Interruption Coding System.

Chapter 7 reports several analyses of political equivocation. In the first instance, criteria were established for identifying what constitute questions, replies and non-replies. These criteria were then used to conduct an assessment of the extent to which politicians fail to reply to questions, based on a set of 33 interviews. The next stage was to investigate the different ways in which politicians equivocate. A typology of equivocation was developed, which was then used to analyse the communicative style of three party political leaders: Margaret Thatcher, Neil Kinnock and John Major.

Chapter 8 is concerned with the reasons why politicians equivocate so extensively in political interviews. It was argued that a principal source of *avoidance–avoidance conflicts* identified by Bavelas *et al.* (1990) as responsible for equivocation are what are termed 'threats to face'. That is to say, politicians will tend to avoid certain kind of responses which may make them look bad. When all the principal ways of responding to a question may make them look bad, they tend to favour equivocation as the least face-threatening option.

To test hypotheses derived from this overall theoretical framework, an analysis was conducted of 18 interviews from the 1992 General Election. A typology was devised which distinguishes between 19 different ways in which questions in political interviews may pose threats to face. An important distinction was made between *avoidance–avoidance conflict* questions, and those where it was considered possible to produce a response which was not threatening to face (*no necessary threat* questions). In the case of the former, equivocation was predicted as the least face-threatening and therefore the most likely response. In the case of the latter, a *no necessary threat* response was predicted as the most likely response.

In Chapter 8, a study is also reported of six interviews from the 2001 General Election. This election was the first in which both the BBC and ITV arranged for the leaders of the three main political parties to be questioned in the same television programme by professional interviewers alongside members of the general public. This offered an excellent opportunity to test the hypothesis that equivocation by politicians is at least in part a function of the questions which they are asked in political interviews. Thus, because of the complex structure of *avoidance–avoidance conflict* questions, it was hypothesised that they are more likely to be posed by professional interviewers than by members of the public. Accordingly, politicians are more likely to equivocate when questioned by professional interviewers because of the nature of the questions which they are asked.

The analysis of the face-threatening structure of questions has important implications for evaluating the interview performance of both interviewers and politicians. In Chapter 9, a study is presented of six interviewers during the 1992 General Election, based on the distinction between *avoidance–avoidance conflict* and *no necessary threat* questions. *Avoidance–avoidance* questions are arguably tougher than those which allow a *no necessary threat* response, because they create pressures on the politician to equivocate. The relative proportion of such questions (referred to as *level of threat*) can be used as a measure of interviewer toughness: the higher the proportion of *avoidance–avoidance* questions, the tougher the interview. *Level of threat* can also used as a means of assessing interviewer neutrality. If it can be shown that an interviewer consistently asks a higher proportion of *avoidance–avoidance* questions to members of one political party rather than another, then it can be argued that this is indicative of interviewer bias.

The analysis of face management also has important implications for evaluating the interview performance of politicians, and this forms the basis of Chapter 10. This chapter was concerned with how politicians handle both *no necessary threat* questions, and questions which create an *avoidance–avoidance conflict*. To the extent that a politician produces a face-damaging response where a *no necessary threat* response was possible, interview performance may be regarded as unskilled – given an adversarial political system in which a politician must seek to present the best possible face. On this basis, an evaluation was conducted of *avoidable face-damaging responses* in interviews broadcast during the 1992 British General Election. An analysis was also conducted of five televised interviews with Tony Blair in the 1997 General Election in which it is argued he showed highly skilled face management in handling questions which create *avoidance–avoidance conflicts*. Both analyses are reported in this chapter.

In the final chapter (Chapter 11), a summary of the main findings is presented. The theoretical significance of the research is also considered, with regard to both Atkinson's (1983, 1984a, 1984b) theory of rhetoric and Bavelas *et al.*'s (1990) theory of equivocation. Finally, the practical significance of the research is considered from a threefold perspective: that of the electorate, the politicians and the professional political interviewers.

Part I

Political speeches

2   The use of hand gestures

Introduction

The study reported in this chapter was concerned with the way in which politicians make use of hand gestures in public speeches (Bull, 1986). It was based on a video-recording of a political rally in St George's Hall, Bradford, West Yorkshire, during the 1983 General Election campaign. One main influence on this study was the extensive research literature on body movement and speech. The second main influence was Atkinson's theory of rhetoric (e.g. Atkinson, 1983, 1984a, 1984b). Each of these approaches is discussed below.

Body movement and speech

According to Condon and Ogston (1966), the body of the speaker moves closely in time with his speech; they called this 'self-synchrony'. Self-synchrony is not simply confined to hand gestures; movements of all parts of the body have been found to be closely co-ordinated with speech. However, this is not to say that *every* bodily movement is related to discourse. For example, in a study of psychotherapy sessions, it was primarily non-contact hand movements (movements that do not involve touching the body or touching an object) which were judged as related to speech (Freedman and Hoffman, 1967).

An important form of self-synchrony is that between body movement and vocal stress. Spoken English is produced in groups of words, typically averaging about five in length, where there is one primary vocal stress, sometimes referred to as the 'tonic' (Halliday, 1970). This primary vocal stress is conveyed principally through changes in pitch, but also through changes in loudness or rhythm. The group of words is referred to as a 'phonemic clause' or 'tone group', and is terminated by a juncture, in which the changes in pitch, rhythm and loudness level off before the beginning of the next phonemic clause (Trager and Smith, 1951). Speakers of English typically accompany their primary stresses with slight jerks of the head or hand (Pittenger *et al.*, 1960). Furthermore, it is not just movements of the head and hands which are related to vocal stress, but movements of all parts of the body (Bull and Connelly, 1985). In fact, most of the tonic stresses (over 90 per cent) in the study by Bull and Connelly were accompanied by some kind of body motion. Typically, these took the form of continuous movements, such as nodding the head or flexing and extending the forearm, where the apex of the movement was timed to occur at the same time as the tonic. So, for example, the downward movement of a head nod might begin before the tonic, the apex of the head nod coinciding with the tonic, the upward movement of the head occurring after the tonic.

Other ways in which body movement is related to speech are through syntax (Lindenfeld, 1971) and meaning (e.g. Scheflen, 1964). From an analysis of the speech of a patient in a psychotherapy session, movements were found to occur principally within the duration of a syntactic clause rather than across clause boundaries (Lindenfeld, 1971). Larger chunks of speech can also be marked out through shifts in posture (Scheflen, 1964, 1973). Changes in what is referred to as the 'position' – corresponding roughly to taking a certain point of view in an interaction – tend to be accompanied by a postural shift involving at least half the body (Scheflen, 1964). Changes of topic are also sometimes accompanied by shifts in posture: in a study of television newsreaders, it was found that the introduction of a different news item was frequently accompanied by a change in hand position (Bull, 1987).

Head movements are also closely related to the meaning of speech. This is not just through signalling 'yes' or 'no', but can occur in a variety of other ways (McClave, 2000). For example, vigorous head shakes may accompany emphatic words such as 'a lot', 'great' or 'really'. A wide sweep of the head may be used to indicate inclusiveness, accompanying such words as 'everyone' or 'everything'. When a person starts to quote directly from someone else's speech, a shift in head orientation may slightly precede or directly accompany the quotation (McClave, 2000).

Body movement is thus clearly co-ordinated with speech, in terms of vocal stress, syntax and meaning. But often it has been studied alone, as if it were a separate and distinct form of communication. Critics of this 'body language' approach have repeatedly stressed the interconnectedness of speech and body movement, and argued that the distinction between them is highly artificial (e.g. Bavelas and Chovil, 2000). Hand and facial gestures in particular may be seen as visible acts of meaning and, hence, should arguably be treated as part of natural language. Bavelas and Chovil (2000) have referred to this as 'face-to-face dialogue', and advocate what they term an integrated message model in which audible and visible communicative acts are treated as a unified whole.

The focus of the study to be reported in this chapter is on hand gestures. According to Kendon (1985), gesture is arguably as fundamental as speech for the representation of meaning; they are joined together only because gesture is used simultaneously for the same purpose. In the organisation of an utterance, speech and gesture are planned at the outset; the encoding of the utterance may occur simultaneously through both speech and gesture. There is considerable evidence consistent with this view (McNeill, 1985). Not only do gestures occur primarily during speech, they are also synchronised with linguistic units; indeed, they have semantic and pragmatic functions that parallel those of speech. In addition, gesture develops simultaneously with speech in children, and dissolves together with speech in aphasia (any disorder of speech resulting from brain damage). Speech and gesture interact with one another in creating meaning. Not only does gesture clarify the meaning of the speech, speech can also clarify the meaning of the gesture (Kelly *et al.*, 1999). In short, gesture may be seen not just as an alternative to speech, but as an additional resource, as part of a multichannel system of communication, which allows the skilled speaker further options through which to convey meaning.

The particular role of gesture can be seen to arise from a number of distinctive features which make it highly suitable for certain kinds of tasks (Kendon, 1985). It is, of course, first and foremost a visual means of communication. As such, it is often easier or quicker, for example, to point to an object than to describe it in words. Again, some gestures are like representative pictures in that they attempt to represent the visual appearance of an object, spatial relationship or bodily action (sometimes referred to as 'physiographic'). In one experiment (Graham and Argyle, 1975), English and Italian students were asked to communicate information about two-dimensional shapes to other students from their own culture, both with and without the use of hand gestures. The decoders drew what they thought the shapes were, the drawings were rated by English and Italian judges for their similarity to the original shapes. When gesture was permitted, the drawings were judged as significantly more accurate, while the Italians also did significantly better than the English under these circumstances. Gesture is, of course, widely believed to be of particular importance in Italian culture.

Because gesture is visual, it is also a silent means of communication. It may be employed when it is difficult or impossible to use speech. The speech channel may be momentarily blocked by noise, but it may also be blocked because it is already in use. Thus, in multiparty conversations, gesture may be employed by people who are not actually talking as a means of commenting on an interaction, without interrupting the flow of speech. This may be done cooperatively or critically, so that the commentator does not have to take a speaking turn (Kendon, 1985).

An additional advantage of gesture is that it can be used without having to enter into the kind of mutual obligation or ritual conduct which seems to be required by conversation. Consequently, it may sometimes be quicker to make a passing comment through gesture rather than through words. It may also be used in situations where the speaker seeks to be less fully bound or committed to what he or she has to say. It may sometimes be adopted as a substitute for speech, where actually to formulate a thought in words might be regarded as too explicit or indelicate (Kendon, 1985).

Gesture is, to some extent, optional. Whereas features like vocalisation, speech rate and amplitude are intrinsic to speech, that is to say, it is impossible to converse without them, it is perfectly possible to converse without the use of gesture. Consequently, the presence or absence of gesture may in itself be seen as a form of communication. Thus, gesture may be used when a person is interested in the topic he or she is talking about, or to accompany certain parts of speech which a person regards as more important. Similarly, it has been found that people attempting to be persuasive used significantly more gesture than when asked to present a message in a neutral fashion (Mehrabian and Williams, 1969). Conversely, an absence of gesture may indicate a lack of desire to communicate. People suffering from depression were found to use significantly fewer illustrative gestures on admission to hospital than on discharge (Kiritz, 1971; cited in Ekman and Friesen, 1974).

Gesture by its very nature is a form of bodily action and this gives it certain advantages in communication. The appearance of an action can never be as adequately described in words as it can be represented through movement. Thus, gesture may be of particular importance in mimicry or in demonstrating how particular skills should be performed. Because gestures can be reminiscent of other physical actions, they may acquire additional forcefulness as a consequence: a clenched fist may convey anger more effectively than a torrent of words. This may give gesture especial importance in the communication of emotions and interpersonal attitudes.

Not only is gesture a visual form of communication, it is *highly* visible, especially in comparison to, say, facial expression or eye contact. In a study of a birthday party, it was observed how people used gesture as an initial salutation to capture one another's attention before entering into conversation (Kendon and Ferber, 1973). In a study of medical consultations, patients were found to use flamboyant gestures to attract the doctor's attention when it was focussed on his or her notes (Heath, 1986). In this context, gesture has the additional advantage of indirectness as well as visibility, since a direct request for attention from a higher-status figure like a doctor might be seen as some sort of challenge to the doctor's authority. There are also differences in visibility between different forms of gesture. More important aspects of speech can be indicated by larger movements (articulated from the shoulder, or indeed involving both arms), and/or by movements involving more than one part of the body.

This is particularly true of a situation like public speaking. For the orator, gesture has distinct advantages over other forms of nonverbal communication such as facial expression or gaze, which may be less discernible to a distant audience. Politicians at public meetings are well known for the flamboyant use of gesture, hence this seemed a particularly good setting in which to examine the relationship of hand gestures to speech. Whereas the author's previous research had been based on conversations between students in a social psychology laboratory (e.g. Bull and Connelly, 1985), the aim of this study was to analyse a naturalistic situation where hand gestures might be expected to occur with a high degree of frequency.

Atkinson's theory of rhetoric

The other major influence on the study reported in this chapter was Atkinson's analysis of the rhetorical devices used by politicians to invite audience applause (e.g. Atkinson, 1983, 1984a, 1984b).

Atkinson pointed out that applause is not random; it occurs in response to a relatively narrow range of actions on the part of the speaker, such as advocating the speaker's own political position or attacking the opposition. The timing of applause is also characterised by a high degree of precision: typically it occurs either just before or immediately after a possible completion point by the speaker. Similarly, speakers usually wait until the applause has finished before starting or continuing to speak. In fact, just as conversationalists take it in turns to speak, so do speaker and audience, although audience 'turns' are essentially limited to gross displays of approval or disapproval (such as cheering or heckling). Indeed, as Atkinson points out, if the audience was not restricted in this way, it is hard to imagine how public meetings could ever take place in the ensuing verbal chaos!

The close synchronisation between speech and applause suggests that audience members are not only paying close attention to the speaker but, in addition, must be able to predict possible completion points in advance of their occurrence. If this were not the case, one would expect to find frequent delays between speech and applause, more instances of applause starting in places other than possible completion points and more incidences of isolated or sporadic applause. The fact that audiences seem for the most part to applaud 'on cue' suggests that there must be some system of signals which enables them to recognise where and when applause is appropriate.

Atkinson's critical insight was to propose that it is features in the construction of talk itself which indicate to the audience when to applaud. He argued that audiences are more likely to respond to statements that are constructed in such a way as to both emphasise and highlight the content, and which project a clear completion point for the message in question. Emphasis naturally calls attention to passages to which the speaker attaches particular significance, but Atkinson argues that emphasis alone is rarely sufficient to ensure a response. Projectability is also important, because audience members must decide not only if they will applaud but when to applaud; if the speech is constructed in such a way as to indicate appropriate applause points, this assists the audience in co-ordinating their behaviour. According to Atkinson (1984a, p. 18), the use of rhetorical devices is in the interest of the audience, because it helps them applaud together rather than risk exposure to public ridicule and humiliation by applauding in isolation.

One of the cues he identified is when a conversation includes a list of three items. In conversation, the completion of a list can signal the completion of an utterance – a point at which another person can or should start talking. Such lists also typically consist of three items, so that once the listener recognises that a list is under way, it is possible to anticipate the completion point and hence the end of the speaker's utterance (Jefferson, 1990). In political speeches, Atkinson proposed that the three-part list may serve a comparable function, but in this case signalling to the audience appropriate places to applaud. For example, Tony Blair (at that time Leader of the Labour Opposition) was duly applauded in his speech to his party's annual conference (1 October, 1996) when he said that 'there is no future for Britain as a low wage, low skills, low technology economy'. He was also applauded for a more famous three-part list in the same speech: 'Ask me my three main priorities for Government, and I tell you: education, education and education.'

Another comparable rhetorical device is the contrast. John Major was duly applauded when he told the Conservative Party conference (11 October, 1996) that 'we are in Europe to help shape it and *not* to be shaped by it'. Contrasts can be used to do a number of things, including boasting about one's own side, attacking the opposition, or doing both things at the same time. To be effective, the second part of the contrast should closely resemble the first in the details of its construction and duration, so that the audience can more easily anticipate the point of completion. If the contrast is too brief, people may have insufficient time to recognise that a completion point is about to be reached, let alone to produce an appropriate response. According to Atkinson, the contrast is by far the most frequently used device for obtaining applause. He also proposed that the skilled use of both contrasts and three-part lists is characteristic of 'charismatic' speakers (Atkinson, 1984a, pp. 86–123), and that such devices are often to be found in those passages of political speeches which are selected for presentation in the news media (Atkinson, 1984a, pp. 124–163).

Given that Atkinson's research was based on the analysis of selected extracts, one possible criticism is that he might have focussed on examples which support his argument but are not necessarily representative of political speech-making as a whole. The only effective answer to this criticism is comprehensive sampling. This was the intention of John Heritage and David Greatbatch (1986), who analysed all the 476 speeches which were televised from the British Conservative, Labour and Liberal Party conferences in 1981 – a truly heroic study! They found that contrasts were associated with no less than 33.2 per cent of the incidences of collective applause during speeches, and lists with 12.6 per cent; hence, almost half the applause occurring during these 476 speeches was associated with the two rhetorical devices originally identified by Atkinson.

Five other rhetorical devices for obtaining applause were identified, referred to as puzzle–solution, headline–punchline, combination, position taking and pursuits (Heritage and Greatbatch, 1986). In the puzzle-solution device, the speaker begins by establishing some kind of puzzle or problem and then, shortly afterwards, offers the solution; this is the important and applaudable part of the message. The puzzle invites the audience to anticipate or guess at its solution, while at the same time listening carefully to the speaker's own solution when it is delivered. Since the delivery of the solution naturally coincides with the completion of the political message, the audience is normally able to anticipate the point at which applause should properly begin. For example, Paddy Ashdown was applauded for the solution to the puzzle posed in this speech to the annual Liberal Democrat Party Conference (24 September, 1996): 'And here's another Conservative solution to the problems of the Health Service. The Private Finance Initiative – PFI. But what the NHS really needs is a different kind of PFI [PUZZLE]. *Patients First Instead*' [SOLUTION].

The headline–punchline device is structurally similar to the puzzle-solution format, although somewhat simpler. Here, the speaker proposes to make a declaration, pledge or announcement and then proceeds to make it. The applaudable part of the message is emphasised by the speaker's calling attention in advance to what he or she is about to say. Thus, the speaker might use headline phrases such as 'I'll tell you what makes it worthwhile...', 'And I'll say why...', 'And I repeat the promise that I made at the election that...', 'And our number one priority is...' or 'And I can announce to you that...' In the following extract from a speech by Tony Blair to the Labour Party Conference (30 September, 1997), he states '*And I tell you that* [HEADLINE] I will never countenance an NHS that departs from its fundamental principle of health care based on need not wealth' [PUNCHLINE]. The punchline 'need not wealth' also contains a contrast, and is duly applauded.

In position taking, the speaker first describes a state of affairs towards which he or she could be expected to take a strongly evaluative stance. The description itself contains little or no evaluation. However, at the end of the description, the speaker overtly and unequivocally either praises or condemns the state of affairs described. Thus, John Major, in his speech to the Conservative Party Conference (11 October, 1996), is applauded for condemning the following state of affairs: 'I still hear too many stories of politically correct absurdities that prevent children being adopted by loving couples who would give them a good home [STATE OF AFFAIRS]. If that is happening we should stop it' [EVALUATIVE STANCE].

All these devices may be combined with one another, with the result that the completion point of the message is further emphasised. The most common form of combination identified by Heritage and Greatbatch links a contrast with a three-part list. The following extract comes from Tony Blair's speech to the Labour Party Conference (1 October, 1996) in which both a contrast (A2, B2) and a three-part list (1, 2, 3) are 'nested' in another contrast (A1, B1):

> (A1) It is sometimes said you know that the Tories are (A2) cruel but they're (B2) efficient.
> (B1) in fact they're the most (1) feckless, (2) irresponsible, (3) incompetent managers of the British economy in this country's history.

If an audience fails to respond to a particular message, speakers may actively pursue applause. A common method of doing so is to recomplete the previous point, as in the following speech by John Major to the Conservative Party Conference (11 October, 1996): 'New Labour, no new services in Glossop or elsewhere. In the most important part of a health service the family doctor's surgery *that's what New Labour would mean.*' John Major failed to receive applause after the contrast 'New Labour no new services in Glossop or elsewhere', consequently he reiterated the point in a slightly different way.

In the 476 speeches analysed by Heritage and Greatbatch (1986), more than two-thirds of the collective applause was associated with these seven rhetorical devices. Most effective were contrasts and lists, the two devices originally identified by Atkinson as significant in inviting applause. Thus, the results of this comprehensive survey of political speeches provided impressive support for Atkinson's original observations. It demonstrated what is, in effect, a strong positive correlation between rhetorical devices and collective applause.

An obvious objection to this whole analysis is that audiences do not simply applaud rhetoric, they also respond to the content of a political speech. This point is readily acknowledged by Atkinson, Heritage and Greatbatch, but they also propose that audiences are much *more* likely to applaud if content is expressed through an appropriate rhetorical device. For example, in an analysis of two debates at the Conservative and Labour Party conferences, Heritage and Greatbatch looked at one particular class of statements the audience might be expected to applaud, referred to as 'external attacks'. These are statements critical of outgroups such as other political parties, which should evoke unambiguous agreement amongst party conference participants. Whereas 71 per cent of external attacks expressed through one of the seven rhetorical devices were applauded, only 29 per cent of external attacks received applause in the absence of rhetorical devices.

In another such analysis, Heritage and Greatbatch looked at political debates characterised by strongly defined majority and minority positions. Two debates were singled out for this investigation: the economic policy debate at the Conservative Party Conference and the defence debate at the Labour Party Conference. In the former, there was a clear consensus in favour of right-wing, Thatcherite policies; in the latter, there was an overwhelming sentiment in favour of unilateral nuclear disarmament. It was found that most of the applauded statements were couched in one or more of the seven rhetorical devices identified by Heritage and Greatbatch (76.3 per cent of the pro-majority statements and 90 per cent of the pro-minority statements). Overall, the pro-majority position was applauded nine times as often as the minority one. While Heritage and Greatbatch acknowledge that applause is clearly related to certain types of speech content, they argue that the chance of that content being applauded is greatly increased if it is expressed in an appropriate rhetorical device.

Applause can also be affected by the speaker's intonation, timing and gesture. The manner in which a message is delivered may strongly complement and reinforce its rhetorical structure, providing further information to the audience that this is a point where applause would be appropriate (Atkinson, 1984a). A sample of speeches formulated in one of the seven basic rhetorical devices was coded in terms of the degree of 'stress' (Heritage and Greatbatch, 1986). Stress was evaluated in terms of whether the speaker was gazing at the audience at or near the completion point of the message, whether the message was delivered more loudly than surrounding speech passages, or with greater pitch or stress variation, or with some kind of rhythmic shift or accompanied by the use of gestures. In the absence of any of these features, the message was coded 'no stress'. One of these features was treated as sufficient for a coding of 'intermediate stress', while the presence of two or more features was categorised as 'full stress'. Over one half of the 'fully stressed' messages were applauded, only one quarter of the 'intermediate' messages attracted a similar response and this figure fell to less than 5 per cent in the case of the 'unstressed' messages. Thus, the manner in which a message is delivered would seem to play a substantial role in influencing audience applause.

From a comprehensive sampling of political speeches, Heritage and Greatbatch provided impressive support in favour of the role of rhetorical devices in inviting applause. Their analysis of the effects of vocal and nonverbal stress also show that delivery is important. But the demands of sampling a large number of speeches means that it is not possible to provide a detailed examination of the way in which vocal and nonverbal features of stress are organised in relation to speech. The alternative is to adopt a case-study approach. This forms the basis of the study to be reported in this chapter, in which three speeches were examined in considerable detail.

Hypotheses of the study

In the analysis of these three speeches, a number of hypotheses were tested concerning the role of hand gestures. These hypotheses were based both on the author's previous research on body movement and speech (Bull and Connelly, 1985) and on Atkinson's theory of rhetoric:

1   a prime function of hand gestures will be to pick out important ele-
    ments of the politician's speech. This was tested by investigating what
    proportion of a speaker's hand gestures were synchronised with vocal
    stress.
2   hand gestures may also serve to pick out phonemic clauses (often
    referred to as 'tone groups'). This was assessed by investigating to what
    extent hand gestures coincide with the duration of tone groups.
3   hand gestures will also be related to rhetorical devices used to invite
    applause.

Method

Speeches

A video-recording was made by the author of a Labour Party rally which
took place in St George's Hall, Bradford, West Yorkshire, on 28 May
during the General Election campaign of 1983. Three speeches were
selected for analysis; the speakers and the duration of their speeches are
listed below:

Martin Leathley	5 minutes 8 seconds
(Labour Party Parliamentary	
candidate, Shipley, West Yorkshire)	
Arthur Scargill	22 minutes 48 seconds
(President, National Union	
of Mineworkers)	
Pat Wall	4 minutes 37 seconds
(Labour Party Parliamentary candidate,	
Bradford North, West Yorkshire)	

At the time of the General Election, Martin Leathley was a schoolteacher
and a local councillor, contesting a safe Conservative seat with a substantial
majority. Pat Wall had something of a national reputation both as a public
speaker and as a consequence of his association with Militant Tendency, a
left-wing group in the Labour Party. Neither of these candidates were
returned to Parliament in the 1983 General Election. The third speech
selected for analysis was by Arthur Scargill, President of the National Union
of Mineworkers. Scargill first came to national prominence as a result of his
involvement in the miners' strikes of 1973 and 1974; he also has a reputation as a highly effective public speaker.

Thus, the three speeches could be seen as representing a continuum:
one speaker (Scargill) a national figure with a good reputation for oratory;
the second speaker (Wall) less well known, but with something of a
national reputation; the third speaker (Leathley) a local councillor
unknown in the national political context. All the speakers delivered their

speeches from the rostrum, and all could be seen to be speaking from notes.

Apparatus

A portable colour video camera mounted on a tripod was used to record the political rally.

Procedure

The political rally was video-recorded with the full consent of the meeting organisers. Care was taken to provide a continuous head and shoulders picture of each speaker so that his hand gestures were always in view of the camera.

Intonation (in terms of both vocal stress and tone group boundaries) was transcribed by a trained phonetician. A reliability check carried out independently by another phonetician on the speech by Pat Wall showed 85 per cent agreement on both vocal stress and tone group boundaries.

Hand gesture was transcribed by the author using the Body Movement Scoring System (Bull, 1987). This system is intended to enable the investigator to describe in detail the visual appearance of body movements. It takes as its basic unit of analysis the single movement act; hence, the system describes gestures as a series of movements rather than as a series of positions. A basic distinction is made between those movements which involve contact with an object or part of the body and those which do not involve any such contact. Body-contact and object-contact acts are described in terms of the way the contact is made (e.g. touching, grasping, scratching), the part of the body which makes the contact and the object or part of the body with which the contact is made. Non-contact acts are described in terms of the various movements which are possible from each of the major joints of the body – in the case of hand/arm movements, from the shoulder, elbow, wrist and finger joints. For example, the forearm can flex, extend, rotate inwards and rotate outwards; these movements can also be performed in combination with one another. Reliability for scoring hand/arm movements was satisfactorily demonstrated in a previous study (Bull and Connelly, 1985) with a k coefficient of 0.81 (Cohen, 1960) between two independent scorers.

A content analysis was carried out on the speech by Arthur Scargill to identify the seven rhetorical devices described by Heritage and Greatbatch as effective in inviting applause. In addition, the speech was classified into different speech acts, following principles for content analysis devised by Thomas *et al.* (1982) in a system called Conversation Exchange Analysis (CEA). In this system, speech is segmented into separate acts, each of which can be seen to represent a single thought or idea. Acts can be further classified along three dimensions: activity, type and focus. The *type* dimension was used in this study to categorise the type of information conveyed in the speech by Arthur Scargill; the categories employed were based on CEA and on the work of Atkinson, Heritage and Greatbatch. A high degree of reliability for CEA has been demonstrated in a previous study: the division into speech acts was achieved with just 3.93 per cent inter-observer disagreement, while a k coefficient (Cohen, 1960) of 0.957 was obtained for the type dimension (Thomas *et al.*, 1982).

The type categories are listed individually below; since a speech act may serve more than one communicative function, these categories were sometimes used in combination with one another:

External attack:	criticisms of other political parties and other external groups.
Internal attack:	criticisms of individuals or factions within the speaker's own party.
Implicit attack:	a statement which can be construed as an attack on another individual or group, although the attack is not explicit.
Positive advocacy:	advocates particular political policies.
Commendation:	commends particular individuals or groups.
Naming:	names particular individuals or groups without commendation.
Address:	addresses the chairman or the audience.
Metastatement:	statements which comment on the nature of the speech.
Personal experience:	refers to past and present experiences of the speaker.
Reply to heckling:	speaker responds to heckling from the audience.

Results and discussion

Hand gesture and intonation

The speeches by Martin Leathley and Pat Wall were transcribed to investigate the relationship between hand gestures and intonation. The results of these analyses are shown in Table 2.1.

In this table, a hand gesture is defined as a single act; this might involve movement from more than one point of articulation, e.g. from the shoulder and the elbow. Where a movement is repeated on a number of occasions, e.g. flexes and extends forearm (five times), this would be scored as five movements. Bilateral gestures are scored as two separate movements; hence, it is possible for two gestures to be related to a single incidence of vocal stress.

The results for both speakers showed that a substantial proportion of their hand gestures were directly related to intonation, in the sense that the movement was timed to occur at the same time as the vocal stress. But not

Table 2.1 Relationship between hand gesture and vocal stress

	Pat Wall (incidences (%))	*Martin Leathley (incidences (%))*
Vocal stresses accompanied by gesture	74 (N= 293)	36 (N= 354)
Gestures directly related to stress	65.5 (N= 362)	49 (N= 266)
Gestures indirectly related to stress:		
(a) Preparatory gestures	3	2
(b) Terminating gestures	9	1
(c) Misplaced gestures in a repeated sequence	10	7
Gestures unrelated to stress	10.5	40
Unscoreable because speech is lost in applause	2	1

all the remaining hand gestures can be dismissed as unrelated to vocal stress. Some can be regarded as preparatory movements, in which, for example, the speaker flexes his forearm before bringing it down to coincide with the stressed word. Other movements can be seen to terminate a clause, where the speaker extends his forearm after a sequence of stress-related movements. A third category consists of movements in a repeated sequence of gestures, where the apex of the movement does not always coincide with the vocal stress; for example, in a sequence of five repeated forearm movements, two may not actually coincide directly with the vocal stress. If gestures indirectly related to vocal stress are included in the total of stress-related movements, the proportion rises to 87.5 per cent for Pat Wall and 59 per cent for Martin Leathley.

In fact, only 10.5 per cent of Pat Wall's hand gestures could be said to be totally unrelated to vocal stress; these comprised mainly contact hand gestures in which Pat Wall shifted his hand on the rostrum (10 per cent of all hand movements). He used only two non-contact gestures (out of 283) which appeared to have no relation to vocal stress: in one of these movements, Pat Wall raised his hands to quell the applause from his audience; the other movement appeared to be a mistake, in which he pointed without saying something, but as if he was going to speak. In the case of Martin Leathley, 40 per cent of his hand gestures appeared to be totally unrelated to vocal stress. Again, these were mainly contact gestures, in which Martin Leathley shifted his hand on the rostrum (30 per cent of all hand movements); but there were also a number of non-contact movements (N= 25, 9 per cent of all hand movements), as well as a couple of movements in which Leathley turned over his notes. However, the majority of his non-contact gestures were related directly or indirectly to vocal stress (83 per cent of all non-contact hand gestures; N= 145).

In both speeches, hand gestures were most commonly related to vocal stress through what were termed 'multiple apex peaks' (Bull and Connelly,

1985). These take the form of a repeated movement, such as flexing and extending the forearm, which can be repeated continuously for two or more occasions, often coinciding with the vocally stressed words. In Pat Wall's speech, 56 of these multiple apex peaks were observed, *none* of which crossed tone group boundaries, i.e. the total length of the gestural sequence occurred within the duration of the tone group. Similarly, in Martin Leathley's speech, there were 15 multiple apex peaks, again none of which violated tone group boundaries. Hence, these multiple apex peaks seemed to serve a dual function: they both picked out stressed words, and demarcated the extent of the tone group. Overall, the majority of hand movements of both speakers were related directly or indirectly to vocal stress; hand movements not related to stress typically took the form of contact movements, where the speaker adjusted the position of his hand on the rostrum.

Hand gestures and the control of applause

From the content analysis of the speech by Arthur Scargill, 25 rhetorical devices were identified. Applause was categorised into collective and isolated applause: collective applause referred to clapping from a substantial proportion of the audience, whereas isolated applause referred to claps from just one or two people. The importance of this distinction is that if rhetorical devices are effective applause invitations, then they should be associated with collective rather than isolated applause. The results showed two-thirds of the instances of collective applause were associated with rhetorical devices (22/33), whereas only two instances of isolated applause (out of a total of 18) occurred in response to rhetorical devices. Thus, rhetorical devices were much more likely to be associated with collective than isolated applause.

Nevertheless, it could still be argued that audience applause occurs in response to the content rather than the form of political speeches. Thus, a further content analysis was carried out of the types of statement used by Arthur Scargill in his speech. The results for collective applause are shown in Table 2.2, for isolated applause in Table 2.3.

These results clearly showed the value of rhetorical devices in inviting applause. A large proportion of Arthur Scargill's speech was made up of external attacks (58 per cent of the total number of speech acts): 86 per cent of rhetorically formatted external attacks received collective applause, in contrast to only 13 per cent of non-rhetorically formatted external attacks. All of the other types of speech act which received collective applause were applauded more when presented in rhetorical devices, with the exception only of replies to heckling (of which there were only three examples in the whole speech). In contrast, isolated applause occurred more frequently in response to speech acts which did not use rhetorical devices, again with the exception only of replies to heckling.

An analysis was then conducted of Arthur Scargill's use of hand gestures

Table 2.2 Collective applause in Arthur Scargill's speech in relation to speech content

Content category	Rhetorical devices*	
	Present	*Absent*
External attacks	86 (7)	13 (91)
Positive advocacy	100 (2)	0 (4)
Positive advocacy/external attack	100 (6)	33 (3)
Implicit attack	67 (3)	0 (6)
Commendation	100 (2)	50 (2)
Internal attack/commendation	100 (1)	(0)
Reply to heckling	0 (1)	100 (2)
Naming	(0)	0 (2)
Address	(0)	0 (2)
Metastatement	(0)	0 (1)
Personal experience	(0)	0 (34)

Note
*The figures given are the percentages of speech acts in each category which received collective applause. Figures in brackets represent the total number of observations in each speech category.

Table 2.3 Isolated applause in Arthur Scargill's speech in relation to speech content

Content category	Rhetorical devices*	
	Present	*Absent*
External attacks	14 (7)	15 (91)
Positive advocacy	0 (2)	25 (4)
Positive advocacy/external attack	0 (6)	0 (3)
Implicit attack	0 (3)	0 (6)
Commendation	0 (2)	50 (2)
Internal attack/commendation	0 (1)	(0)
Reply to heckling	100 (1)	0 (2)
Naming	(0)	100 (2)
Address	(0)	0 (2)
Metastatement	(0)	0 (1)
Personal experience	(0)	0 (34)

Note
*The figures given are the percentages of speech acts in each category which received isolated applause. Figures in brackets represent the total number of observations in each speech category.

in relation to rhetorical devices. The three most commonly occurring devices in the speech were contrasts, three-part lists and headline–punch-lines. (NB It should be noted that rhetorical devices are sometimes used in combination with one another; for example, the second part of a contrast might take the form of a three-part list. In the preceding analysis of rhetorical devices in relation to applause, such a combination would be regarded as part of one rhetorical device; but in the ensuing analysis of gesture, this would be treated as an example of both a contrast and a three-part list. Hence, the number of examples in the gesture analysis comes to more than the 25 rhetorical devices discussed above, p. 38).

Of the ten contrasts which occurred during the course of the speech, eight were followed by collective applause, one by isolated applause. In the case of contrasts, Arthur Scargill made use of a particularly interesting device, that of ambidextrous gesturing. In eight out of the ten contrasts, he illustrated one part of the contrast with one hand, the other part of the contrast with the other hand. However, this should not be seen as a device which is simply confined to illustrating contrasts. Switching from one hand to the other is a characteristic feature of Arthur Scargill's speaking style; in fact, in this speech it occurred on no less than 80 occasions. Contrasts typically involve a transition from one syntactic clause to another (eight out of the ten contrasts in this speech), and an examination of the speech as a whole showed that 62.5 per cent of the hand switches occurred at clause boundaries. The other incidences of hand switching also occurred at syntactic boundaries: at the end of a prepositional phrase (12.5%), at a subject/verb boundary (5%), at a verb/object boundary (5%) and to separate items in a list (14%). Thus, it seems that the use of ambidextrous gesturing to illustrate contrasts is merely a special example of the way in which Arthur Scargill seemed to use this device to mark out syntax.

During the course of the speech, there were also nine three-part lists, six of which were followed by collective applause, one by isolated applause. The three items in a list were also marked out by carefully synchronised gestures. Where a three-part list comprised three words, each was stressed vocally and accompanied by a single hand gesture. Where a three-part list included a phrase or a clause with more than one vocal stress, then a repeated hand movement was typically employed, picking out two or more vocal stresses and terminating at the end of the list item; a new gesture would then start on the next item. Scargill typically used non-contact gestures in the form of single or multiple apex peaks to pick out words, phrases or clauses, but on one occasion he actually smacked one hand on the other on each of the stressed words in the three phrases which made up the list.

The headline–punchline device was used on seven occasions, and each time it was greeted with collective applause. On three occasions, the final part of the punchline was delivered with a gesture using both hands. Although bilateral gestures occurred frequently throughout the speech, they are only used on one other occasion in conjunction with a rhetorical device. In association with a punchline, they seemed to have the effect of bringing the message to a climax, highlighting that here was an appropriate point for the audience to applaud.

If Scargill's hand gesture were closely intertwined with rhetorical devices which invite applause, they also played a significant role in the way in which he attempted to control applause. Where incidences of isolated applause occurred ($N = 18$), he consistently talked through them; on four of these occasions, he also held up his hand to suppress the applause, either with a hand or a finger outstretched. Collective applause was often interruptive, the audience starting to applaud before Scargill had finished his sentence (21/33 instances of collective applause). Nevertheless, he still continued to speak into the applause, even though on a number of occasions he became completely inaudible (9/21 interruptions). In every instance of collective applause, he started speaking before the applause ended (except of course in the final ovation!). Typically, he would resume speaking as the applause tailed off (18/33 instances), but sometimes he attempted to interrupt after a brief pause (11/33), and on three occasions he simply continued talking. On eight occasions, he gestured to stop the applause, typically with hand/hands outstretched.

Further analysis was carried out of the points in the speech where these 12 applause-suppressing gestures occurred. On four occasions, they occurred at the end of a long burst of collective applause, presumably because Arthur Scargill simply wished to continue with his speech. However, on the other eight occasions, these gestures occurred just before a point in the speech where applause might be considered more appropriate, typically when Arthur Scargill was about to invite applause through one of the rhetorical devices discussed above (p. 40).

Thus, Arthur Scargill created the impression of overwhelming popularity, continually struggling to make his message audible, both by speaking into the applause and by using gestures to restrain it. At the same time, he whipped up applause by using rhetorical devices, the structure of which was articulated by the carefully synchronised use of hand gestures. These gestures singled out pairs of statements in a contrast, picked out the items in three-part lists and highlighted climaxes. In fact, Arthur Scargill actually seemed to conduct his audience: his gestures not only accompanied rhetorical devices which invited applause, but also curtailed the applause once it had been invited – even to the extent of indicating points at which applause was or was not appropriate.

Conclusions

The purpose of this study was to investigate the functions of gesture in political speeches. The results showed that gesture was related both to intonation (in terms of vocal stress and tone group boundaries). It was also shown how hand gesture was used both to articulate the structure of rhetorical devices and to control applause. As such, this study added to the research literature demonstrating a close relationship between body movement and speech.

3   Do audiences applaud only 'claptrap' in political speeches?

Introduction

The previous chapter introduced Atkinson's theory of how rhetorical devices are used to invite applause. This analysis proved invaluable in helping to understand how hand gestures can both articulate the structure of applause invitations, as well as refuse applause when it occurs at inappropriate points during a speech. Atkinson's theory has, in fact, proved remarkably influential and provides some compelling insights into the stage management of political speeches. As such, it has become widely accepted, although it has always been open to criticism on a number of counts. Nevertheless, since the time when the original research was conducted in the 1980s, the theory has never been subjected to any systematic re-evaluation. In this and the next two chapters, a series of studies are presented which were intended to do precisely this – to test the validity of Atkinson's theory of rhetoric.

When people are introduced to this theory, they often object that it is the actual political content of a speech which audiences applaud, not just rhetorical devices. This issue of content has already been discussed in the previous chapter, but needs further consideration here. Atkinson (1984a), it should be noted, pointed out that there are a restricted number of messages which can be regarded as applaudable: favourable references to individual people, favourable references to 'us', unfavourable references to 'them'. In one sample, Atkinson (1984a, p. 44) found that these three categories accounted for 95 per cent of the bursts of applause at British political party conferences. Heritage and Greatbatch (1986) also performed a number of content analyses, and similarly found that applause was reserved for a relatively narrow range of message types. They further proposed that the likelihood of these message types receiving applause was greatly increased by rhetorical devices. When negative attacks (criticisms of policies and/or their proponents) were rhetorically formatted, they were about twice as likely to evoke applause as when not rhetorically formatted; the comparable analysis for positive assertions showed that they were between three and five times more effective when rhetorically formatted. Heritage and Greatbatch concluded that, although applause is clearly related to certain types of speech content, it is far more likely to occur if a statement is expressed using an appropriate rhetorical device.

Why do audiences reserve their applause for such a restricted range of message types? Heritage and Greatbatch (1986, p. 145) propose that audiences simply applaud statements with which they agree. However, it is by no means self-evident that audiences applaud only to express agreement. People may applaud at political meetings to show solidarity with the party and the speaker, or even just to be polite (for example, simply because the speaker is clearly inviting applause).

A further problem is that not all political messages are of comparable importance. An attack on the opposition may be much more likely to receive applause if it is couched in clever and witty language; indeed, it may fall quite flat if it does *not* make use of effective rhetorical devices. Conversely, a policy statement with which the audience passionately agrees may be applauded, however it is formatted, or even if it is not expressed in a rhetorical device at all. Indeed, the mere mention of one or two words associated with a highly emotive issue might be enough to draw a round of applause. Heritage and Greatbatch's categories of 'negative attacks' and 'positive assertions' are arguably far too general and bland to pick up subtle and potentially highly important differences in content between different political messages.

If the role of speech content is one major issue in evaluating Atkinson's theory of rhetoric, a second is that of synchronisation. Atkinson observes that applause is typically very finely synchronised with speech: in the vast majority of cases, it tends to start either just before or immediately after the speaker reaches a completion point, such as the end of a sentence (Atkinson 1984a, p. 33). He further reports that it reaches its maximum volume very quickly, typically after the first second (Atkinson 1984a, p. 24), again suggesting that the audience are able to predict the appropriate place to applaud. Heritage and Greatbatch (1986, p. 112) found that most applause was typically initiated within 0.3 seconds of the precipitating item.

According to Atkinson, it would be quite impossible for audiences to synchronise their applause unless the speaker provides clear signals as to appropriate applause points:

> If displays of approval are seldom delayed for more than a split second after a completion point, and frequently start just before one is reached, it means that speakers must be supplying their audiences with advance notice as to precisely when they should start clapping. Otherwise, it is quite impossible to see how anyone would ever be able to respond so promptly...
>
> (Atkinson, 1984a, pp. 33–34)

The importance of rhetorical devices is, of course, that they provide precisely his kind of advance notice. Indeed, Atkinson (1984a, p. 18) argued that the use of rhetorical devices is in the interest of the audience, because it helps them applaud together rather than risk exposure to public ridicule and humiliation by applauding in isolation.

But if it is so difficult for audiences to co-ordinate their behaviour, some explanation is also required of how audience applause is organised in response to statements which are not couched in rhetorical devices. Although Heritage and Greatbatch note that just over two-thirds of the collective applause in their 476 speeches was associated with seven rhetorical devices, no account is provided of how audience applause occurred in response to the other (slightly less than one-third) of applauded statements. To effectively test the validity of Atkinson's theory of rhetoric, an analysis is also required of non-rhetorically formatted statements which receive applause. This was the purpose of the study to be presented in this chapter (Bull, 2000a).

Thus, a detailed analysis is reported of three political speeches delivered by the leaders of the principal British political parties (Conservative, Labour and Liberal Democrat) to their respective autumn conferences in 1996. The particular focus of the study was on statements which received collective applause in the absence of rhetorical devices. There were two principal forms of analysis:

1   completion points. The principal evidence cited in support of the close synchronisation between speech and applause is that collective applause typically occurs at or near a completion point. Hence, an analysis was conducted of the extent to which collective applause in response to non-rhetorically formatted statements occurs at completion points.
2   speech content. Given the concerns expressed above regarding the role of speech content in relation to applause, a detailed content analysis was conducted of each of the statements which received collective applause in the absence of rhetorical devices.

Method

Speeches

Three speeches delivered by the leaders of the principal British political parties (Conservative, Labour and Liberal Democrat) to their respective autumn conferences in 1996 were analysed:

11 October   John Major (51 minutes 8 seconds)
1 October   Tony Blair (65 minutes 37 seconds)
24 September   Paddy Ashdown (57 minutes 30 seconds)

Apparatus

Transcripts of the speeches were obtained from the respective party head-quarters, put through an optical scanner and converted into a word process-ing package. Each speech was then checked for accuracy against the video-recording, and amended accordingly.

Procedure

Incidences of applause were marked on each transcript. Following Atkinson's (1984a) notation, the use of small and large crosses was used to represent the changing intensity of applause (e.g. xxxxXXXX), a dash on either side of a cross represented an isolated clap (-x-) and several in a row represented hesitant or spasmodic clapping (-x-x-x-).

Statements were identified which received collective applause, but did not employ any of the seven rhetorical devices reported by Atkinson, Heritage and Greatbatch. These statements were analysed in terms of both content and whether collective applause occurred at completion points.

Results

Synchronisation

Over the three speeches, 15 instances were identified of statements which received collective applause but did not use any of the seven rhetorical devices analysed by Atkinson, Heritage and Greatbatch. These 15 statements were divided into three categories: applause at or near a possible completion point; applause not at a possible completion point; speaker interrupted by applause.

In 40 per cent of these statements, the applause did not occur at a possible completion point. An example is given below from the speech by Tony Blair:

> We will put a roof over the heads of the homeless
> by releasing those capital receipts from the sale of council
> houses and let homes be built for our people
>   xxxxxxxxxxxxxxxxxxxxxxxxxxxxxxxxxxxxXXXXXXXXXXXX
>   (CHEERS)   (3 seconds)

In this instance, the applause starts a clear three seconds before Blair actually reaches the completion point. In all six examples, there is a mean two-and-a-half seconds of applause before Blair reaches his completion point. On every occasion, the applause only reaches its full intensity after the completion point has been reached, a considerably longer duration than the one second observed by Atkinson (1984a, p. 24).

In a further 20 per cent of these statements, Tony Blair is actually interrupted by the applause (these examples are presented below, pp. 50–51). Although it must be acknowledged that these three interruptions occur at what the audience might have mistakenly assumed were completion points, nevertheless the fact that they are interruptive still shows a lack of synchrony between speaker and audience. In only 40 per cent of the statements did applause occur at or near a possible completion point.

Thus, the majority of these 15 incidents of collective applause (60 per cent) showed a lack of synchrony between speaker and audience. This is quite contrary to the pattern observed by Atkinson in response to statements where applause is invited through rhetorical devices.

Content analysis

The content analysis of all 15 statements showed a further distinguishing feature: in every instance, they constituted a statement of policy. This contrasted markedly with the pattern reported by Atkinson (1984a) in relation to rhetorically formatted statements, where 95 per cent of his sample constituted favourable references to specific individuals, favourable references to 'us' and unfavourable references to 'them'. Heritage and Greatbatch (1986) do include advocacy of particular policy positions as one type of applaudable message; however, they comprised only 9.3 per cent of the rhetorical formatted statements which received applause. Each of the 15 non-rhetorically formatted statements is discussed in detail below.

Applause at or near completion point

John Major

1   Many people in our country build up savings long after they've enough for their own needs. And one reason they do that is to pass on the fruits of their life's work to their children and to their grandchildren. This is a powerful, human emotion so over time our next target is to remove the burden of inheritance tax entirely.

xxxxxxXXXXXXXXX

Inheritance tax has traditionally been unpopular with certain sections of the Conservative Party; the proposal to abolish it completely is a radical one, given that inheritance tax in Britain has existed in its modern form since its introduction by the government of Lord North in 1779!

2   ...this autumn, Stephen Dorrell will introduce a Bill to do just that giving family doctors greater freedom to develop local services in their surgeries, creating a new generation of cottage hospitals all over Britain

(1 second) xxxxxxxXXXXX

This is the one example in these 15 statements which seems to evoke a relatively lukewarm response (witness the one-second delay between the end of the statement and the applause), possibly because the statement is rather confusing. The traditional cottage hospital was a small institution without resident medical staff served by local general practitioners. Many such hospitals were closed down as a result of changes initiated by the Conservative Government (1979–1997); in this speech, Major held them up as an object of praise.

Tony Blair

3 And what are they? They're merely the due claim of civilisation. A statutory minimum wage. Like every other industrial country the world over we will have one under a Labour government in Britain

xxxxxXXXXXXX

The statutory minimum wage was in the Labour manifesto throughout the 1980s, and the 1992 Manifesto proposed a figure of £3.40. The policy commitment was renewed in the 1997 Manifesto, although no specific figure was mentioned. Low pay is a traditional concern of the Labour Party and especially its traditional supporters, the trade unions. The policy of a minimum wage was widely regarded as having been driven by the unions, effectively as a quid pro quo for their continued support of what has become known as the 'modernisation' of the Labour Party.

4 ...and if a majority of the workforce want it for the union to represent those people
xxxxXXXXXXX

On 25 January, 1984, 7,000 workers at the high security government communications centre GCHQ (General Communication Head Quarters) had been banned by the Conservative Government 'in the interests of national security' from belonging to a trade union or taking industrial action. This decision was immensely unpopular with the trade union movement and with the Labour Party. Blair's statement is an important re-affirmation of the Labour Party's commitment to the principle of the right to union representation.

5 You saw in that film a review of the year the day when John Major and I visited Dunblane together. It was a searing and chilling and dreadful day. Conservative MPs complain that our response has been 'emotional' – well, if they had been in that gym, if they had talked to those parents, sitting on those tiny chairs where once their children sat, they would have been emotional too. I believe that we should ban the private ownership and possession of handguns.
xxxxXXXXXXXXXXXXXXXXX

This particular policy proposal has to be understood in the context of the massacre at a school in Dunblane, Scotland (13 March, 1996), where 16 children and their teacher were shot dead by a lone gunman. Following this event, there was widespread support amongst both the general public and the Labour Party for a blanket ban on the private ownership of handguns. This policy proposal was enacted by the Labour Government in the Firearms Amendment Act, which received the Royal Assent on 27 November, 1997.

6   A directly elected authority for London our capital city
                                    CHEERSxxxxxxxxxxxx
         XXXXXXXXXXXXXXXXX

During the early 1980s, the Labour-controlled Greater London Council (GLC), led by Ken Livingstone, had been a focal point of opposition against the government of Margaret Thatcher; she eventually had it abolished in 1986. Hence, the commitment to the restoration of a directly elected authority for London was immensely popular with the Labour Party.

Applause not at completion point

Tony Blair

7   And we will ask that Nolan Committee to investigate political funding
    and we will legislate so as to make the Tories tell us where the money
    comes from for these negative and deceitful advertising campaigns
                                    xxxxxxxxxxxxxxxxxxxxXXX
         XXXXXX
         (2 seconds)

The Nolan Committee was set up by John Major (25 October 1994) to 'examine the current concern about standards of conduct of all holders of public office'. Tony Blair's criticism of 'negative and deceitful advertising campaigns' can be understood in the context of a Conservative Party poster campaign, which showed an adulterated picture of him with red, demonic-looking eyes. A complaint against this poster was upheld by the Advertising Standards Authority in 1996.

8   And we'll give Britain the modern integrated transport network, built
    in partnership between public and private finance and restoring a uni-
    fied system of railways with a publicly owned,
    publicly accountable British Rail at its core
                 xxxxxxxxxxxxxxxxxxxxxxxxxXXXXXXXXXX
         (2 seconds)

The privatisation of parts of British Rail was one of the last of a series of privatisations by the Conservative Government. It was deeply unpopular with the Labour movement, hence the importance of Blair's commitment to a 'publicly owned publicly accountable British Rail'.

9   We will put a roof over the heads of the homeless by releasing those capital receipts from the sale of council houses and let homes be built
          xxxxxxxxxxxxxxxxxxxxx

    for our people
          xxxxxxxxxxxXXXXXXXXX
          (CHEERS)   (3 seconds)

Council tenants had been given the right to buy council houses where they lived by the Housing Act of 1980. But receipts from these sales were kept locked up in reserve funds, hence the Conservative Government was widely criticised for failing in its duty to provide homes for the homeless. Labour's policy proposal has the advantage of proposing a remedy for homelessness (a traditional concern of the Labour Party) without necessitating any increases in direct taxation.

10   The review that we have announced will be set up under a Labour Government on the terms we have announced to see how we fulfil that duty for modern times and it will review also the whole issue of community care where those elderly people have to sell their homes to pay the costs of nursing care.
          xxxxxxxxxxxxxxxxxxxxxxxxxxxxXXXXXXXXXXXX
          (3 seconds)

The implementation of the Community Care Act of 1990 led to a tightening of financial control by central government over local authority provision for the elderly. One key consequence was that some elderly people (who previously would have received long-term hospital care through the National Health Service) ended up having to sell their homes to pay the costs of nursing care – a consequence for which the Conservative Government was widely criticised.

11   So local people decide how to run local services. A Parliament for Scotland an Assembly for Wales legislated for in the first year of a Labour
          xxxxxxxxxxxxxxxxxxxxxx xxxx

    Government
          xxxxxxxxXXXXXXXXX
          (3 seconds)

Under the Labour Government of Jim Callaghan (1976–1979), referenda to introduce devolution in both Scotland and Wales failed to secure the necessary majority of the popular vote. The Labour Party has traditionally drawn widespread support in both Scotland and Wales, hence the increasing success of both the Scottish Nationalist Party and Plaid Cymru (the Welsh nationalist party) has presented it with a serious electoral threat. This policy of devolution was widely believed to be a means of countering that danger to the Labour Party.

12 Ending the greatest symbol of privilege in any democracy in the world by ensuring that hereditary peers aren't voting in the House of Lords

xxxxxxxxxxxxxxxxxxxxXXXX

XXXXXXXXX

(2 seconds)   (CHEERS)

The House of Lords has traditionally been a target of Labour Party conferences, most famously in 1980 when Tony Benn made what became known as his Thousand Peers Speech, in which he proposed that a Labour government would need to create a thousand peers to abolish the House of Lords in its entirety. Blair's more limited policy was to abolish the voting rights of hereditary peers who have a right to vote in the Upper Chamber only as a consequence of birth.

Interruptive applause

13 We will be part of the European Social Chapter as every other government Tory or Labour is in the rest of Europe. And there will be a right for any individual to join a trade union and if...

xxxxXXXXXXXXXX

The importance of the right to join a trade union has already been discussed above (p. 47). Here, the audience interrupt Tony Blair to express their support for that principle.

14 Tomorrow David Blunkett will set out how to ensure that every primary school child leaves school able to read to the adequate standard

xxxxxXXXXXXX

This example is considered interruptive because Tony Blair was still gesturing after the phrase '...to the adequate standard', suggesting that he intended to continue speaking, but then gives way until after the applause. Literacy targets had been recommended as part of a report produced in 1994 by the Labour Party's Commission of Social Justice.

15 I vow that we will have cut the numbers of long-term unemployed and cut by over a half the number of young people unemployed.   I vow...   I vow

xxxxxxxxxxxxxxxxxxxxxxxx

Combating unemployment has always been a traditional Labour value. The audience interrupts Tony Blair to express their support for this policy commitment.

In the analysis above, detailed consideration has been given to the policy issues enshrined in each of the 15 non-rhetorically formatted statements. With the possible exception only of John Major's statement about cottage hospitals, all these examples of applause can be seen as occurring in response to substantive policy issues, which were of central concern to the respective party conferences.

Discussion

The major implication of this analysis is that neither rhetorical devices nor synchronisation between speaker and audience are necessary for collective applause to occur in political speeches. Synchronisation plays a central role in Atkinson's theory of rhetoric, the problems of synchronisation underlie the need for speakers to use rhetorical devices. But as has been shown above (pp. 45–51), applause is often not synchronised with speech, indeed it may be quite disruptive. So how does the audience succeed in producing this kind of collective applause?

Clayman (1993) proposed that there are two principal ways in which an audience can co-ordinate its behaviour. There is what he calls 'independent decision-making', whereby individual audience members may act independently of one another yet still manage to co-ordinate their actions – through, for example, applause in response to the rhetorical devices identified by Atkinson, Heritage and Greatbatch. There is also what Clayman calls mutual monitoring, whereby individual response decisions may be guided (at least in part) by reference to the behaviour of other audience members. Thus, once it becomes evident that some people are starting to applaud, this drastically alters the expected payoff for other audience members: fear of responding in isolation will be reduced, while not applauding can increasingly become an isolating experience. Clayman points out that responses organised primarily by independent decision-making should begin with a 'burst' that quickly builds to maximum intensity, as many audience members begin to respond together. Mutual monitoring in contrast should result in a 'staggered' onset as the initial reactions of a few audience members prompt others to respond.

What is interesting about Clayman's observations is that staggered onset was typical of much of the applause to the non-rhetorically formatted statements analysed here, especially the six examples not occurring at a completion point. It should be noted that Clayman's analysis was based on booing, and he concluded (1993, p. 124) that 'clappers usually act promptly and independently, while booers tend to wait until other audience behaviours are underway'. The staggered onset of clapping observed in this study suggests that mutual monitoring may also be involved in applause. Given that

all the 15 non-rhetorically formatted statements in this study involved substantive policy issues, applause may have been initiated by some members of
the audience specifically in response to the content of the speech, its take-up
by other members of the audience being facilitated by mutual monitoring.

From the occurrence of staggered clapping, it is proposed that there are
not one but two processes whereby applause occurs in political speeches.
There is the process analysed by Atkinson, in which the speaker indicates
through the rhetorical structure when and where applause is appropriate.
Since this process is effectively initiated by the speaker, it might be referred
to as 'invited applause'. There is also the process analysed here, whereby
applause in the absence of rhetorical devices may be seen as a direct response
to specific aspects of speech content. Since this process appears to be initiated by the audience (or certain sectors of it), it might be referred to as
'uninvited applause'. Whereas invited applause is typically closely synchronised with speech, this is not necessarily the case with uninvited applause,
which can occur through the process of mutual monitoring described by
Clayman.

The proposal that there are two principal modes of applause generation
has a number of interesting implications with regard to Atkinson's theory of
rhetoric. One implication is that Atkinson has overestimated the importance of synchronisation. He argues that rhetorical devices assist the audience
to behave in a co-ordinated fashion rather than risk exposure to public
ridicule through solitary applause. This seems to ignore the possibility that
political activists may be willing to take such risks to endorse publicly a
policy or cause for which they wish to attract wider support. Whereas
invited applause may be closely synchronised with speech, this would not
appear to be the case for uninvited applause.

Another implication concerns the role of speech content. The most frequently voiced criticism of Atkinson, Heritage and Greatbatch is that they
underestimate the role of speech content – that is to say, people applaud
because they agree with what is being said, irrespective of the role of
presentation. Heritage and Greatbatch reject this criticism, arguing that a
message with applaudable content is much more likely to be applauded if it
is presented using rhetorical devices. The problem with this argument is
that there may be certain political statements which are so popular with the
audience that they will be applauded irrespective of rhetorical devices. In
this study, Tony Blair's policy statement in favour of 'A directly elected
authority for London our capital city' earns not only collective applause but
cheers. Again, there is a similar response to Tony Blair's statement, 'I believe
we should ban the private ownership and possession of handguns.' Neither
of these statements make use of the rhetorical devices identified by Atkinson, Heritage and Greatbatch, yet they are greeted with rapturous applause;
these policies would appear to be so popular that they would have been
applauded irrespective of how they were presented. Such statements seriously call into question Heritage and Greatbatch's argument that a message

with applaudable content is much more likely to be applauded if it is presented using rhetorical devices. It would also suggest that there is considerable justice to the criticism that Atkinson, Heritage and Greatbatch have simply underestimated the significance of speech content.

A further implication concerns the occurrence of spontaneous applause, which is regarded with considerable scepticism by Atkinson. He writes: 'Professional politicians would no doubt prefer us to think of displays of approval as wholly spontaneous responses to the depth and wisdom of their words. Unfortunately, however, the available evidence provides few grounds for so doing' (Atkinson, 1984a, pp. 45–46). In fact, uninvited applause, as identified in this chapter, does appear to be much more spontaneous than applause which is invited by the speaker, and might be seen as more reflective of genuine audience enthusiasm than speaker-invited applause. Of course, it would be naïve to assume that uninvited applause is invariably spontaneous: the existence of claques, for example, in nineteenth-century French theatre is well documented, and there is no reason why political activists should not collude in similar ways. Nevertheless, it is interesting to note that most of the uninvited applause (87 per cent) observed in this study occurred in the speech by Tony Blair, who went on to win a landslide Labour victory in the 1997 General Election; hence, the high proportion of uninvited applause to Blair's speech might simply have reflected his greater popularity at that time.

The analysis presented in this chapter was intended to address a fundamental criticism of the theory of rhetoric presented by Atkinson, and elaborated by Heritage and Greatbatch. The results suggest that the failure to analyse collective applause in relation to non-rhetorically formatted statements is an important omission from Atkinson's theory; that he underestimates the role of speech content; and is overly dismissive of the concept of spontaneous applause. In brief, applause is not invariably orchestrated by the speaker, it may also be initiated independently by the audience; it is not only 'claptrap' which is applauded in political speeches.

4   The mistiming of applause

Introduction

In the previous two chapters, a detailed description has been given of Atkinson's theory of rhetoric. In this theory, the synchronisation of speech and applause plays a central role. Atkinson observed that applause is typically very finely synchronised with speech: in the vast majority of cases, it tends to start either just before or immediately after the speaker reaches a completion point, such as the end of a sentence (Atkinson, 1984a, p. 33). Furthermore, he argued that synchronisation is in itself good evidence for the effectiveness of rhetorical devices used to invite applause. In order for the audience to time their applause with such a fine degree of precision, the speaker must in some way be providing them with advance notice of when and where to clap; this is exactly what rhetorical devices achieve.

In assessing the validity of Atkinson's theory of rhetoric, the synchronisation of speech and applause is thus of considerable interest. If incidences of asynchrony occur with considerable frequency, this would suggest at the very least that rhetorical devices do not function as effectively as Atkinson has argued, or more fundamentally, that they are not as important as Atkinson proposes. Indeed, in the study reported in the last chapter, it was found that in the absence of rhetorical devices, collective applause was typically asynchronous. This latter finding calls into question Atkinson's observation that applause is 'typically' synchronised with speech. It also highlights the need for a more systematic investigation of failures in synchronisation, referred to here as 'mismatches'. In this chapter, an analysis of mismatches is reported, based on six speeches delivered by the three leaders of the principal British political parties to their respective party conferences in 1996 and 1997. The study was intended to assess both the frequency of mismatches, and the different ways in which they may occur (Bull and Noordhuizen, 2000).

At first sight, it would appear that there are at least four ways in which lack of synchronisation may occur between speech and audience applause. One form of mismatch is isolated applause (claps from one or two people), which Heritage and Greatbatch (1986) distinguish from collective applause.

Given that isolated applause does not involve a co-ordinated response from the audience as a whole or a substantial section of it, isolated applause may be regarded as a mismatch. Another form of mismatch may occur if there is an extended silence between the speaker's utterance and audience applause. Silence suggests that the speaker was expecting applause, but for some reason the audience failed to respond appropriately, hence a failure of synchronisation between speaker and audience, just as an extended silence in conversation may also be considered 'awkward'.

Just as incidences of simultaneous speech in conversation can be regarded as a failure in turn-taking, incidences of applause simultaneous with the politician's speech may also be regarded as mismatches. Such incidences may be initiated either by the speaker or the audience. The audience may interrupt the speaker by applauding; this can be regarded as a mismatch, whether or not the speaker completes what he was saying. Conversely, the speaker may interrupt the audience's applause by starting to speak again before the applause has subsided. However, brief overlaps where the audience starts to applaud just before the speaker completes an utterance, or the speaker resumes the speech as the audience applause dies down would not be regarded as mismatches, because they suggest that either the speaker or the audience are anticipating a completion point – just as a brief overlap in conversation between one speaker and another would not be regarded as interruptive.

Interruptions of applause by the speaker, it should be noted, differ in certain important respects from the other three types of mismatch. In particular, whereas the other three categories are focussed on the audience, this is the only category which deals with the behaviour of the speaker. Furthermore, as Atkinson (1985) pointed out, a charismatic orator, by speaking into the applause, may create an impression of overwhelming popularity, struggling to be heard while at the same time inhibiting and frustrating the audience. When the speaker does finally allow the audience an opportunity to respond, they may be literally bursting to applaud, thereby the speaker is seen as receiving a 'rapturous reception'. As such, interruptions of applause by the speaker may be strategic, inciting the audience to ever greater enthusiasm. However, there is no reason to believe that *every* incidence of the speaker interrupting applause is necessarily strategic in the way which Atkinson describes. Audience applause can simply go on for so long that the speaker has to interrupt in order to continue with the speech. Thus 'speaker interrupts audience applause' is regarded as a mismatch, but one of a special kind.

The above analysis would suggest that there are at least four different ways in which mismatches between speech and applause can occur. In the light of the above discussion, the first three categories (isolated applause, delayed applause, audience interrupts speaker) were referred to as 'audience mismatches', the fourth category (speaker interrupts audience) as 'speaker mismatches'. To test the validity of these distinctions, it was decided to construct a typology of mismatches based on the detailed analysis of a number of political speeches. An investigation was then conducted of both the frequency and the manner in which mismatches occur, thereby to consider their significance for Atkinson's theory of rhetoric.

Method

Speeches

The study was based on the three speeches used in the previous study, and on a further three speeches delivered by the leaders of the three principal British political parties to their annual conferences in 1997. Thus, three of the speeches were delivered at the last party conferences before the General Election of 1997, the other three at the first party conferences after that election. The speeches from 1997 were as follows:

24 September   Paddy Ashdown (56 minutes 10 seconds)
30 September   Tony Blair (59 minutes 4 seconds)
10 October   William Hague (58 minutes 41 seconds)

The speeches from 1996 were as listed in the previous chapter.

Apparatus

Transcripts of the 1997 speeches were downloaded from each party's website and converted into a word processing package. The text was then checked for accuracy against the video-recording, and amended accordingly.

Procedure

Incidences of applause were marked on each transcript following Atkinson's (1984a) notation as described in Chapter 3. Two parts of a contrast were identified with the letters 'A' and 'B'. The three elements of a three-part list were numbered from 1 to 3. Nonverbal and vocal features of delivery were also noted if they were considered to affect the judgement of a mismatch.

A typology of mismatches was devised from detailed analysis of the 1997 speeches by Paddy Ashdown and Tony Blair. Four categories of mismatch were distinguished, and all six speeches were coded in terms of this typology. In settling on the final categories of mismatch for all six speeches, any disagreements were resolved by discussion.

To test the reliability of this coding system, two studies were conducted. The first was intended to assess the identification of mismatches, the second the coding of the four mismatch categories. In the first study, two raters independently coded all incidences of applause in the four speeches by Hague (1997), Blair (1996), Major (1996) and Ashdown (1996) as either synchronised or unsynchronised. In the second study, two raters independently coded all the mismatches from those same four speeches in terms of the four categories in the mismatch typology.

Results

Typology of mismatches

The results of the two reliability studies were as follows: identification of mismatches 0.87 (Phi coefficient); coding of the four categories in the mismatch typology 0.77 (Cohen's *k*; Cohen, 1960).

It was found that all instances of mismatches observed in all six speeches could be subsumed within the four mismatch categories. The full mismatch typology is presented below. It is based on a distinction between three different types of audience mismatch (isolated applause, delayed applause, audience applause interrupts speaker) and a fourth category of speaker mismatches (speaker interrupts audience applause). It should be noted that these four categories are not mutually exclusive: for example, isolated applause may not only be interruptive, it may also be delayed.

Audience mismatches

1 *Isolated applause.* Refers to clapping by one or two people, as distinct from collective applause by all of the audience or a substantial section of it. Isolated applause is always coded as a mismatch unless it constitutes part of a wider collective audience response (e.g. isolated claps which occur amidst collective laughter would not be regarded as a mismatch).

2 *Delayed applause.* There is a discernible silence between the end of the speaker's utterance and the onset of applause (typically of at least one second).

3 *Audience applause interrupts speaker.* Applause is regarded as interruptive if the onset occurs at a point where it is not possible to project the completion point of the speaker's utterance. If the audience start to applaud at a possible completion point, but it is clear that the speaker intended to continue, this would also be regarded as interruptive.

If the audience starts to applaud just before the speaker completes an utterance (where the completion point is projectable), this is regarded not as a mismatch but as an overlap. Brief overlaps suggest that the audience is anticipating a completion point, just as a brief overlap in conversation between one speaker and another is not typically regarded as interruptive (Roger *et al.*, 1988).

Speaker mismatches

> *Speaker interrupts audience applause.* If the speaker resumes the speech before the end of the applause, this is regarded as a mismatch, unless the audience applause is already dying down, where it would be regarded as an overlap. In the latter case, it would appear that the speaker is anticipating the end of the applause, not interrupting it.

Note: In deciding whether it is the audience who interrupt the speaker, or whether the speaker interrupts the audience, it depends who has the turn at that point. If the onset of applause occurs before the speaker has finished the utterance, then it is regarded as an interruption by the audience. But if the speaker has already relinquished the turn to audience applause, and then tries to resume the speech before the applause has died down, it is regarded as an interruption by the speaker.

Proportion of mismatches

Table 4.1 shows the frequency with which different types of applause occurred in the six speeches analysed in this study. These results show that mismatches between speech and applause are a common occurrence. Across all six speeches, audience mismatches accounted for a mean 29.2 per cent of applause events, speaker mismatches for 12.9 per cent. Only a mean 61 per cent of applause incidences were fully synchronised with speech. By far the most frequently occurring type of mismatch is applause where the audience interrupts the speaker (mean: 17.8 per cent), followed by incidences where the speaker interrupts the audience applause (mean: 12.9 per cent). Isolated applause (mean: 4.7 per cent) was the least frequently occurring type of mismatch.

It should also be noted that there is considerable variability between the speakers in the extent to which they show different types of mismatch, especially with regard to incidences where the speaker interrupts the applause (standard deviation: 18.8 per cent) and incidences where the audience interrupt the speaker (standard deviation: 10.9 per cent). Furthermore, there was considerable variability between the speakers in the extent to which mismatches occur. For example, the proportion of applause events synchronised with speech for John Major was 80.3 per cent, whereas in Paddy Ashdown's two speeches this was only 33.3 per cent and 50.9 per cent, respectively. Over all six speeches, the standard deviation was 17.3 per cent.

In evaluating the significance of mismatches for Atkinson's theory of rhetoric, it was not sufficient simply to present frequency counts for each type of mismatch. Consideration needs also to be given to the ways in which each of the four principal types of mismatch are related to rhetorical devices, and for this reason a qualitative analysis was conducted. The results are reported in the following section.

Table 4.1 Frequency of different types of applause

	Audience mismatches				Speaker mismatches (Speaker interrupts audience)	Synchronous applause	Total incidents of applause
	Isolated applause	Delayed applause	Audience interrupts speaker	Total			
1996							
Paddy Ashdown	0.6 (0)	6 (16.7)	8 (22.2)	13 (36)	16 (44.4)	12 (33.3)	36
Tony Blair	2 (2.4)	4 (4.7)	27 (31.8)	32 (37.6)	4 (4.7)	50 (58.8)	85
John Major	2 (2.6)	7 (9.2)	6 (7.9)	15 (19.7)	0 (0)	61 (80.3)	76
1997							
Paddy Ashdown	3 (5.7)	3 (5.7)	7 (13.2)	13 (24.5)	15 (28.3)	27 (50.9)	53
Tony Blair	4 (5.1)	1 (1.3)	21 (26.9)	26 (33.3)	1 (1.3)	52 (66.7)	78
William Hague	8 (12.1)	5 (7.6)	3 (4.5)	16 (24.2)	0 (0)	50 (75.8)	66
M (%)	4.7	7.5	17.8	29.2	12.9	61	
SDs	4.2	5.2	10.9	7.4	18.8	17.3	

Notes
Percentages are in parentheses.
Totals cannot be derived directly from individual scores because one incident of applause may involve more than one category of mismatch.
M = means; SD = standard deviations.

How mismatches occur

Each of the four major types of mismatch can occur for a variety of reasons:

Audience mismatches

Isolated applause
1 *Misreading of cues.* The speaker employs a rhetorical device, but some members of the audience fail to accurately predict the completion point. The following example from William Hague can be seen in Heritage and Greatbatch's terms as a puzzle-solution:

> And what about the minimum wage? Wasn't it John Prescott who said that of course a minimum wage destroys jobs; any silly fool knows that he said [PUZZLE] Well, now Margaret Beckett is planning to introduce one
> LAUGHTER-x-
> (2 seconds)

Apparently not every silly fool knows that! [SOLUTION]
                                        xxXXXXXXXXXXxx
                                        LAUGHTER

In this example, the statement of one leading Labour politician (John Prescott) is used to pose a puzzle, but also to imply that another leading Labour politician (Margaret Beckett) is a silly fool (solution). The isolated applause after the first part of the solution seems to be a misreading of cues, because the statement ('Well, now Margaret Beckett is planning to introduce one') could well have been taken as the solution to the puzzle: there is already the clear implication that, according to John Prescott's statement, Margaret Beckett is a silly fool. Hague's two-second pause at this point might be taken to indicate that this is the solution. However, the pause might also have been for dramatic effect, and it is only when Hague goes on to complete the solution that it wins extensive collective applause.

2 *Failure of rhetoric.* In some instances, the speaker employs a rhetorical device but fails to win collective applause from the audience. The example below from William Hague might also be seen in Heritage and Greatbatch's terms as a puzzle-solution device:

This government is like a hologram [PUZZLE]
It looks so real. But when you reach out to touch it, there's nothing there [SOLUTION]
(1.5 seconds) -x-

However, Hague's delivery of this solution is somewhat confusing. The pause suggests that he might have been expecting applause at this point, but also keeps his right hand raised as if he wishes to continue speaking.

3 *Speaker overshoots completion point.* The speaker employs a rhetorical device, but fails to leave the audience sufficient opportunity to applaud. In the next example, William Hague is clearly using a contrast but by continuing to speak ('The prospect...'), the applause is not allowed to develop:

A The great danger is not that Britain will be left behind in Europe
B but that Europe will be left behind in the world
                                        x-x-x-x
                                        The
prospect the prospect of a single currency may present this country with one of the most momentous decisions in its history.

4 *Isolated applause in the absence of rhetorical devices.* In some instances, isolated applause seems to occur in response to the content of the speech alone. So in the following extract from John Major, the isolated applause seems to be a direct reaction to the reference to 'grammar schools in every town' before any rhetorical formulation by Major:

And if parents want grammar schools in every town well then so do I

        x x

and they shall have them

Delayed applause

1 *Poorly constructed rhetoric.* The following extract comes from Tony Blair's (1997) speech in which he uses a three-part list, but one which is poorly constructed:

> And parents will have to play their part
> (1) There will be home school contracts for all pupils
> I say sign them
> (2) There will be new measures to tackle truancy and disruptive children, new homework requirements
> Support them
> (3) And when a school disciplines a child why
> not back the teacher
>   (1 second) xxxxxxxxXXXXXXXXXXXXX

In this example, it is clear that Blair is inviting applause not only because he uses the rhetorical device of a three-part list, but also because when the applause fails to come, he stands there silently nodding his head (after 'why not back the teacher') until the audience start to applaud. Whereas the first two items of the list use the same rhetorical structure in which Blair describes what is going to happen ('There will be...'), and then makes a recommendation as to the appropriate course of action, the third item departs from that format ('And when a school disciplines a child...'). Because of this lack of symmetry, the completion point may not be fully projectable.

2 *Absence of rhetorical devices.* In the absence of a rhetorical device, the audience may not know that the speaker was expecting applause, hence there is a pause while he waits for them to applaud the statement. In this example from William Hague's speech, the language is highly emotive, but there are no obvious signals in the rhetorical structure that he is inviting the audience to applaud. His delivery at this point is confusing. The long pause at the end of the sentence suggests that he might have been expecting applause, but simultaneous with the onset of the applause he opens his mouth as if to start speaking again, only to close it as the applause gathers pace.

> Education needs the Conservative Party now. For if Labour gives way to dogmatic attacks on choice and betrays our nation's children then they will face the implacable opposition of the Conservative Party and deserve the condemnation of the country.
>   (1.5 seconds) xxxxxxxXXXXXX

It should be noted that, although delayed applause is typically treated as an indication of lack of synchrony between speaker and audience, there was one notable exception in this corpus of data. In the following example from Paddy Ashdown's 1997 speech, delayed applause seems entirely appropriate:

> The extraordinary response to the death of Diana was in part at least a cry for a
> (1) more caring
> (2) more decent
> (3) and more compassionate society
> (1 second) xxxxxxxxXXXXXX

The speech was delivered on 24 September, less than a month after the death of Princess Diana in a car accident (31 August, 1997), and in not responding immediately to Ashdown's three-part list, the audience applause seems not to be unsynchronised with speech but to be showing respect for the dead Princess.

Audience interrupts speaker

1 *Misreading of cues.* The speaker uses a rhetorical device (or devices), but the audience misjudges when the completion point occurs. In the next example, Blair (1997) uses a complex rhetorical device which involves both a headline–punchline and two three part-lists (the second list forming the third item of the first list). But the audience appear to project the completion point at the third item of the first list, starting to applaud after 'it can be done'; this is understandable, given that the first two items seem to imply that 'it can't be done'.

> And you know when people say to me sorry that's too ambitious sorry it can't be done I say [HEADLINE]:
> (1) This is not a sorry country
> (2) We are not a sorry people
> (3) It can be done if we have the (1) will and (2) courage and
>   [xxxxxxXXXXXXXXXXXXXXXXXXXXXX
>   (3) determination to do it
>   XXXXXXXXXXXXXXXXXXXXXXXXXxxxxxxx

2 *Poorly constructed rhetoric.* Rhetoric may be poorly constructed, such that the audience does not applaud at the appropriate completion point. The following is an example from Tony Blair's 1997 speech of what Atkinson (1984a, p. 49) refers to as 'projecting a name', where the speaker identifies someone in the audience for commendation. However, as Atkinson (1984a, pp. 54–57) points out, there are a number of ways in which such 'namings' can go wrong such that the applause does not occur at the right moment. In the example below, the naming occurs too soon. Blair names Neil Kinnock before expressing his tribute to him, so that the audience applaud twice – once after hearing Neil Kinnock's name, and a second time after hearing the

tribute to him. Although Blair pauses after stating Neil Kinnock's name, the rising intonation and the tribute which follows strongly suggests that he intended to continue at this point, and that the applause was interruptive:

> And let me pay thanks to those that led our party before me.
> To Neil Kinnock
>   xxxXXXXXXXXXXXXXXXXXXXXXXX
> XXXXXxxxx
>   the mantle of Prime Minister was never his but I know that without him it would never have been mine
>   xxxxxXXXXXXXX
> XXXXXXXXXXXXXXXXXXXXXxxxxxxxxxxx

3 *Failure of rhetoric.* Applause does not occur immediately in response to a rhetorical device, so the speaker continues as the audience starts to applaud – hence, the applause becomes interruptive. In the following example, Ashdown (1996) uses what Heritage and Greatbatch term a 'position taking'. Because the audience do not applaud immediately, he continues with his speech just as the applause gets under way:

> Now my fear my urgent fear is this.
> That we'll see we shall see an election, and maybe a change of government – but we shall not see a change of direction. We Britain shall still be starved of clear vision, a commitment to change, the courage to face up to what must be done. It is the very first crucial role of this Party our primary role to ensure that that does not happen [POSITION TAKING] [With the
>   xxxxxxxxxXXXXXXXXXXxxxxxxx
> xxxxxxx
>   With the Liberal Democrats strong in the next Parliament
> Britain will face the challenges that confront us

4 *Speaker overshoots completion point.* The speaker employs a rhetorical device, but fails to give the audience an opportunity to applaud. In the following example, Blair (1997) uses a three-part list to which the audience responds with collective applause. Blair continues the speech with the phrase 'Now people…' almost exactly at the same time as the applause begins, but then breaks off, hence he is interrupted by the applause:

> (1) Teacher training will be reformed
> (2) Headteachers will have a proper qualification
> (3) And poor teachers will go [Now people…
>   xxxxxxxxxxxxxxxxxXXXXXXXXXXXxx
> xxxxxxxxxx
>   And I'll say why. People say my job is pressurised. So is teaching

5 *Absence of rhetorical devices.* Interruptive applause may occur in the absence of rhetorical devices, in which case the audience seem to be responding directly to the content of the speech. In the following example from Blair (1996), the audience interrupt with applause to endorse Blair's commitment to the principle of trade union representation:

> We will be part of the European Social Chapter as every other government Tory or Labour is in the rest of Europe. And there will be a right for any individual to join a trade union and if . . .
>   xxxxXXXXXXX

Speaker mismatches – speaker interrupts audience

The speaker may interrupt audience applause either successfully or unsuccessfully.

1 *Successful interruption.* In the following example from Ashdown (1997), the applause seems to be unenthusiastic, so Ashdown continues with the speech:

> Now I know I know not in many of your council chambers but in Westminster at least socialism and all it stood for has been consigned to a quiet burial in an unmarked grave
>   xxx-xx-xx-xx-x
>   [But it isn't just old party boundaries that are shifting. Ideas are finding new homes too.

On other occasions, the applause seems to be so enthusiastic that Ashdown has to curtail it in order to continue with the speech. In response to the following extract from Ashdown's (1997) speech, the applause continues for a full 24 seconds before Ashdown eventually intervenes in order to continue:

> So where shall we be, we Liberal Democrats, as this historic game is played out in the months and years ahead? Some say that we should be satisfied with our local strength and concede that Westminster will always be a side-show for us. Some say that we should be content to be a good conventional opposition, and that is enough. Well no doubt our opponents would like to see us satisfied with such limited ambitions. But I am not. And I hope that you will not be, either. I have bigger ambitions for the Liberal Democrats. I accept no glass ceilings for this Party.
>   xxxxxxXXXXXXXXXXXXXXXX

2 *Unsuccessful interruption.* In the following example from Ashdown (1997), he attempts to interrupt the applause unsuccessfully ('So...'), then waits for the applause to die down before continuing with the speech:

A Where we should cooperate we will do so wholeheartedly
B Where we must oppose we will do so unflinchingly
   xxxxXXXXXXXXXXXXXXXXXXXXXXXXXXXXxxxxxxx
                  [So   So
here's my prayer for the Parliament ahead
here's my prayer for the next four or five years

Discussion

Mismatches in audience applause are relatively commonplace during political speeches, according to the results of this study. Across all six speeches, audience mismatches accounted for a mean 29.2 per cent of applause events. This contrasts with Atkinson's statement that 'displays of approval are seldom delayed for more than a split second after a completion point, and frequently start just before one is reached' (Atkinson, 1984a, p. 33). Speaker mismatches also accounted for a mean 12.9 per cent of applause events. Only a mean 61 per cent of applause events across all six speeches were found to be fully synchronised with speech Of the four principal types of mismatch identified in this study, only one (isolated applause) is discussed in any detail by Atkinson, Heritage and Greatbatch. Given that isolated applause occurred the least frequently of the four types of mismatch (mean: 4.6 per cent of applause incidences), it is perhaps not surprising that Atkinson's research underestimates the frequency of mismatches.

A detailed qualitative analysis showed that each of these four principal types of mismatch may occur either in the presence or absence of rhetorical devices. Mismatches associated with rhetorical devices can occur in a variety of ways. If the speaker does not allow the audience sufficient time to applaud at a possible completion point and continues to speak, the audience applause may become interruptive. If the rhetorical device is complex, the audience may start to applaud before the speaker has reached the projected completion point, thereby interrupting the flow of the speech. If the rhetorical device is poorly constructed, applause may be delayed until the audience recognises that a completion point has been reached, or interruptive, if the audience anticipates the completion point because it has not been predicted sufficiently well. Each of the above forms of mismatch may take the form of either collective or isolated applause. Finally, the speaker may interrupt applause which occurs in response to a rhetorical device.

All the above forms of mismatch show different ways in which rhetorical devices may break down. However, it is possible to accommodate these different forms of mismatch within Atkinson's existing theoretical framework, if one accepts that speakers may differ in the skill with which they deploy these devices. If the speaker uses poorly constructed devices, if the rhetorical structure is complex, if the speaker's timing is poor, these may all result in incidences of mistimed applause. But this does not undermine the concept of rhetorical devices, it simply means that speakers do not always use them to full effect.

Of much greater significance for Atkinson's theory are mismatches which occur in the absence of rhetorical devices. In the case of delayed applause, it is possible that if the speaker pauses for the audience to respond, the pause itself may function as a kind of clumsy invitation to applaud. But when interruptive applause occurs in the absence of rhetorical devices, there is no reason to believe that in any sense the speaker is inviting applause. It can be much more easily understood in terms of the concept of uninvited applause. The study presented in the previous chapter included all instances of inter-ruptive collective applause to non-rhetorically formatted statements in three of the speeches analysed here (those from 1996). From a content analysis, it was argued that applause was initiated by the audience specifically in response to statements of policy; thus, the audience was applauding the content of the speech, regardless of the fact that these messages were not rhetorically formatted. Whereas Heritage and Greatbatch (1986, p. 146) state that 'audience agreement may be a necessary condition for the genera-tion of applause, but it is not generally a sufficient one', this analysis of uninvited applause in response to specific policy statements would suggest that audience agreement alone can indeed be a sufficient condition for collective applause.

The concept of uninvited applause can also be extended to incidences of isolated applause. In the previous chapter, it was argued that collective unin-vited applause need not be synchronised with speech, but may be charac-terised by a staggered onset, through the process of what has been termed 'mutual monitoring' (Clayman, 1993). In this instance, the initial reactions of a few audience members may prompt others to join in, resulting in collective applause. From this perspective, isolated applause in the absence of rhetorical devices may be seen as the response of a few audience members to some aspect of the content of the speech, but one which fails to draw in sufficient numbers of the audience to turn it into collective applause. Indeed, the speaker may interrupt such applause in order to move on with the speech. Thus, the results of this study overall are consistent with the proposal put forward in the previous chapter that two types of applause can be distinguished in political speeches, namely, invited and uninvited applause.

Audience applause undoubtedly occurs as a result of an interaction between speaker, message and audience, but that interaction will depend upon whether the applause is invited or uninvited. In the case of invited applause, the speaker encodes applaudable content in rhetorical structures which, if decoded appropriately, will result in a high degree of synchrony between speech and applause. Mismatches may occur if the rhetorical structures are poorly encoded, or if the audience misreads the signals. In the case of uninvited applause, members of the audience are not responding to invitations to applaud but are initiating applause in response to specific aspects of speech content. Thus, frequent mismatches might be expected to characterise uninvited applause; interaction occurs in terms of the audience's response to speech content, and also between different sections of the audience, if the applause is taken up through mutual monitoring.

When taken together, the analyses in this and the preceding chapter can be seen as highlighting a principal weakness in Atkinson's research: that is, a failure to examine negative examples which might prove inconsistent with his theory. Whereas Atkinson, Heritage and Greatbatch have produced a great detail of data to show what is in effect a strong positive correlation between rhetorical devices and collective applause, they do not analyse non-rhetorically formatted statements which receive collective applause, nor instances where applause is asynchronous with speech. Analyses of such negative instances are consistent with the view proposed in the previous chapter that not all applause in political speeches is invited through rhetorical devices. It may also be uninvited, unsynchronised with speech, initiated by a few members of the audience in direct response to speech content and sometimes taken up by the audience as a whole; in short, it may be a direct reaction to the content of the speech itself.

5   A model of invited and uninvited applause

Introduction

The studies reported in the previous two chapters raised a number of significant questions about the validity of Atkinson's theory of rhetoric. It was found that applause may occur uninvited in the absence of rhetorical devices. It was also found that only a mean 61 per cent of applause instances in six political speeches were fully synchronised with speech. But in this latter study, only a global figure for the proportion of mismatches was reported; these were not analysed in terms of the distinction between invited and uninvited applause. Nor indeed do we have any idea of the relative distribution of invited and uninvited applause in political speeches. Hence, it was decided to conduct a further study in which synchrony could be investigated in relation to the distinction between invited and uninvited applause (Bull and Wells, 2002a).

The concept of invited applause used in this study is heavily indebted to Atkinson's analysis of rhetorical devices, but it should be noted that it also differs in a number of important respects. In the first instance, there is no reason to believe that the seven rhetorical devices identified by Atkinson, Heritage and Greatbatch are necessarily exhaustive; there may be other ways in which speakers invite applause. On the other hand, the presence of rhetorical devices does not always automatically constitute in itself an invitation to applaud; the delivery of the message is also important. Atkinson was well aware of this, and argued that appropriate delivery increases the chance of a rhetorical device being applauded (Atkinson, 1984a, p. 84).

An alternative point of view is that delivery is important in indicating whether *or not* the message should be seen as constituting an invitation to applaud. For example, a speaker may articulate each element of a three-part list with a closely synchronised gesture to stress that this is an applause invitation. But if the speaker continues to gesture beyond the three-part list, this might convey just the reverse, that the speaker does not want applause at that point, but has more things to say before inviting applause later in the speech. Again, if the delivery is unclear, it may also be unclear to the audience what the speaker's intentions are, and this may result in a mismatch between speech and applause. For this reason, the presence or absence of rhetorical devices was coded independently of whether the utterance was considered an invitation to applaud.

The measure of synchronisation also differs slightly from that employed in the previous chapter. In this study, asynchrony was coded only in terms of three audience mismatches (isolated, delayed and interruptive applause). The fourth type of mismatch (speaker interrupts audience) was omitted, on the grounds that this is not a measure of audience synchronisation, rather a measure of speaker synchronisation with audience applause. It was the other three forms of mismatch which were considered the most appropriate to test Atkinson's claim that audience applause is closely synchronised with speech.

The study as a whole was based on 15 speeches delivered by the leaders of the three principal British political parties to their annual party conferences between 1996 and 2000. Each incidence of applause which occurred during a speech was coded in terms of three dimensions: invited/uninvited; presence/absence of rhetorical devices; synchronous/asynchronous.

On the basis of the concepts of invited and uninvited applause, two predictions were made.

1   From Atkinson's analysis, the most commonly occurring form of applause should be that which is invited through rhetorical devices and synchronous with speech.
2   From the analysis reported in Chapter 3, uninvited applause should typically occur in the absence of rhetorical devices and be asynchronous with speech.

In addition to testing these specific predictions, it was also intended to obtain some basic information on the overall relationship between the three dimensions, and on the relative distribution of invited and uninvited applause.

Method

Speeches

The study was based on 15 speeches delivered by the leaders of the three principal British political parties to their annual conferences between 1996 and 2000. Details of the 1996 and 1997 speeches have already been given in the preceding two chapters. The nine speeches from 1998–2000 were as follows:

2000   21 September   Charles Kennedy (30 minutes 45 seconds)
       26 September   Tony Blair (56 minutes 35 seconds)
       5 October   William Hague (49 minutes 23 seconds)

1999	23 September	Charles Kennedy (49 minutes 31 seconds)
	28 September	Tony Blair (53 minutes 50 seconds)
	7 October	William Hague (57 minutes 32 seconds)
1998	24 September	Paddy Ashdown (60 minutes 22 seconds)
	29 September	Tony Blair (49 minutes 24 seconds)
	8 October	William Hague (61 minutes 26 seconds)

Apparatus

Details of transcripts for the 1996 and 1997 speeches have already been given in the preceding two chapters. The speeches from 1998–2000 were downloaded from each party's website, and converted into a word processing package. The text of each speech was then checked for accuracy against the video-recording, and amended accordingly.

Procedure

Incidents of applause were marked on each transcript following Atkinson's (1984a) notation, as described in Chapter 3.

Each incident of applause was coded in terms of three dimensions (invited/uninvited, rhetorical/non-rhetorical, synchronous/asynchronous). The criteria for each dimension are:

1   *invited/uninvited.* Invitations to applaud were identified by the use of rhetorical devices and by delivery. Delivery includes both vocal features (change in pitch, speed or intonation) and non-vocal features (stance, gaze or gesture). Thus, in deciding whether applause was invited, the presence of rhetorical devices was not in itself sufficient, the delivery also had to be consistent with an applause invitation. For example, if the speaker was visibly taking in another breath (to continue speaking), continuing to gesture, or even simply starting another sentence, the applause would not be judged as invited, because it was clear that the speaker had intended to continue with the speech.

2   *rhetorical/non-rhetorical.* Rhetorical devices were identified on the basis of the seven listed by Heritage and Greatbatch (1986). In addition, it was found necessary to include two extra devices – *jokes,* and what was referred to as *negative naming.*

   Jokes receive applause as well as laughter, so need to be included amongst the devices which speakers use to invite an audience response. *Negative naming* is a variant on what Atkinson calls naming. In naming, the audience is invited to applaud a person (typically in the audience) who has been named and praised by the speaker. In *negative naming,* the audience are invited to applaud the abuse or ridicule of a named person – typically a politician of an opposing political party.

3   *synchrony/asynchrony.* Applause was coded as asynchronous if it was iso-

lated, delayed or interruptive, and also classified in terms of these three sub-categories of asynchrony. The criteria for identifying each sub-category were presented in the previous chapter.

The transcript of each speech was coded independently by the two authors. In settling on the final categories for each incident of applause, any disagreements were resolved by discussion. Reliability studies were conducted to check the coding of the three dimensions under analysis (invited/uninvited, rhetorical/non-rhetorical, synchronous/asynchronous), and also to check the coding of the three sub-categories of asynchrony. For this purpose, the two authors independently coded all the speeches from 1997 (Blair, Hague and Ashdown).

Results

Reliability

The results of the reliability studies were as follows: invited/uninvited 0.94; synchronous/asynchronous 0.90 (both Phi coefficients); coding of the sub-categories in the mismatch typology 0.89 (Cohen's k, Cohen, 1960).

With regard to the coding of rhetorical/non-rhetorical, it was not possible to calculate a meaningful Phi correlation coefficient, because most applause incidents were associated with rhetorical devices (95 per cent in the three speeches in the reliability sample, as well as in the total set of 15 speeches). Inter-observer agreement for coding rhetorical/non-rhetorical in the three speeches in the reliability sample was 94 per cent.

Analysis of data

Overall, the results showed that most of the applause was associated with rhetorical devices (94.8 per cent, $N = 917$), most of the applause was invited (86.2 per cent, $N = 834$), and that applause was also typically synchronous (66.1 per cent, $N = 639$). The full breakdown for all eight possible combinations of applause type is shown in Table 5.1.

To test the two specific hypotheses formulated in the Introduction, a three-way repeated measures analysis of variance was conducted (invited/uninvited $\times$ rhetorical/non-rhetorical $\times$ synchronous/asynchronous). Results are shown in Table 5.2.

All three main effects were significant, as were the three two-way interactions, and the three-way interaction (all $p < 0.0001$). All significant effects were interpreted in the context of the significant three-way interaction, for which pairwise comparison t tests were used to make all possible comparisons (see Table 5.3).

Using the Bonferroni adjustment for multiple comparisons, results need to be significant at the $p < 0.002$ level. The results of the significant pairwise

Table 5.1 Incidents of applause for the eight possible combinations of applause

Invited				Uninvited			
Rhetorical		Non-rhetorical		Rhetorical		Non-rhetorical	
S	AS	S	AS	S	AS	S	AS
64.7	19.5	1.0	0.9	0.2	10.3	0.1	3.1
(626)	(189)	(10)	(9)	(2)	(100)	(1)	(30)

Notes
S = synchronous; AS = asynchronous.
Figures are percentages, raw scores are in parentheses.

Table 5.2 Analysis of variance for applause incidents

Source	df	F
	Within speeches	
Invited (I)	1	166.677*
Rhetoric (R)	1	294.541*
Synchrony (S)	1	38.286*
I × R	1	224.28*
I × S	1	100.03*
R × S	1	46.474*
I × R × S	1	77.731*
Within group error	14	(33.560)

Notes
$*p < 0.0001$.
Value enclosed in parentheses represents mean square error.

Table 5.3 Pairwise comparison *t* values for all eight types of applause

	I/R/S	I/R/AS	U/R/AS	U/R/S	I/NR/S	I/NR/AS	U/NR/S	U/NR/AS
I/R/S	–	8.428**	11.711**	14.472**	13.897**	14.369**	14.380**	13.371**
I/R/AS		–	0.013	8.011**	8.064**	8.086**	7.980**	6.021**
U/R/AS			–	7.140**	5.628**	5.658**	6.709**	4.248*
U/R/S				–	0.077	0.130	0.723	0.012
I/NR/S					–	0.707	0.064	0.065
I/NR/AS						–	0.064	0.057
U/NR/S							–	0.007

Notes
$*p < 0.001$; $**p < 0.0001$.
I = invited; U = uninvited; R = rhetorically formatted; NR = non-rhetorically formatted; S = synchronous; AS = asynchronous.

comparisons are summarised below in relation to the two main hypotheses formulated in the Introduction.

   Hypothesis 1: the most frequently occurring form of applause should be invited, synchronous and rhetorically formatted. This hypothesis received strong support. This combination occurred significantly more frequently

than all the other seven possible combinations of applause type
($p<0.0001$), and accounted for 64.7 per cent of all applause observations.
However, it is noteworthy that invited, *asynchronous*, rhetorically formatted
applause accounted for a further 19.5 per cent of all applause observations,
and occurred significantly more frequently than five other possible combinations of applause type (all comparisons $p<0.0001$). Further analysis of
the subcategories of mismatch associated with this combination (in-
vited/asynchronous/rhetorical) showed that interruptions predominated:
interruptions 87.5 per cent; delayed applause 12.5 per cent; isolated
applause 0 per cent.

   *Hypothesis 2: uninvited applause will typically occur in the absence of rhe-
torical devices and be asynchronous with speech.* This hypothesis was only partially confirmed. Although uninvited applause as predicted was typically
asynchronous (97.7 per cent of all observations of uninvited applause), it
occurred most frequently *in conjunction with* rhetorical devices (75.2 per
cent of all incidents of uninvited applause). This combination occurred
significantly more often than five applause types (four comparisons
$p<0.0001$, one comparison $p<0.001$). There were no significant differences with two applause types: applause invited through rhetorical devices
(both synchronous and asynchronous). Further analysis of the subcategories
of mismatch associated with uninvited/asynchronous/rhetorical applause
showed that interruptions predominated: interruptions 69.3 per cent; isolated applause 29.7 per cent; delayed applause 1.0 per cent.

Discussion

Overall, the results provided strong support for the distinction between
invited and uninvited applause in political speeches. Whereas applause
invited through rhetorical devices was significantly more likely to be synchronous than asynchronous, uninvited applause was almost exclusively
asynchronous; however, uninvited applause occurred more often in the
presence of rhetorical devices than in their absence. These results have
significant implications for the concepts of both invited and uninvited
applause, which are discussed in the following paragraph.

   By far the most frequently occurring applause type was invited, rhetorical
and synchronous (64.7 per cent of all applause incidents). These were what
Atkinson believed to be the main characteristics of applause in political
speeches, and provided strong support for his original observations. Nevertheless, this combination only accounts for just under two-thirds of all
applause incidents in this study. Although Atkinson (1984a, p. 33) claimed
that applause is typically closely synchronised with speech, the results of this
study showed that over a third of all applause incidents were asynchronous
(33.9 per cent).

   Even when applause was invited through rhetorical devices, it was not
always synchronous: 19.5 per cent of all applause observations took this

form. Further analysis of the different forms of asynchrony showed that these were predominantly incidents of interruptive applause (87.5 per cent of observations), i.e. audiences were starting to applaud before the speaker had reached the completion point. This form of applause might be understood as indicative of audience enthusiasm: audiences are so keen to endorse what the speaker is saying that they start to applaud before the end of the utterance. Conversely, in delayed applause (the remaining 12.5 per cent of observations), the audience are either less enthusiastic about what the speaker has just said, or possibly the speaker's signals are less clear as to whether applause is being invited. It is noteworthy that when applause was invited, it was never isolated. Thus, when speakers invited applause through rhetorical devices accompanied by appropriate delivery, the audience always produced collective applause. Most often, it occurred at the projected completion point, sometimes it was interruptive, less often it was delayed.

These results would suggest that the synchronisation of applause with speech is less important than Atkinson would have us believe. Audience members may oblige the speaker by applauding at the appropriate completion point, but are perfectly capable of applauding before or after it is reached. It is possible that, through varying the timing of their applause, they may be sending the speaker more subtly modulated signals of approval or disapproval. At the same time, by always producing collective applause when it is invited, they comply with the overall wishes of the speaker. However, in this context, it should be noted that all 15 speeches were delivered by party political leaders to their respective annual conferences. Hence, the fact that applause was invariably produced when invited by the speaker may be in part due to their leadership roles. Audiences might not be so obliging in responding to applause invitations with other political speakers who do not enjoy the same status.

The remaining 13.8 per cent of all applause incidents were considered to be uninvited. On the basis of the analysis presented in Chapter 3, it was hypothesised that uninvited applause will typically be asynchronous and occur in the absence of rhetorical devices. This hypothesis was only partially confirmed. Although uninvited applause was almost exclusively asynchronous (97.7 per cent of all incidents of uninvited applause), it occurred most frequently in conjunction *with* rhetorical devices (76.7 per cent of all incidents of uninvited applause). The association of uninvited applause with rhetorical devices was not considered in the study reported in Chapter 3, because that analysis was based exclusively on applause which occurred in the absence of rhetorical devices. In this study, uninvited applause in the absence of rhetorical devices was comparatively rare, accounting for only 3.2 per cent of all applause incidents.

The association of uninvited applause with rhetorical devices stems directly from the analysis of delivery used in this study. Whereas Atkinson argued that appropriate delivery increases the chance of a rhetorical device receiving applause, this analysis was based on the proposition that delivery is important in indicating whether *or not* the message constitutes an invitation to applaud. Thus, for a rhetorical device to be considered to be an applause invitation, it had to be accompanied by delivery which suggested that the speaker was inviting applause. For example, Tony Blair, in the following extract from his 2000 speech, used a three-part list in which each list item was marked out by an accompanying gesture. At the end of the third item, there was also a clear fall in pitch, whereupon the audience duly applauded (list items have been numbered (1) to (3)):

> But I believe that when people reflect on those big fundamentals that determine our future – the economy, jobs, public services – (1) they will know we are doing the right thing (2) we are on the right track for Britain (3) and the last thing this country needs is ever a return to Tory government.

Conversely, if a speaker used a rhetorical device, but the delivery indicated that the speech was intended to continue, then the applause was judged to be uninvited. For example, William Hague in his 1999 speech received applause when he said, 'What annoys me most about today's Labour politicians is not their beliefs – they're entitled to those – but their sheer, unadulterated hypocrisy. They say one thing and they do another.' In this extract, Hague used the rhetorical device of a contrast twice in quick succession ('beliefs' are contrasted with 'hypocrisy,' 'saying one thing' is contrasted with 'doing another'). However, Hague also showed a very clear and visible intake of breath following the phrase 'they do another', which suggested that his intention had been to continue, and that he had not been seeking applause at that point. Hence, the applause which occurred after '...they do another' was judged to have been uninvited.

There are a number of possible reasons why uninvited applause might occur in this way. One possibility is that the delivery may be insufficiently clear or visible for the audience to perceive that the speaker is not inviting applause at this point. Although detailed microanalysis of a video-recording may show clear signals that the speaker was intending to continue (for example, by taking a breath), these cues may not necessarily be easily perceptible to the audience.

Another possibility is that audiences simply misread the signals. As the speaker starts to use a rhetorical device, the audience may mistakenly anticipate that a completion point is about to be reached. Some rhetorical devices can be extremely complex, the speaker piling one device upon another; in such circumstances, the audience may start to applaud before the final completion point is reached. It is interesting to note that when asynchronous applause was associated with rhetorical devices, it was predominantly interruptive, irrespective of whether applause was invited or uninvited (uninvited 69.3 per cent; invited 87.5 per cent). This frequent occurrence of interruptions suggests the possibility that audiences are anticipating completion points by applauding early. In the case of invited applause, they anticipate the speaker's intentions accurately; in the case of uninvited applause, they misread the speaker's intentions.

A further possibility is that what appears in some instances to be uninvited applause may actually be a stratagem on the part of the speaker. A speaker may use rhetorical devices to whip up the responses of the audience, but then deny them the opportunity to applaud, as Atkinson (1985) argued in his analysis of refusing invited applause. From this perspective, what appears to be uninvited applause may in fact be the result of messages which are deliberately ambiguous and contradictory. At present, the data do not allow us to choose between these different interpretations.

But the results do suggest that considerably more attention needs to be given to the role of delivery in political speeches. In this study, for a rhetorical device to be regarded as an applause invitation, it had to be accompanied by appropriate delivery. Of particular interest is the finding that synchronous applause occurred almost exclusively in response to rhetorical devices judged to be applause invitations (98.0 per cent of observations of synchronous applause). Applause in response to rhetorical devices not considered to be applause invitations (on account of the associated delivery) was almost invariably asynchronous (98.0 per cent of observations of uninvited applause associated with rhetorical devices). Whereas Atkinson claimed that most applause in political speeches is synchronous with speech, these results showed that synchrony only occurred when rhetorical devices were accompanied by delivery appropriate for inviting applause. Thus, by making a clear conceptual distinction between rhetorical devices and what constitutes an applause invitation, this analysis suggests that delivery may be of much greater importance than was originally recognised by Atkinson. Indeed, given that all the 15 speeches analysed here were delivered by party political leaders, it might be the case that delivery is even more important for political speakers who do not enjoy the same status in achieving effective applause invitations.

Conclusions

The study presented in this chapter is the first to make a comprehensive analysis of all incidents of applause in political speeches in the context of the distinction between invited and uninvited applause. By far the most frequently occurring applause type was invited, rhetorical and synchronous (64.7 per cent of all applause incidents). These were what Atkinson believed to be the main characteristics of applause in political speeches and provided strong support for his original observations. The case study reported in Chapter 2 also showed the value of Atkinson's theoretical framework in helping to understand the role of hand gestures both in articulating the structure of applause invitations, as well as in refusing applause when it occurs at inappropriate points during a speech.

At the same time, the studies reported in this and the previous two chapters have highlighted a number of problems with Atkinson's theory, in particular the importance of other features such as delivery, speech content and uninvited applause. A detailed consideration of the implications of all of these studies for Atkinson's theory is presented in the final chapter (Chapter 11). The second part of the book (Chapters 6–10) is concerned with the other main strand of the author's research, that on televised political interviews.

Part II
Televised political interviews

6   Interruptions

Introduction

The author's analyses of televised political interviews arose initially out of an interest in the role of interruptive speech. Interruptions became a popular research topic as part of a wider concern with how people take turns in conversation, commonly referred to as 'turn-taking'. Conversation (or at least American and English conversation) is characteristically organised in terms of an orderly exchange of turns, following the basic rule of one speaker at a time. Considerable attention has been paid to how this is achieved in instances when turn-taking is not pre-arranged. Of particular importance was a seminal paper by Sacks *et al.* (1974), who identified a number of distinctive features considered to characterise turn-taking, and proposed a system of rules to account for the way in which turn-taking is organised.

Interest was also stimulated in what happens when the exchange of speaking turns is disorderly: excessive interruptions can be seen as a breakdown in conversational turn-taking. For example, a tendency to interrupt can be seen as a way of attempting to dominate conversation, so a number of studies investigated the relationship between interruption rate and the personality trait of dominance. In one experiment, students who had been pre-selected on the basis of a personality questionnaire conversed in pairs where the members of each pair were either high or low on dominance. When the students in a pair were both high on dominance, they tended to interrupt one another significantly more as the conversation progressed, suggesting that a tendency to interrupt is indeed related to personality (Roger and Schumacher, 1983).

A number of studies have focussed on gender differences. According to some analysts, the use of interruptions is a characteristic feature of men's conversational style, a means whereby they seek to maintain social control and deny women equal rights as conversational partners. In conversations between members of the same sex, it was found that interruptions appeared to be symmetrically distributed between speakers, whereas in conversations between members of the opposite sex, almost all the interruptions were initiated by men (Zimmerman and West, 1975).

Not surprisingly, this study proved extremely controversial, not least because these gender differences were not always replicated by other observers. For example, in another study (Murray and Covelli, 1988) just the opposite results were found: women interrupted men twice as often as men interrupted women. This study is directly comparable to that by Zimmerman and West, because the tapes were made in the same historical period (mid-1970s), so that differences in the results should not be due to the effects of social change. In addition, the same coding procedures were employed, but on a much wider sample of conversations with a much larger corpus of interruptions (400 as opposed to 55). Furthermore, comparisons were also made of different speech settings, and this was found to be a much more significant factor which overrode any differences due to gender.

Opposing conclusions on gender and interruptions were also reached by the authors of several narrative reviews. Whereas Holmes (1995) argues that men initiate interruptions more than women, other reviewers maintain that there are no consistent gender differences (James and Clarke, 1993; Aries, 1996). One way of tackling these competing claims is through the techniques of meta-analysis. Meta-analysis is a statistical technique whereby the data from a number of different studies can be pooled. This procedure is employed because the spread of a set of scores can vary from one study to another, hence a direct comparison of data from different studies can be misleading. This problem can be corrected through the use of a measure of effect size (d), which standardises mean differences between any two groups according to the amount of variation in the samples (Cohen, 1969). Effect sizes can be calculated for each of the studies collated in the meta-analysis, which are then directly comparable with one another.

Forty-three published studies of gender and interruptions were examined in a meta-analysis by Anderson and Leaper (1998). Their results showed that although men were significantly more likely than women to initiate interruptions, the effect size ($d = 0.15$) was insubstantial. But when the analysis was restricted to what were termed 'intrusive interruptions' (attempts by one speaker to usurp the other's speaking turn), then the effect size was much larger ($d = 0.33$). However, the results were also affected by situational factors: the effect was more pronounced when the observations were made in naturalistic as opposed to laboratory settings, and in groups of three or more persons rather than pairs of conversationalists. But overall, it does appear that men are significantly more likely than women to initiate interruptions.

Methodology

Early research on interruptions used relatively simple forms of classification, although it soon became apparent that these could not satisfactorily represent the full complexity of interruptive speech. So, for example, Mishler and

Waxler (1968) made a distinction between successful and unsuccessful interruptions, but Ferguson (1977) argued that so broad a classification combined forms of interruption which are empirically discriminable. She presented an alternative system, comprising four categories: simple interruptions, butting-in interruptions, silent interruptions and overlaps. Each of these categories may be contrasted with what Ferguson called a perfect speaker-switch, which occurs when there is no simultaneous speech, and the previous speaker's utterance appears to be complete in every way. Thus, a simple interruption differs from a perfect speaker-switch because it involves both simultaneous speech and a break in continuity: the second speaker takes over the turn by preventing the first from completing an utterance. In an overlap, the second speaker starts speaking just before the first speaker completes the utterance, so that simultaneous speech does occur. In a butting-in interruption, simultaneous speech occurs, but the interruptor is unsuccessful in attempting to take over the turn. In a silent interruption, the first speaker's utterance is incomplete, but there is a pause before the second speaker takes over, so there is no simultaneous speech: hence the term, 'silent interruption'.

Unfortunately, Ferguson's fourfold categorisation was also open to serious criticism. Simple and butting-in interruptions correspond closely to Mishler and Waxler's successful and unsuccessful interruption types; they do not represent any substantial modification of their work. Overlaps, although potentially disruptive to the smooth flow of conversation, are not necessarily interruptive. One conversationalist, anticipating that another is about to finish talking, may start to speak just before the turn is completed, thus producing a brief burst of simultaneous speech. This is not necessarily interruptive, if it is clear that the first speaker's utterance was almost complete; indeed, it may be indicative of the other speaker's enthusiasm and involvement.

Ferguson's final category, that of silent interruptions, presents special problems, since it is based on the assumption that because an utterance is incomplete, the speaker intended to continue. However, conversations do not strictly follow the rules of standard grammar, and speakers may simply tail off because they have finished what they want to say. In fact, in one study, it was shown that people do not necessarily regard such utterances as interruptive. Participants took part in conversations in a social psychology laboratory, which were video-recorded; they then observed themselves on videotape (Roger and Nesshoever, 1987). When questioned about 'silent interruptions', it was clear that participants frequently saw the second speaker's utterance not as disruptive but as cooperative, seeking to provide help when they were uncertain as to how to finish what they were going to say.

In view of these problems, it was decided to develop a new system for the classification of interruptions (Roger *et al.*, 1988); this system is described in the following section.

The Interruption Coding System (ICS) (Roger *et al.*, 1988)

The ICS was based on two experiments conducted in the social psychology laboratory in York (UK), devised with the specific intention of maximising the number of interruptions which might occur. Participants were initially asked to respond to a questionnaire, which comprised a series of statements about contentious political and social issues. They were then asked to discuss a number of these issues with another person, and to try to convince that person of their own point of view. The other person was always a confederate of the experimenter, acting under instructions. In one experiment, the confederate spoke for as much of the time as possible; hence, in order to get a word in edgeways, it was necessary for the participants to interrupt. In the second experiment, the confederate interrupted as frequently as possible; hence, it was also necessary for the participants to interrupt in order to put over their own point of view. Both confederates received detailed training prior to the actual experiments, and became highly skilled in these behaviours.

All the conversations were video-recorded. From a detailed analysis of all incidences of interruptions and simultaneous speech, a new classificatory system was constructed. Its aim was to enable the investigator to categorise interruptions and incidences of simultaneous speech. To decide on the classification of each such event, the investigator asked a series of questions which were presented in the form of a binary flow chart (Figure 6.1). The system can best be applied by working through each level of the chart in sequence.

In the first instance, it is necessary to establish which conversationalist has the speaking turn. Hence, the initial question is whether a first and a second speaker can be identified. If the answer to this question is 'no', then the event is labelled a false start, or unintended simultaneous speech. Such events are typically followed by some form of repair. For example, there may be a pause followed by an apology on the part of one or both speakers, before they decide on who is to take the turn.

If a first and second speaker can be identified, then the next step is to ask whether the second speaker disrupted the first speaker's utterance. If the answer to this question is 'no', then the chart leads into non-interruptive simultaneous speech, the form of which is determined by whether the first speaker continues with the utterance. If the first speaker does not continue, the event is classified as an overlap. If the first speaker does continue, then the event is classified as either a listener response (brief or extended) or as an afterthought. Listener responses are simply acknowledgement or attention signals, such as 'yeah', 'right', 'uh-huh', 'that's fine'. An afterthought represents a sort of coda attached to the first speaker's utterance in the form of phrases such as 'or something' or 'well, anyway'.

If the observer does consider that the second speaker disrupted the first speaker's utterance, then the event is classified as an interruptive. A basic

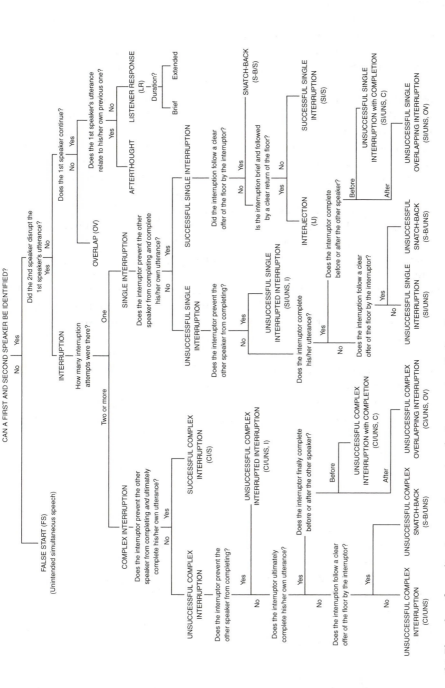

Figure 6.1 Flow chart for coding interruptions using the Interruption Coding System.

distinction is then made between single and complex interruptions, where complex interruptions involve two or more consecutive interruption attempts. Complex interruptions occur particularly in arguments where one person is determined to interrupt while the other speaker is equally determined not to give way. Another basic distinction can be made between successful and unsuccessful interruptions. In a successful interruption, the interruptor both prevents the speaker from completing an utterance and makes a complete utterance of his or her own. In an unsuccessful interruption, the interruptor may fail to prevent the speaker completing an utterance and/or fail to make a complete utterance of his or her own.

Hence, interruptions can be successful or unsuccessful, single or complex. Within this framework, it is possible to make further distinctions between different types of successful interruption. One type of successful single interruption has been dubbed the 'snatchback'. The first speaker offers the second speaker a turn (for example, by asking a question) and then starts to speak again before the other's response is complete, thereby literally 'snatching' back the turn. Another type of successful single interruption is the 'interjection', whereby the second speaker interrupts the first speaker with a brief but complete utterance (such as 'like what?' or 'so?'). Leaving the previous utterance incomplete, the first speaker now responds to the second speaker's interjection. Interjections are interesting, because their function seems to be not to take over the speaking turn but in some way to influence the content of what the first speaker is saying. Thus, to be successful, interruptions do not necessarily have to result in an exchange of speaking turns. If the event is neither a snatchback nor an interjection, but the interruptor does make both a complete utterance and prevents the other speaker from completing, then it is simply classified as a successful interruption. This can be either single or complex, depending upon the number of interruption attempts.

A number of distinctions can also be made between different types of unsuccessful interruption. An interrupted interruption is one in which an interruption attempt is interrupted by the other speaker. However, if both speakers complete their utterances, then the event is classified according to whether the interruptor completes either before the other speaker (unsuccessful single overlapping interruption) or afterwards (unsuccessful single interruption with completion). If the interruptor neither completes an utterance nor prevents the first speaker from completing, then the event is simply classified as an unsuccessful interruption. The only exception to this is if the interruption attempt followed a clear offer of the turn by the interruptor, in which case it would be classified as an unsuccessful snatchback. All of these categories of unsuccessful interruption can be either single or complex.

Compared with the typology devised by Ferguson, this system allows the researcher to make many more distinctions between different types of interruption. For example, in Ferguson's system, there is no way of distinguishing between single and complex interruptions. Repeated attempts at interruption have to be treated as independent events, which fails to capture the fact that they are interrelated and constitute part of a sequence. In the ICS, both single and complex interruptions are distinguished, giving a total of 14 different interruption types. One advantage of being able to make these fine distinctions is that it then becomes possible to correlate the pattern of interruptions between individuals. This enables the investigator to assess whether these individuals both interrupt and are interrupted in similar kinds of ways.

The ICS was based on two experiments conducted in a social psychology laboratory. Although the intention of using confederates was to maximise the frequency and variety of interruptions, this kind of investigation is always open to the charge of artificiality. That is to say, behaviours which occur in laboratory-based experiments may not be typical of those which occur in the outside world. Hence, the best form of validation was to apply the system to a non-experimental situation where interruptions occur with a high degree of frequency.

For this purpose, the televised political interview seemed ideal. Beattie (1982) reported that interruptions accounted for 45.2 per cent of all attempted exchanges of turn in political interviews, compared with 10.6 per cent of turn exchanges in university tutorials and 6.3 per cent for telephone conversations. Furthermore, because such interviews are specifically intended for television, the cameras are an integral part of the social context. Hence, unlike situations video-recorded specifically for the purposes of research, there is no particular problem about camera awareness. For all these reasons, political interviews represented an excellent setting in which to extend the author's previous work on interruptions. The next section reports an empirical study of interruptions based on eight televised interviews with Margaret Thatcher and Neil Kinnock during the 1987 General Election.

Interruptions in political interviews

Introduction

A number of observers have commented on the distinctive nature of turn-taking in political interviews. Typically, the interviewer both begins and ends the interview; he or she is also expected to ask questions while the interviewee is expected to provide replies (e.g. Clayman, 1989; Greatbatch, 1988; Heritage, Clayman and Zimmerman, 1988). Even when the interviewer departs from the question/answer format (for example by making a statement), that statement will typically be followed with a question or concluded with a tag in the form of 'isn't it?' or 'wasn't it?' Thus, the question/answer format is the principal means of interaction used by the participants, although interviewers may engage in non-questioning actions in order to open and close interviews (Heritage and Greatbatch, 1991).

The opening sequence of a news interview differs from ordinary conversation in a number of important respects. In particular, the primary task of the opening is to project the agenda for the interview, whereas topics in ordinary conversation are not predetermined but developed during the course of the interaction (Clayman, 1991). The way in which news interviews are terminated is also significantly affected by the pattern of turn-taking (Clayman, 1989). Given that interviewees are not expected to speak unless the interviewer has asked them to do so, termination can be accomplished in a unilateral fashion by the interviewer; this is in contrast to ordinary conversation, where it is jointly managed by the participants.

Another distinctive feature of turn-taking in political interviews is the high frequency of interruptions. Turn-taking in political interviews may break down if interruptions are excessive. A detailed analysis was conducted of interruptions in two political interviews from the 1979 British General Election (Beattie, 1982). One interview was between Denis Tuohy and Margaret Thatcher (at that time Leader of the Conservative Opposition), the other was between Llew Gardner and Jim Callaghan (at that time Labour Prime Minister). Whereas Margaret Thatcher was interrupted by her interviewer almost twice as often as she interrupted him, the pattern for Jim Callaghan was the reverse: he interrupted his interviewer more than he was interrupted.

Beattie went on to put forward an explanation of why Margaret Thatcher was interrupted so often. This was based on Duncan's analysis of turn-taking in informal conversation (e.g. Duncan, 1972; Duncan and Fiske, 1977). Duncan had identified what he called turn-yielding cues – signals which indicate that the speaker is ready to offer the speaking turn to the other person. Duncan's (1972) analysis revealed six turn-yielding cues: a rise or fall in pitch at the end of a clause, a drawl on the final syllable, the termination of hand gestures, the completion of a grammatical clause, stereotyped expressions such as 'but uh' or 'you know', and a drop in pitch or loudness associated with one of these stereotyped expressions. Beattie found that Margaret Thatcher was often interrupted following the display of these turn-yielding cues, in particular at the ends of clauses associated with a drawl on the stressed syllable and falling intonation. These turn-yielding cues were in effect misleading, giving the interviewer the impression that she had completed her utterance. The interviewer would then attempt to take over the turn, whereupon Margaret Thatcher would continue speaking. This, it was proposed, was why Margaret Thatcher was excessively interrupted in political interviews (Beattie, 1982).

Beattie subsequently carried out an experiment in which undergraduate students rated extracts from the Denis Tuohy interview (Beattie *et al.*, 1982). Specifically, they were asked to indicate in each case whether they considered that Margaret Thatcher had completed her utterance. Ten of these extracts were turn-final (that is, utterances at the end of a turn immediately preceding a smooth speaker switch), twenty were turn-medial (utterances from within a turn), and the remaining ten were turn-disputed (utterances immediately preceding an interruption from Tuohy). These extracts were presented to different groups of participants on video, audio, vision only and in the form of a typescript. Turn-disputed utterances were significantly more likely than turn-medial utterances to be judged as complete in the video, audio and vision-only conditions. This supported Beattie's proposal that Margaret Thatcher was frequently interrupted because of misleading turn-yielding cues.

Beattie's work became very widely known, but the original study (Beattie, 1982) suffered from some very obvious flaws. It was based on only one interview, with Denis Tuohy; the comparison interview was between James Callaghan and a different interviewer, Llew Gardner. Hence, Margaret Thatcher may have been interrupted more frequently simply because Denis Tuohy had a tendency to interrupt more frequently than Llew Gardner! Nor do we know on how many occasions Margaret Thatcher gave misleading turn-yielding cues: Beattie simply observed that 'many' of the interruptions in the interview occurred after the display of turn-yielding cues.

There were also problems with Beattie's statistical analysis. The statistical test he employed was inappropriate. He made use of chi square, which requires the use of independent observations. Given that all the interruptions were taken from the same politician in the same interview, these observations cannot be assumed to be independent. Furthermore, the coding system which Beattie employed was the one devised by Ferguson (1977), which distinguishes between just four different interruption types. However, as was pointed out above, it is debatable whether two of the categories which Ferguson employs ('overlaps' and 'silent interruptions') are really interruptions at all.

The other study reported by Beattie (Beattie *et al.*, 1982) was also open to serious criticism. The obvious flaw in the experiment is the lack of an appropriate control, i.e. a comparison with another politician. Although the results showed that Margaret Thatcher's turn-disputed utterances were judged as significantly more complete than turn-medial utterances, it is possible that exactly the same results might also be found with another politician. In this case, the results of the experiment might reflect not the peculiarities of Margaret Thatcher's interview style, but the way in which interviewers go about interrupting in political interviews. It may be that interviewers tend to interrupt at points where it appears that the politician has reached the end of an utterance, since this is the most convenient and appropriate place for them to do so. This would have obvious advantages for interviewers who have to be careful about how they interrupt, since they may be criticised – indeed reprimanded – if they appear too rude or aggressive. Soon after the 1987 General Election, a report to precisely this effect appeared on the front page of the *Observer* newspaper (Brooks, 1987).

Beattie's hypothesis that Margaret Thatcher was frequently interrupted because of her misleading turn-yielding cues was interesting and provocative. Yet, as can be seen from the argument above, it was clearly open to alternative interpretations. Hence, it was decided to make a much more systematic analysis of interruptions in interviews with Margaret Thatcher. In this instance, the comparison was with Neil Kinnock. Eight televised interviews were video-recorded during the 1987 General Election campaign with four different interviewers, who each interviewed both politicians. Thus, by using the same interviewers for each politician, it was possible to control for any differences in interruption rate which might have been due to the interviewer rather than the politician. All eight interviews were then categorised using the Interruption Coding System (Bull and Mayer, 1988).

Method

Interviews

The politicians observed in this study were Margaret Thatcher and Neil Kinnock. The television interviewers were Sir Robin Day, Jonathan Dimbleby, David Dimbleby and David Frost, who each interviewed both politicians. Interview durations were: Sir Robin Day, 50 minutes; Jonathan Dimbleby, 25 minutes; David Dimbleby, 7 minutes; David Frost, 25 minutes.

Procedure

Interruptions and incidences of simultaneous speech were categorised according to the ICS. Roger *et al.* (1988) reported a reliability study based on six conversations, which showed agreement of 75–97 per cent on eight major event categories in the ICS. In the study presented below (Bull and Mayer, 1988), all coding was carried out initially by the second author and subsequently checked by the senior author, any disagreements being resolved by discussion.

To make a direct test of the misleading turn-yielding cue hypothesis, each interruption of a politician was coded according to whether it was considered that the politician had finished speaking. The cues used in making these judgements were speech content, continuation of speech, intake of breath, use of hand gestures and trunk movements. In addition, the number of turn-yielding cues the politician displayed at interruptions was noted on the basis of Duncan's (1972) typology. Finally, a content analysis was performed on each interruption in order to provide an account of why interruptions occur in political interviews. All this coding was carried out by both authors working together, any disagreements being resolved by discussion.

Results and discussion

Interruptions were calculated as a rate over partner speaking time for both politicians and interviewers. Margaret Thatcher was interrupted at a slightly slower rate than Neil Kinnock and tended to interrupt at a slightly quicker rate, but none of the differences between the politicians was statistically significant (all comparisons using *t*-tests, correlated samples; see Table 6.1).

An obvious problem in using *t*-tests with such a small sample is that any significant difference has to be extremely powerful to be demonstrated in these circumstances. An alternative is to investigate the degree of similarity in the pattern of interruptions between the two politicians: if significant similarities can be demonstrated, it can safely be concluded that the two politicians do not differ in the way in which they interrupt or are interrupted.

In this respect, the ICS is particularly useful because it distinguishes between an extensive range of interruption types. Hence, it was possible to correlate the interruption profiles of the two party leaders. Correlations (Pearson's *r*) between Margaret Thatcher and Neil Kinnock were performed for single and complex interruptions by both interviewers and politicians. The total number of interruptions in each category was calculated as a rate over partner speaking time. All the correlations were positive and statistically significant (see Table 6.2). Hence, Margaret Thatcher neither

Table 6.1 Interruption rates with Margaret Thatcher and Neil Kinnock

	Margaret Thatcher	*Neil Kinnock*	t *values*
Interruptions received			
Total interruptions	52.9	44.8	1.10
Successful interruptions	135.3	111.5	0.70
Unsuccessful interruptions	87.0	75.0	1.12
Interruptions made			
Total interruptions	38.7	41.9	0.35
Successful interruptions	131.1	141.0	0.94
Unsuccessful interruptions	55.0	59.6	0.03

Notes
$df = 3$ for all *t*-tests.
Figures show the rate per second at which interruptions occur, e.g. Margaret Thatcher was interrupted at a total rate of one interruption every 52.9 seconds of speaking time.

Table 6.2 Correlations between interruptions for Margaret Thatcher and Neil Kinnock

Complex interruptions by the politicians	0.99**
Complex interruptions to the politicians	0.92**
Single interruptions by the politicians	0.67*
Single interruptions to the politicians	0.82**

Note
*$p < 0.05$; **$p < 0.01$.

interrupted nor was interrupted more than Neil Kinnock. Indeed, the pattern of interruptions between the two politicians was highly similar.

In order to carry out a direct test of the misleading turn-yielding cue hypothesis, each interruption of a politician had been coded according to whether it was considered that the politician had finished speaking. On most of the occasions on which Margaret Thatcher was interrupted (73 per cent), it was perfectly clear that she intended to continue speaking. The comparable figure for Neil Kinnock was 89 per cent: however, this difference does not reach statistical significance ($t = 2.52$, $df = 3$). On those interruptions which occurred when Margaret Thatcher could have finished what she was saying, she displayed on average 2.08 turn-yielding cues (in terms of Duncan's typology). The comparable figure for Neil Kinnock was 2.16; this difference is not statistically significant ($t = 1.43$, $df = 3$).

Thus, these results provided no evidence to support the proposal that Margaret Thatcher was frequently interrupted in political interviews because she gave misleading turn-yielding cues. In order to provide an alternative account of why interruptions occur in political interviews, a content analysis was performed; the results are shown in Table 6.3.

Of those interruptions which could be coded, the most common reason for interviewer interruptions was to re-formulate a question. The most common reason for politician interruptions was to disagree with the inter-

Table 6.3 Reasons for interruptions in political interviews

	Interviewer	Politician
Reformulation of question	24.2	1.0
Offer of information	0.9	9.6
Request for information	9.2	2.2
Self-justification	11.6	–
Reply	0.2	9.3
Consent	0.3	6.5
Dissent	14.7	27.6
Apology	0.2	0.8
Topic change/topic control	2.6	0.7
New question	0.2	–
Correction	–	4.6
Metacommunication	0.6	–
Dissent/modification	0.6	–
Modification	0.6	–
Accusation	–	0.7
Acknowledgement	0.6	–
Completion of question	1.8	–
Dissent/reply	–	3.1
Unscoreable	31.7	33.9

Note
Figures are mean percentages across all eight interviews. Where an interruption was incomplete or inaudible because of simultaneous speech, it was classified as unscoreable.

viewer; disagreement was also the second most common reason for interviewer interruptions.

This analysis provided the basis for an alternative rationale for why interruptions occur so frequently in political interviews. Politicians are frequently criticised for evasiveness. If a politician gives a lengthy but equivocal response, the interviewer has to be able to interrupt effectively in order to get the politician to address the question. This may be why the most frequent reason for interviewer interruptions is to re-formulate questions. The association of interruptions with disagreements can also be interpreted relatively easily, given that political interviews are typically adversarial. In such a situation, disagreement is best expressed at the time the other person is saying something with which you disagree, rather than later on when the conversation may have moved on to a different topic. Hence, to disagree effectively, it may be necessary to interrupt. In short, there may be perfectly good situational reasons for the high frequency of interruptions in political interviews without the need for an explanation in terms of misleading turn-yielding cues.

Overall, the results showed a striking similarity between Margaret Thatcher and Neil Kinnock both in the way in which they interrupt and in the way in which they were interrupted. But there was one interesting difference – that is, in the extent to which they commented on interruptions. Margaret Thatcher objected much more frequently to being interrupted, in two instances where there was no indication that the interviewer was about to interrupt! On one of these occasions, the interviewer (Jonathan Dimbleby) openly protested that he was not about to interrupt. Thus, it is easy to receive the impression that Margaret Thatcher was frequently interrupted, simply because of her frequent objections. All the explicit comments concerning interruptions made by the two politicians are summarised in Tables 6.4 and 6.5.

Margaret Thatcher's tendency to comment explicitly on interruptions can be related to a number of other aspects of her interview style. One feature was a tendency to reformulate questions and criticism as accusations; another a tendency to personalise issues. Both features can be illustrated in the following excerpt from the interview with Jonathan Dimbleby:

Dimbleby:　. . . if the National Health Service is only safe in your hands wouldn't it be a good idea to demonstrate that, and a way of demonstrating that might be to use it some people would say.

Thatcher:　don't you think that you'd have *got at me* very much had I said, look I've got to be in on a certain day and I've got to be out on a certain day, you'd *accuse me* of queue jumping and *you'd have been the first to have done so.*

Dimbleby:　certainly not

Another feature of Margaret Thatcher's style was the way in which she frequently addressed the interviewer formally by title and surname. On two

Table 6.4 Margaret Thatcher's comments on interruptions

no please let me go on
may I just finish
one moment
I must beg of you
please may I
let me finish it
can I just finish it
will you give me time
may I say something else
may I now and then say a word in my own defence
please may I say
just let me get this
I would love to go on
but can I just go on
yes but one moment
one moment
please there's just one other thing
one moment er hold on
no don't stop me
no let me stand up for my own government
but please

Table 6.5 Neil Kinnock's comments on interruptions

if I can just finish
if I can tell you why
we'll do without the heckling
wait a minute
I'm going to stop you then
if I can just finish the point
hold on a second
you prolong my answer by the interjection

occasions, she actually used the incorrect title with Sir Robin Day: 'Mr Day I think you're asking me I think you're I'm so sorry I made that mistake last time I won't do it again Sir Robin...' She then repeated the mistake on a subsequent occasion in the middle of one of her answers with 'but Mr Sir Robin...' None of these tactics were employed by Neil Kinnock.

All these devices can be interpreted as ways of wrong-footing the interviewer. Margaret Thatcher's explicit comments on interruptions gave the impression that the interviewer was somehow behaving badly by continually interrupting, whereas the objective evidence showed a striking and significant degree of similarity in the use of interruptions between the two political leaders. Similarly, personalising issues and taking questions and criticisms as accusations again gave the impression that the interviewers were behaving badly, whereas they might say they were simply trying to do their job: namely, to ask questions and put forward political arguments.

Finally, the device of naming the interviewers gave the impression that the interviewers need to be called to account for misdemeanours – misdemeanours which, as this analysis showed, they were not actually perpetrating. Misnaming the interviewer did more than this. Failing to use Sir Robin Day's title can be construed as an overt put-down, especially given that it was Margaret Thatcher who had been responsible for awarding him the knighthood in the first place (in 1981). With Jonathan Dimbleby, she used a different form of put-down. She asked him: 'Do you remember Harold Wilson? Well perhaps you don't you're too young.' There can be no doubt at all that Jonathan Dimbleby was old enough to remember the former Labour Prime Minister Harold Wilson – as Margaret Thatcher well knew.

One of the interviewers (Sir Robin Day) made several explicit references to these tactics. On one occasion, he said: 'I didn't accuse you of anything Prime Minister, you keep on accusing me of accusing you of things.' On another occasion (after trying unsuccessfully to interrupt Margaret Thatcher on several occasions): 'We're not having a party political broadcast here we're having an interview which must depend on me asking some questions occasionally.' The fact that such an experienced and eminent interviewer as Sir Robin Day should have had to justify his role in this way is a very striking example of the way in which Margaret Thatcher's tactics put the interviewer on the defensive. Jonathan Dimbleby was actually reduced to apologising for asking a question, which can be seen in the following interchange. Margaret Thatcher was responding to a question about whether she would rule out extending Value Added Tax to, for example, children's clothes, books, newspapers, fuel and fares:

Thatcher:	I'm not going any further than that Mr Dimbleby for a very good reason yes people like you will try to go on and on and the moment we say one thing you'll find another and then another
Dimbleby:	well
Thatcher:	one moment
Dimbleby:	the viewer might be interested Prime Minister
Thatcher:	well hold on and then another but you see a Chancellor of the Exchequer has to govern according to the circumstances and no responsible minister would constrain him no responsible minister yes there are so
Dimbleby:	the one you didn't mention were books and magazines to does that mean that they're the ones you're
Thatcher:	no you're going to tr no you're going yes *that's exactly a typical question*
Dimbleby:	I'm sorry

In conclusion, the results of the study provided no evidence to support the hypothesis that Margaret Thatcher was frequently interrupted because she gave misleading turn-yielding cues. Her interruptive style was unusual only in that she voiced frequent interruptions to being interrupted, although the objective evidence showed a striking degree of similarity in the way in which the politicians interrupted and were interrupted by the interviewers. The impression that she was badly treated was compounded by her tendency to personalise issues, to take questions and criticisms as accusations, and frequently to address the interviewers formally by title and surname, as if they needed to be called to account for misdemeanours. In fact, far from lacking basic conversational skills as the misleading turn-yielding cue hypothesis seems to imply, Margaret Thatcher showed a striking mastery of the arts of political one-upmanship. She continually wrong-footed her interviewers and put them on the defensive, such that they felt obliged to justify and even apologise for their role as interviewers.

A debate over interruptions

Unsurprisingly, this study of interruptions in interviews with Margaret Thatcher proved highly controversial. Beattie was given the opportunity by the *Journal of Language and Social Psychology* to respond to the criticisms of his work (Beattie, 1989a); Bull and Mayer (1989) responded to Beattie's response, and Beattie also responded to Bull and Mayer's response (Beattie, 1989b). The ensuing debate ranged over a number of issues, not only over Margaret Thatcher's interview style, but also over more basic concerns as to how to conduct research on interruptions. The main points are summarised below.

Statistics

One of the main criticisms of Beattie's (1982) analysis of the interview between Margaret Thatcher and Jim Callaghan was the inappropriate use of the chi square statistical test. This test is based on the assumption that the data are independent, whereas Bull and Mayer (1988) argued that observations all taken from the same interview are not independent. Beattie (1989a, p. 332) replied to Bull and Mayer as follows:

> In my study the responses were from the same subject, but they were spread out in time. Were these therefore dependent or independent? Who knows, but given the limited way I was trying to extrapolate my data I felt that the chi square was justified.

However, to assume that interruptions all taken from the same interview are independent – even if they are spread out in time – is seriously open to question. For example, if an interviewer interrupts successfully, he may attempt further interruptions; if his attempted interruptions are persistently unsuccessful, he may give up interrupting altogether. The usual statistical convention with chi square to ensure independence is to take only one observation from each participant. There seemed no good reason to abandon this practice in this analysis of just the one interview between Denis Tuohy and Margaret Thatcher.

An important point that emerged from the debate over statistical analysis was the use of different methods to quantify interruptions. Beattie's technique was to calculate the proportion of turn exchanges which took place through interruptions. Bull and Mayer's technique was to calculate the rate at which interruptions occurred as a proportion of the partner's speaking time. These are both perfectly valid techniques of analysis, but they may produce very different results. Thus, calculating the proportion of turn exchanges mediated by interruptions does not necessarily tell us who is being interrupted most frequently. One problem is that this presumably rules out unsuccessful interruptions, which do not result in an exchange of turns. If one politician typically yielded the turn when interrupted, while another typically resisted the interruption, it might appear from this method of calculation that the first politician was being interrupted more frequently, although this would not necessarily be the case.

Using appropriate controls

Beattie's second study (Beattie *et al.*, 1982) demonstrated that significantly more of Margaret Thatcher's turn-disputed utterances were judged as complete than were those taken from the middle of a speaking turn. Bull and Mayer's main criticism of this experiment was the lack of an appropriate control, i.e. another politician. Beattie (1989a) subsequently pointed out that there were insufficient turn-disputed utterances in the 1979 interview with Jim Callaghan to be able to make systematic comparisons.

Nevertheless, a control is still essential. If it can be shown that interviewers interrupt at possible completion points with other politicians, then this would not appear to be an idiosyncratic feature of Margaret Thatcher's interview style. Rather, it would suggest that this is a tactic which interviewers employ to interrupt politicians.

The Interruption Coding System

The ICS was criticised by Beattie (1989a) on a number of grounds. He claimed that it dealt only with simultaneous speech and ignores what Ferguson (1977) called 'silent interruptions'. This was actually a misunderstanding, because the system categorises interruptions irrespective of whether or not they involve simultaneous speech.

Beattie also pointed out that the definition of an overlap in the ICS differs from his own. In the ICS, an overlap is coded if the first speaker completes the utterance, but the second speaker starts before the first has finished, so that simultaneous speech occurs. Beattie (1989a) pointed out that in his own research, an overlap was regarded as occurring when the first speaker reaches a *possible* completion point; this might be after a protracted battle with the second speaker entering right in the middle of a turn (Beattie, 1989a). Hence, there would be no reason for excluding this form of overlap from the general category of interruptions.

Finally, Beattie (1989a) criticised Bull and Mayer for failing to carry out a reliability study. In a typical reliability study, a sample of observations from one scorer are categorised independently by another observer, and their codings are then correlated. In the Bull and Mayer (1988) study, all the scoring was carried out initially by the second author, and then checked by the first author – a much more meticulous procedure. Furthermore, a conventional reliability study using the ICS had already shown high inter-observer agreement (Roger *et al.*, 1988). This study included data from three dyadic conversations between someone who suffered from a stammer and a fluent speaker. Speech dysfluencies make conversation remarkably difficult to categorise, hence they constituted a powerful test of the robustness of the ICS.

Direct test of the misleading turn-yielding cue hypothesis

Bull and Mayer (1988) found highly significant positive correlations between the two politicians in the way in which they both interrupted and were interrupted. A direct test of the misleading turn-yielding cue hypothesis was also conducted, which showed that in 73 per cent of the instances on which Margaret Thatcher was interrupted, it was perfectly clear that she intended to continue speaking. Beattie (1989a) criticised this analysis for a failure to use independent judges and for a lack of technical sophistication, given that in his second study acoustic analyses were also conducted of Margaret Thatcher's intonation (Beattie *et al.*, 1982).

However, these criticisms rather seem to miss the point. If Margaret Thatcher, when interrupted, was still talking and still gesturing, or if there was an audible inhalation of breath, it would seem perfectly clear that she intended to continue speaking. These were the kinds of cue used by Bull and Mayer (1988) in their analysis; from this perspective, more technically sophisticated acoustic measurements were hardly necessary to establish whether Margaret Thatcher had finished talking (Bull and Mayer, 1989).

Sample size

The most basic criticism of Beattie's (1982) study is that it is based on only one interview, and the comparison interview with a different politician was also with a different interviewer. Bull and Mayer's analysis was based on eight interviews, with four interviewers who each interviewed both politicians for exactly the same length of time. Hence, it was possible to make much more systematic comparisons between the two politicians.

However, whereas the interview analysed by Beattie was broadcast during the 1979 General Election campaign, those analysed by Bull and Mayer were all broadcast during the 1987 General Election campaign. It is of course always possible that Margaret Thatcher's interview style had simply changed during the course of those eight years. Bull and Mayer's point was that, after a much more systematic analysis of political interviews and review of the evidence, the alleged idiosyncrasies of Margaret Thatcher's interview style had never really been satisfactorily demonstrated.

Conclusions

Despite all the disagreements, claims and counter-claims covered here, it must immediately be acknowledged that Beattie's (1982) paper did much to stimulate interest in the topic of interruptions of political interviews. The hypothesis about misleading turn-yielding cues was interesting and provocative, it suggested that there was much to learn about a politician's communicative style from detailed 'microanalysis' of conversation.

Beattie's analysis also suggested that there was something distinctive about the kind of discourse which occurs in political interviews, in this instance the high frequency of interruptions. But why do interruptions occur so often in this context? Bull and Mayer (1988) found that the most frequent reason for interviewer interruptions was to re-formulate questions. They argued that one possible reason for this is that politicians are notoriously evasive, hence interviewers may need to interrupt in order to get the politician to address a particular question. Stereotypically, evasiveness is another feature which characterises the discourse of political interviews, although there was little hard evidence on this point. Hence the next set of studies were intended to address the issue of equivocation in political interviews.

7   Equivocation

Introduction

In this chapter, three studies of equivocation are reported, based on televised political interviews with Margaret Thatcher, Neil Kinnock, John Major and Paddy Ashdown. The study of Margaret Thatcher and Neil Kinnock (Bull and Mayer, 1993) was based on the set of eight interviews from the 1987 General Election, which had already been used in the analysis of interruptions reported in the previous chapter. The second set of seven interviews were all conducted with John Major (Bull and Mayer, 1991). Four of these took place in 1990 when he was Chancellor of the Exchequer; the other three were broadcast during 1991, following his appointment (28 November, 1990) as Prime Minister. The final set of 18 interviews with John Major, Neil Kinnock and Paddy Ashdown were broadcast during the 1992 General Election (Bull *et al.*, 1996).

These studies of equivocation were a direct sequel to those on interruptions reported in the previous chapter. They were focussed on a number of issues. In the first instance, criteria were established for identifying what constitute questions, replies and non-replies (Bull, 1994). These criteria were then used to conduct an assessment of the extent to which politicians fail to reply to questions (Bull, 1994). Politicians are notoriously evasive, but this could be just a stereotype; hence, the need for some basic facts on equivocation. The next stage was to investigate the different ways in which politicians equivocate. A typology of equivocation was developed, based on the 1987 interviews with Margaret Thatcher and Neil Kinnock (Bull and Mayer, 1993) and the 1990/1991 interviews with John Major (Bull and Mayer, 1991). Finally, this typology was used to conduct an analysis of the communicative style of these three party leaders (Bull and Mayer, 1991, 1993).

Method

Interviews

The first set of eight interviews with Margaret Thatcher and Neil Kinnock came from the 1987 General Election; full details have already been given in Chapter 6.

The second set of seven interviews were with John Major. Interviewers and interview durations (to the nearest minute) of the four interviews when he was Chancellor of the Exchequer (1990) were as follows:

Brian Walden	28
Peter Jay	38
Jonathan Dimbleby	34 (25 March)
	28 (25 November)

Interviewers and interview durations of the three interviews from 1991, following John Major's appointment as Prime Minister, were as follows:

David Frost	53
Sue Lawley	24
Brian Walden	62

The third set of 18 interviews were from the 1992 British General Election. Six of these interviews were with John Major, six were with Neil Kinnock and six with Paddy Ashdown. Each politician was interviewed by Sir Robin Day, David Dimbleby, Jonathan Dimbleby, David Frost, Jeremy Paxman and Brian Walden. Interview durations (to the nearest minute) were:

	John Major	Neil Kinnock	Paddy Ashdown
Sir Robin Day	25	25	25
David Dimbleby	39	40	38
Jonathan Dimbleby	20	20	17
David Frost	39	15	14
Jeremy Paxman	19	17	17
Brian Walden	42	42	42

Procedure

Transcripts were made of each interview. Questions were defined functionally as requests for information, replies as responses in which the information requested is given. The term 'non-reply' was coined to refer to those responses in which the politician failed to provide any of the information requested in the question. There were also certain utterances which, for a variety of reasons, fell somewhere between replies and non-replies; these were referred to as 'intermediate replies'.

Criteria were then established for identifying questions and responses to questions (replies, intermediate replies and non-replies). In addition, a typology was devised for identifying different forms of equivocation. The two coding systems will be discussed now.

Identifying questions

Defining a question is by no means self-evident. If questions are defined simply according to syntax (i.e. questions are those utterances that take the interrogative form), then there is no problem. But if a question is defined functionally as a request for information, then it does not necessarily require interrogative syntax. Quirk *et al.* (1985) describe what they call 'declarative questions': a type of question identical in form to a declarative statement, except for the final rising question intonation (e.g. 'You realise what the risks are?'; 'They've spoken to the ambassador, of course?'). Indeed, some declarative questions may not even be accompanied by rising intonation, although the function of the utterance is still clearly to request information.

On the other hand, the interrogative can also be used to pose a question that one not only expects to remain unanswered but that one expects to be unanswerable. For example, if a latecomer is greeted with the utterance, 'So what sort of time do you call this then?', it is clearly not a request to tell the time, but a reprimand. Such rhetorical questions are like strong statements and certainly should not be regarded as requests for information.

Quirk *et al.* (1985) distinguished between three different types of question that, although taking the interrogative form, vary according to the type of reply expected. Those that expect affirmation or negation (e.g. 'Have you finished the book?') are called 'yes–no questions'. Those that expect as the reply one of two or more options presented in the question (e.g. 'Would you like to go for a walk or stay at home?') are referred to as alternative questions (sometimes also as disjunctive questions). Those that typically expect a reply from an open range of replies (e.g. 'What is your name?' or 'When are you going out?') are referred to as wh-questions, because they begin with the words 'what,' 'when,' 'why,' 'who' and 'which' (Quirk *et al.*, 1985). It should be noted that Quirk *et al.* do not include 'where' as a question word, but do include 'how' (which of course does not begin with 'wh-'). Thus, because the term 'wh-question' is somewhat confusing, the term 'interrogative word question' may be regarded as preferable (Bull, 2002).

Utterances identified as questions were coded according to the four categories presented by Quirk *et al.* (1985) (yes–no questions, wh-questions, disjunctive questions, declarative questions). In conducting this analysis, it was found necessary to introduce two additional categories: indirect questions and what have been referred to by Jucker (1986) as 'moodless' questions (questions that do not have a finite verb).

A good example of a moodless question can be seen in the following interchange between Sir Robin Day and Neil Kinnock:

Day: Under a Labour government would the trade unions recover much of their pre-Thatcher power?

Kinnock: We've made the propositions and we will put into effect those propositions that there is universal balloting that there is a system er of industrial tribunals that er the membership shall be in control

Day: [interrupts] *Secondary picketing?*

Kinnock: of the trade union and there will be no flying pickets what we will have of course

Day: [interrupts] *Secondary picketing?*

Kinnock: I'll explain what we will have of course is a legal procedure that ensures that British trade unions and British employees have the same civil rights as exist on the other side of the Channel in the rest of the European Community and that means there can be no sac secondary action unless it is directly related to a primary action.

In this example, Day could be understood as asking whether a Labour government would restore the right to secondary picketing, although the question was not couched in the interrogative, nor does it even have a verb. (Secondary action is action by workers whose employer is not a party to the trade dispute that the action relates to [Department of Employment Code of Practice on Picketing.] The right to secondary action was abolished by the Conservative government under the Employment Act of 1982).

Indirect questions, in which the force of the question is expressed in a subordinate clause, were also used on occasion by interviewers as a means of posing questions to politicians. For example, the following extract comes from an interview between Robin Day and Margaret Thatcher (1987 General Election):

Day: What this er remarkable man with the tremendous brain Mr Powell says

Thatcher: mm

Day: in his latest utterance he says it almost defies belief that grown men and women should seriously propose so crazy a scenario which he says is this Russia invades Germany or northern Norway perhaps the United States declines to commit suicide so he says Britain fires a nuclear salvo at Moscow and Leningrad and he asks the question how balmy do you have to be to believe that or believe that the Kremlin believes that.

Thatcher: Yes but you see so many of Enoch's arguments stem from the
starting place he chose and the starting place he chose isn't the
right one.

In this extract, Day could be understood as using the reported speech of
Powell as a means of posing a question to Thatcher; hence, it would be
coded as an indirect question.

The addition of indirect and moodless questions to the four categories
identified by Quirk *et al.* (1985) creates a typology of six major question
types; the frequency of each category is shown in Table 7.1.

Because the data are based on three distinct groups of interviews, broadcast at three different points in time, the results for each set of interviews are
presented separately as well as together for this and the ensuing tables. In
Table 7.1, it should be noted that three of the question types (yes–no, interrogative word and disjunctive) take interrogative syntax, whereas the other
three types (declarative, moodless, and indirect) do not. The results clearly
showed that most (78.8 per cent) of the utterances coded as questions in
these 33 political interviews employed interrogative syntax. The most frequent form of non-interrogative question was the declarative (18 per cent).

Table 7.1 Distribution of question types

	General Election 1987	John Major 1990–1991	General Election 1992	Totals
Interrogative questions				
Yes–no	11.4 (119)	16.1 (169)	26.0 (271)	53.5 (559)
Interrogative word	4.9 (51)	4.6 (48)	13.7 (144)	23.2 (243)
What	2.6 (27)	2.8 (29)	3.5 (37)	8.9 (93)
Who	0.0 (0)	0.0 (0)	0.4 (4)	0.4 (4)
How	0.5 (5)	0.9 (10)	2.5 (26)	3.9 (41)
Why	1.6 (17)	0.4 (4)	6.8 (71)	8.8 (92)
When	0.0 (0)	0.3 (3)	0.1 (1)	0.4 (4)
Where	0.1 (1)	0.2 (2)	0.3 (3)	0.6 (6)
Which	0.1 (1)	0.0 (0)	0.2 (2)	0.3 (3)
Disjunctive	0.7 (7)	0.9 (10)	0.4 (5)	2.1 (22)
Totals	16.9 (177)	21.7 (227)	40.2 (420)	78.8 (824)
Non-interrogative questions				
Declarative	1.9 (20)	4.1 (43)	12.0 (126)	18.0 (189)
Moodless	0.0 (0)	0.4 (4)	2.0 (20)	2.4 (24)
Indirect	0.3 (3)	0.1 (1)	0.4 (4)	0.8 (8)
Totals	2.2 (23)	4.6 (48)	14.3 (150)	21.1 (221)

Notes
Figures in percentages, raw scores in parentheses.
Total no. of questions = 1,045.

All the questions identified in these 33 political interviews could be classified in terms of one of these six categories.

Identifying replies and non-replies

At first sight, what constitutes a reply to a question might seem unproblematic: thus, in the case of yes–no questions, an appropriate reply would be either 'yes' or 'no'. However, a reply to a yes–no question does not always have to be in the form of only 'yes' or 'no'. If someone is asked, 'Do you like Honolulu?' and replies, 'Only a little', this would seem to constitute a perfectly acceptable reply, even though neither yes nor no accompanied 'Only a little' (Bolinger, 1978). Similarly, in the case of disjunctive questions, if a person chooses one or other of two alternatives, this would constitute a reply, but many choices are not necessarily reducible to two alternatives even if presented as such. If in response to the question, 'Would you like to go for a walk or stay at home?' someone said, 'I would rather go out for a drive', this would seem a perfectly acceptable reply, even though neither of the two alternatives has been chosen.

The typology proposed by Quirk *et al.* is useful not only in characterising what utterances should be regarded as questions. It also has significant implications for identifying what utterances should be regarded as replies, because the criteria for deciding what constitutes a reply vary according to the structure of the question. The criteria employed for each type of question are presented below.

INTERROGATIVE-WORD QUESTIONS

Interrogative-word questions ask for a missing variable, and if the politician supplied that missing variable, he or she can be seen as having answered the question. Quirk *et al.* (1985) recognise six major types of wh-questions (what, when, why, who, how and which). The criteria for defining what constitutes a reply to each of these six categories were based on their customary dictionary definition. So, 'what' asks for a selection from an indefinite number of possibilities, or for the specification of amount, number or kind. 'When' asks at what time, on what occasion, in what case or circumstance. 'Why' asks on what grounds, for what reason or with what purpose. 'Who' asks what or which person(s). 'How' asks in what way or to what extent. 'Which' asks what one(s) of a stated or implied set of persons, things for alternatives. However, in addition to the six types of wh-question identified by Quirk *et al.* (1985), it was found necessary to include 'where' as a seventh interrogative word. Again, an appropriate reply is constituted in terms of the dictionary definition of 'where' – at or in what place, position or circumstances.

If the politician gave the information in response to an interrogative-word question as specified, then the response was coded as a reply. If the politician failed to provide that information, then the response was coded as a non-reply, as in the following example from an interview between Robin Day and John Major (1992 General Election):

Major: Well I find it interesting that you should say that er I spent half my time being told by some people that I've suddenly become too aggressive and half my time being told by other people that I ought to be more aggressive I rather suspect in the midst of that I've got it right

Day: Who told you you got

Major: but the but the

Day: who told you you got too aggressive?

Major: (laughs) Well I rather fancy that a number of people have but the poi the important issue is really not just the question of style it's substance it's whether we're raising the issues that really matter to people in this election and that really matters for their futures that's what the election's about.

In this sequence, Major is asked who (i.e. what or which persons) told him he got too aggressive. In giving his response, he failed to specify the persons; hence, the response is coded as a non-reply.

YES–NO QUESTIONS

Yes–no questions invite the answer 'yes' or 'no', and if this response is given, it can be seen as constituting a reply. However, affirmation and negation may be conveyed by words or expressions other than 'yes' or 'no', e.g. 'certainly', 'of course', 'not at all', 'never' (Quirk *et al.*, 1985). In the following extract from the 1992 General Election, it is perfectly clear that Neil Kinnock has answered the question from Sir Robin Day, although he does not use either of the words yes or no:

Day: er you have your own views about PR at Westminster don't you?

Kinnock: I do.

Yes–no questions may also be answered by replies that lie somewhere along a scale of affirmation–negation, e.g. 'probably', 'perhaps', 'it appears so', 'to some extent', 'occasionally', 'very often'. The following example comes from an interview in the 1992 General Election between Jeremy Paxman and Neil Kinnock:

Paxman: Now on the question of PR Roy Hattersley said on *Newsnight* last night that not only this election but the election after this one will be fought on first past the post system do you agree with him?

Kinnock: Oh I think that's quite probable...

Another example comes from the same interview:

Paxman: You're committed to a Scottish Parliament if by any chance that
            Scottish Parliament should have at some stage a majority of SNP
            members could it declare independence?
Kinnock: I suppose it could...

In responding to both these questions, Neil Kinnock is clearly giving a
reply, although he uses neither the words 'yes' or 'no' in doing so.

Conversely, responding with either 'yes' or 'no' does not always constitute a reply. Thus, 'yes' may be used simply to acknowledge the question
rather than reply to it, as in the following example from an interview
between David Dimbleby and Neil Kinnock (1987 General Election):

Dimbleby: What about your attitude to trade unions you've said you're
             going to give a massive return of power to trade unions if
             Labour comes back isn't that something again that people are
             fearful of that is going to lose you votes?
Kinnock: Yes I haven't said by the way that we're going to give massive
             return of power I've never used such a phrase in my life.

In saying 'yes', Neil Kinnock is not replying to the question but simply
acknowledging it; in fact, he goes on to attack the question by claiming that
he has been misquoted.

Similarly, 'no' may precede an attack on the question, rather than signalling a negative reply, as in the following extract from an interview
between David Frost and Neil Kinnock (1987 General Election):

Frost: ...if the situation were to emerge where in fact there was no tac-
             tical voting and as a result of that Mrs T. was returned with a
             majority or a situation in which there was some tactical voting
             and so she was not ret returned with a majority you would rather
             have stayed pure and lost?
Kinnock: No no it isn't a question of purity it's a question of pers percep-
             tion...

In saying no, Neil Kinnock is not replying to the question but attacking it,
objecting to the use of the word 'purity'.

There are also questions which are couched in a yes/no format, but for
which either 'yes' or 'no' may not be a sufficient reply. The following
example comes from an interview between David Dimbleby and Margaret
Thatcher (1987 General Election):

Dimbleby: Were you to be returned tomorrow and come back as Prime
             Minister is there anything you've learnt during this campaign

any lessons you've learnt during this campaign that you would apply in a next period of Thatcher government?

Thatcher: Perhaps you've taught me one that it's not enough actually to do things which result in caring you also have to talk about it but we have done them and I have done them as you know personally although we don't talk about that either.

If Margaret Thatcher answered 'no' to this question, then this would be a sufficient reply; however, if she answered 'yes', then there would also be an expectation that she should identify what it is she had learnt during the election campaign. In this sense, an affirmative answer can be seen as posing an implied interrogative-word question, and it is to this implied interrogative-word question which Margaret Thatcher addressed her reply. Because of this problem, the question has to be regarded both as a yes–no question, and as an interrogative-word question; an affirmative response by the politician would only be categorised as a reply if the politician identified what it is that he or she has learned during the campaign.

DISJUNCTIVE QUESTIONS

Disjunctive questions pose the politician with a choice between two or more alternatives. If the politician chooses one of the alternatives, then this can be seen as constituting a reply. However, it is possible to present an additional alternative, which might also be regarded as a reply. The following extract comes from an interview between David Frost and Paddy Ashdown (1992 General Election):

Frost: ...can you get a feeling of whether as some of the people say Labour's support is stronger and firmer than Tory support or do you think they're both equally if there is such a word wavery?

Ashdown: I think the mood of the country is one of some gloom disappointment...

In making this response, Paddy Ashdown did not actually choose either of the alternatives presented by the interviewer, but at the same time he clearly gave a reply to the question.

Conversely, if the politician does not choose between the alternatives posed by the interviewer, nor offers another alternative, then the response is regarded as a non-reply. This is well illustrated in this extract from an interview between Sir Robin Day and Margaret Thatcher (1987 General Election):

Day: Which would you regard as a greater evil a coalition between Thatcherism and the Alliance and others or letting in a Thatch a a Kinnock minority government committed to socialism and unilateral disarmament?

Thatcher: I do not accept I do not accept that that is the alternative.

NON-INTERROGATIVE SYNTAX

Moodless, declarative and indirect questions might seem to present a problem for this way of analysing replies, because they lack interrogative syntax. However, because moodless and declarative utterances are typically put forward for agreement or disagreement by the interviewee, they can in most cases be treated as a form of yes–no question (Harris, 1991). For example, Jonathan Dimbleby asks Margaret Thatcher (1987 General Election) 'So you expect the proportion in the National Health Service to shift across the private sector in the same way?' (a declarative question which seeks the answer 'yes' or 'no').

To check on this proposal, all the questions which did not take interrogative syntax were coded according to whether they could be regarded for purposes of replies as yes–no, interrogative-word or disjunctive questions. The results of this analysis are shown in Table 7.2. It was found that 92 per cent of all such questions could be regarded as yes–no questions; the remaining questions could be regarded as either disjunctive or as interrogative-word questions. Thus, it would appear that the criteria for deciding what constitutes a reply to yes–no, interrogative-word questions and disjunctive questions can also be applied to those questions which do not take interrogative syntax.

Table 7.2 Forms of reply appropriate for questions that do not take interrogative syntax

	Yes–No	*Disjunctive*	*Interrogative word*	*Totals*
The 1987 General Election				
Declarative	73.91 (17)	8.69 (2)	0.0 (0)	82.6 (19)
Moodless	0.0 (0)	0.0 (0)	0.0 (0)	0.0 (0)
Indirect	4.34 (1)	0.0 (0)	13.04 (3)	17.39 (4)
Totals	78.26 (18)	8.69 (2)	13.04 (3)	100 (23)
John Major 1990–91				
Declarative	82.0 (41)	6.0 (3)	0.0 (0)	88 (44)
Moodless	10.0 (5)	0.0 (0)	0.0 (0)	10 (5)
Indirect	2.0 (1)	0.0 (0)	0.0 (0)	2 (1)
Totals	94.0 (47)	6.0 (3)	0.0 (0)	100 (50)
The 1992 General Election				
Declarative	78.66 (118)	4.66 (7)	0.66 (1)	84 (126)
Moodless	12.6 (19)	0.66 (1)	0.0 (0)	13.33 (20)
Indirect	2.0 (3)	0.0 (0)	0.66 (1)	2.66 (4)
Totals	93.33 (140)	5.33 (8)	1.33 (2)	100 (150)
All three data sets combined				
Declarative	78.92 (176)	5.38 (12)	0.44 (1)	84.75 (189)
Moodless	10.76 (24)	0.44 (1)	0.0 (0)	11.21 (25)
Indirect	2.24 (5)	0.0 (0)	1.79 (4)	4.03 (9)
Totals	91.92 (205)	5.82 (13)	5.82 (13)	100 (223)

Note
Figures in percentages, raw scores in parentheses.

Intermediate replies

In identifying replies and non-replies to questions, there are certain utterances which cannot be regarded as either replies or non-replies. For example, a reply may be implied in the politician's response, but not explicitly stated. Again, a politician may answer a question, but only in part. Furthermore, a response to the question may be interrupted by the interviewer, such that it is not possible to say whether or not a reply would have been given. In each case, the politician cannot be said to have given a full reply to the question, but nor can he or she be said not to have given any reply at all. As a consequence, a third superordinate category of 'intermediate replies' was distinguished. In an independent study of a different set of political interviews, Harris (1991) reached a similar conclusion, referring to what she called 'indirect answers', which can be placed midway on a scale of evasiveness between direct answers and outright evasion.

Three major types of intermediate response were distinguished. The first is the answer by implication, in which the politician makes his or her views clear but without explicitly stating them. So, for example, Sir Robin Day asked Margaret Thatcher (1987 General Election) if the Labour Party won the Election and decommissioned Polaris, whether she thought it would be the duty of the Chiefs of Staff to resign. In an extended answer, Margaret Thatcher stated: 'I know what I would do I just could not be responsible for the men under me under those circumstances it wouldn't be fair to put them in the a field if other people had nuclear weapons . . . but they are free to make their decision that's a fundamental part of the way of life in which I believe.' In giving this answer, Margaret Thatcher made her own views quite clear without ever explicitly stating that she thought it would be the duty of the Chiefs of Staff to resign.

The second type of intermediate response is the incomplete reply. Three sub-categories of intermediate response are distinguished: partial replies, half-answers and fractional replies. If the interviewer is in effect asking two questions (a double-barrelled question), and the politician only answers one of the questions, then this is referred to as a half-answer. The following example comes from an interview between David Frost and Margaret Thatcher (1987 General Election):

Frost: But do you regret the leaking of that letter? Was that a black mark against the government?

Thatcher: Well I indeed I indeed I indeed said that I regretted the the leaking of that letter I said so at the time.

This is regarded as a half-answer, because Thatcher only replied to the first question, she never said whether or not she considered the leaking of the letter was a black mark against the government.

Similarly, in a fractional reply, the politician answers only part of a multi-barrelled question. The following example comes from an interview between Sir Robin Day and Paddy Ashdown (1992 General Election):

Day: Many people reading that may say to themselves how so what on earth is the relevance of PR to better schools curbing inflation unemployment homelessness or any of our other problems?

Ashdown: Let me take that urm absolutely urm better schools would we not have better schools if we'd not had this ridiculous dogmatic argument by Labour and Tories on the basis of less than 50 per cent of the vote the one helping private schools the other helping but underfunding public schools...

In replying to this multi-barrelled question, Paddy Ashdown chose to focus on education without discussing inflation, unemployment or homelessness; hence, it is regarded as a fractional reply.

In a partial answer, the politician replies to only part of a single-barrelled question. The following example is taken from an interview between David Dimbleby and Neil Kinnock (1987 General Election):

Dimbleby: Is it still your position that nobody earning under five hundred pounds a week is going to be damaged in any way financially by the return of a Labour government in terms of tax?

Kinnock: They won't be worse off in income tax that's for certain.

Dimbleby: Well that's not the full answer because income tax is only one part of the tax people pay.

Dimbleby, in his response, made it clear that he did not regard Kinnock's response as a complete answer, because he only dealt with direct taxation, he made no reference to indirect taxation.

The third major type of intermediate response is the interrupted reply, where it is not possible to say whether the politician would have replied to the question or not because of an interruption by the interviewer. The following example comes from an interview between Sir Robin Day and Neil Kinnock (1992 General Election):

Day: Yeah but many many voters may ask this you see why is it that you wanted to scrap our nuclear weapons when the Soviet Union er was our potential enemy and had and had them of their own yet you now want to keep them when the Soviet Union doesn't exist and isn't a danger to us?

Kinnock: Well through those years as I candidly acknowledge and I have since...

Day: [interrupts] You made a mistake.

In this sequence, Kinnock was simply not given the opportunity to respond to the question posed by Day.

The equivocation typology

All 33 interviews were analysed in terms of the above criteria for identifying questions, replies and non-replies. In addition, a coding system was devised for identifying different forms of equivocation. This typology was based on the eight interviews with Margaret Thatcher and Neil Kinnock from 1987, and the seven interviews with John Major from 1990/1991. It was developed inductively on the basis of responses in which the politicians failed to provide the information requested by the interviewers; it was intended to provide the 'best fit' in terms of characterising these responses.

All responses coded as non-replies in the 15 interviews with Thatcher, Kinnock and Major were analysed in terms of the typology, as well as those intermediate replies which took the form of incomplete replies (partial replies, half answers, fractional replies). Incomplete replies fail to provide the full information requested by the interviewer; hence, their inclusion in the typology as forms of equivocation. The full typology is presented below in the 'Results' section.

Coding and reliability

The coding both for the equivocation typology and for identifying questions, replies and non-replies was carried out by at least two researchers working together, one of whom was always the author of this book. Any disagreements were resolved by discussion. In addition, a reliability study was carried out in which the author and another scorer independently coded two of the 1990/1991 interviews with John Major. Reliability was assessed both for the coding of questions, replies and non-replies, and for the categories in the equivocation coding system.

Results and discussion

Reliability

The results, using Cohen's (1960) kappa, showed $k = 0.82$ on the scoring of question-replies/non-replies; $k = 0.75$ on the equivocation typology.

Reply rates

The distribution of replies, intermediate replies and non-replies for each of the three sets of political interviews is presented in Table 7.3. Results for all three data sets combined (33 interviews; 1,026 questions) showed an overall reply rate of 46 per cent, intermediate replies 14 per cent, non-replies

Table 7.3 Distribution of replies, intermediate replies and non-replies

The 1987 General Election	*Kinnock*	*Thatcher*
Replies	38.0 (35)	38.9 (35)
Intermediate replies	6.5 (6)	10.0 (9)
Incomplete answers:	3.3 (3)	2.2 (2)
Partial	1.1 (1)	0.0 (0)
Fractional	0.0 (0)	0.0 (0)
Half	2.2 (2)	2.2 (2)
Answers by implication	0.0 (0)	5.6 (5)
Interrupted	0.0 (0)	0.0 (0)
Non-replies	58.7 (54)	53.3 (48)
Total number of questions	92	90

John Major 1990–1991	*Major*
Replies	41.3 (111)
Intermediate replies	8.9 (24)
Incomplete answers:	1.9 (5)
Partial	0.4 (1)
Fractional	0.0 (0)
Half	1.5 (4)
Answers by implication	4.5 (12)
Interrupted	0.7 (2)
Non-replies	51.7 (139)
Total number of questions	269

The 1992 General Election	*Major*	*Kinnock*	*Ashdown*
Replies	38.9 (70)	47.3 (80)	62.2 (125)
Intermediate replies	21.1 (38)	20.7 (35)	13.9 (28)
Incomplete answers:	3.3 (6)	3.6 (6)	1.5 (3)
Partial	0.6 (1)	1.2 (2)	0.0 (0)
Fractional	0.6 (1)	0.0 (0)	0.5 (1)
Half	2.2 (4)	2.4 (4)	1.0 (2)
Answers by implication	12.2 (22)	11.2 (19)	7.5 (15)
Interrupted	2.2 (4)	2.4 (4)	3.5 (7)
Non-replies	43.3 (78)	35.5 (60)	25.4 (51)
Total number of questions	180	169	201

All three data sets combined	
Replies	45.6 (456)
Intermediate replies	14.0 (140)
Incomplete answers:	2.5 (25)
Partial	0.5 (5)
Fractional	0.2 (2)
Half	1.8 (18)
Answers by implication	7.3 (73)
Interrupted	1.7 (17)
Non-replies	43.0 (430)
Total number of questions	1,001

Note
Figures in percentages, raw scores in parentheses.

43 per cent. These results are very similar to those of a completely independent study by Harris (1991), who found with a different set of political interviews (principally with Margaret Thatcher and Neil Kinnock) that the politicians gave direct answers to just over 39 per cent of questions.

In comparison, it is interesting to consider reply rates in televised interviews with people who are not politicians. The late Diana, Princess of Wales, in her celebrated interview with Martin Bashir (20 November, 1995), replied to 78 per cent of the questions put to her (Bull, 1997). Louise Woodward, the British au-pair who was convicted of the manslaughter of eight-month-old Matthew Eappen, in an interview with Martin Bashir (22 June, 1998), replied to 70 per cent of the questions (Bull, 2000b). Monica Lewinsky replied to 89 per cent of questions posed by Jon Snow (4 March, 1999) in an interview concerning her affair with President Clinton (Bull, 2000b). The mean reply rate of 79 per cent across all three interviews is significantly higher than the mean reply rate of 46 per cent for each of the three sets of political interviews discussed in this chapter (Mann Whitney $U = 0$, $p < 0.05$ for each data set).

Equivocation typology

Thus, the results of all these studies supported the popular stereotype of politicians as evasive. The different ways in which politicians equivocate is presented in the typology below. It is organised in terms of both superordinate and subordinate categories, identifying in total 35 different forms of equivocation.

1 Ignores the question

The politician simply ignores the question without making any attempt to answer it or even to acknowledge that the interviewer has asked a question, for example:

Thatcher: ...that is the only power you have the power from the ballot box at every election you submit yourself to the judgement of your people on your stewardism
Frost: But that back on January 27th though why did you say that?
Thatcher: and then don't forget I also have another submission to make to the judgement of my party and that is every single year I'm the first leader to whom that's happened...

(In this example, Margaret Thatcher simply continued talking without even acknowledging that the interviewer has asked a question, let alone attempting to reply to it – hence, she ignored the question.)

2 Acknowledges the question without answering it
The politician acknowledges that the interviewer has asked a question but then fails to give an answer, for example:

Thatcher:	. . . they also will get housing benefit which meets their rent they will also get rate rebate and also may I point out that when er we come to . . .
Dimbleby, J.:	[interrupts] Would you accept they live in poverty Prime Minister?
Thatcher:	please there's just one other thing when we get bad weather the Labour Party only gave 90 million pounds a year on heating allowances with us it's up over 400 million . . .

(In this example, Margaret Thatcher did acknowledge that Jonathan Dimbleby had asked a question ['please there's just one other thing'] but continued her response to the previous question.)

3 Questions the question
Two different ways of questioning the question are distinguished:

(a) Request for clarification. The politician asks for further information about the question. For example:

Dimbleby, J.:	. . . and I should be glad if you would ask Mrs Thatcher what advice she can give me in order to spend the extra 15p she awarded me in the budget to my best advantage what is your advice to her?
Thatcher:	The 15p awarded in the budget?
Dimbleby, J.:	I thi I think she was probably referring to the April uprating in practice which in fact gives her I think 11p a day

(b) Reflects the question back to the interviewer, for example:

Day:	If you have an overall majority Mr Kinnock say with about 350 MPs what proportion of those will be on the hard left?
Kinnock:	Well you tell me

4 Attacks the question
The politician attacks or criticises the question; eight different reasons for attacking the question are distinguished:

(a) The question fails to tackle the important issue, for example:

Day:	But do you accept that Western freedom the freedom of Western Europe is ultimately assured by the nuclear weapons behind NATO?

Kinnock: I think the fact that nuclear weapons exist and they're a fact of life and that there are two superpowers each co counterpoised against each other is the predominant issue

(b) The question is hypothetical or speculative, for example:

Frost: But given that scenario there I mean could Labour cope if if that came true could you cope or would you be shot out of the water in in a guff of wind?

Kinnock: It's the stuff of which novels are made I don't think that it could be or should be regarded as a serious proposition...

(c) The question is based on a false premise, for example:

Day: ...and he asks the question how balmy do you have to be to believe that or believe that the Kremlin believes that?

Thatcher: Yes but you see so many of Enoch's arguments stem from the starting place he chose and the starting place he chose isn't the right one this has always been one of Enoch's problems...

(d) The question is factually inaccurate, for example:

Dimbleby, J.: In the present circumstances do you think that those 2 million or so pensioners who rely on the basic state pension have enough to live a decent life?

Thatcher: But they don't have to rely on the basic state pension

(e) The question includes a misquotation, for example:

Dimbleby, D.: What about your attitude to trade unions you've said you're going to give a massive return of power to trade unions if Labour come back isn't that something again that people are fearful of that is going to lose you votes?

Kinnock: Yes I haven't said by the way that we're going to give massive return of power I've never used such a phrase in my life

(f) The question includes a quotation taken out of context, for example:

Dimbleby, J.: What do you make of this statement if I can quote it to you irrespective of whether or not we win the election there's a major struggle coming about the kind of Labour Party we want to see

Kinnock: I've read the piece and you've got it out of context

(g) The question is objectionable, for example:

Dimbleby, J.: The one you didn't mention were books and magazines does that mean they're the ones that might be...

Thatcher: No you're going to tr you're going yes and that's exactly a typical question

(h) The question is based on a false alternative, for example:

Day: Which would you regard as a greater evil a coalition between Thatcherism and the Alliance and others or letting in a Thatch a a Kinnock minority government committed to socialism and unilateral disarmament?

Thatcher: I do not accept I do not accept that that is the alternative

Day: Supposing it was?

Thatcher: I think you have possibly posed a false alternative.

5 Attacks the interviewer

Criticises the interviewer as distinct from attacking the question, for example:

Thatcher: Look if anyone tried to put Value Added Tax on children's clothes and shoes they would never never never get it through the House er

Dimbleby, J.: So that's out?

Thatcher: ...now I'm not going any further than that Mr Dimbleby for a very good reason yes people like you will try to go on and on and the moment we say one thing you'll find another and then another

6 Declines to answer

Five different ways of declining to answer a question can be distinguished:

(a) Refusal on grounds of inability, for example:

Day: If you're reelected for another four or five years will inflation be brought down to zero?

Thatcher: It will be our aim to bring down inflation further we shall run our financial policies in that way I wish I could promise it would be brought down to zero I can't

(b) Unwillingness to answer, for example:

Day: The hypothesis I was discussing wouldn't you regard that as a defeat?

Thatcher: I am not going to prophesy what will happen

(c) I can't speak for someone else, for example:

Day: If Labour wins Prime Minister and decommissions Polaris immediately as Mr Kinnock has announced his intention of doing what do you think is the duty of the Chiefs of Staff to resign if they disagree with that order or to obey the orders of the democratically elected Queen's first minister?

Thatcher: The Chiefs of Staff have to make up their own mind each person is responsible for what he decides it'll be for the Chiefs of Staff to decide . . .

(d) Deferred answer. It is not possible to answer the question for the time being, for example:

Walden: . . . is that what you're telling me?

Major: Brian I'm telling you to wait for the consultation document which will be published very shortly

Walden: Will I will I then see that you have changed your mind or see that you haven't?

Major: Wait for the consultation document Brian and then you can make up your own mind

(e) Pleads ignorance, for example:

Walden: Let me put it to you Mr Major that at least one other candidate I say at least because I don't want to bring Mr Hurd into this at the moment but at least one other candidate in this election Mr Heseltine would not accept that view would he?

Major: Well I don't know whether Michael would accept that view at all on Thursday and I'm not going to be tempted along this route

7 Makes political point

Eight different ways of making political points are distinguished:

(a) External attack – attacks opposition or other rival groups, for example:

Dimbleby, D.:   . . . are you saying that a third of the people are supporting a party that is revolutionary and quite different and militant and unacceptable in the way the Labour Party used to be that they've all been conned?

Thatcher: They have done everything possible to hide their militants and to hide their real plans during this election

(b) Presents policy, for example:

Day: That is why I'm asking what you would do
Kinnock: ...it is a government a Labour government that is committed to combating inflation to fighting poverty...

(c) Justifies policy, for example:

Dimbleby, J.: Well what sense of negotiations is that then?
Kinnock: ...Cruise weapons have never enjoyed the majority support of the British people they don't enhance our security they're weapons of first use

(d) Gives reassurance, for example:

Day: ...don't you think some of them are worried about some of the people on the hard left wing of the Labour Party who advocate things that disgust many ordinary people?
Kinnock: ...I think the British people have come to know me well enough to know that there is nobody on what you describe as the hard left or any of those elements that may or may not be in or around the Labour Party that exercises any influence

(e) Appeals to nationalism, for example:

Dimbleby, J.: Wouldn't it lead to they should have the right to do so as well?
Thatcher: No I'm not talking about the logic I'm talking about Britain's history I'm talking about the fact that Britain hung on when the rest of Europe surrendered I'm talking about the fact that Britain was right in the beginning of the atomic weapon

(f) Offers political analysis, for example:

Dimbleby, J.: ...wages are running at seven per cent at the moment do you regard that as too high from the point of wages?
Kinnock: ...where does inflation come from most of our inflation is imported in er inflation it comes from movements in commodity and import prices and the effects of our currency

(g) Self-justification, for example:

Day: Does it surprise you or upset you when you see yourself or hear yourself described as a hard woman uncaring and out of touch with the the feelings of ordinary folk?

Thatcher: …I certainly hope they would not level it at me personally because as you know both Dennis and I spend a great deal of time working for our own favourite causes my my own the National Society for Prevention of Cruelty to Children

(h) Talks up one's own side, for example:

Dimbleby, D.: Do you think it does you political damage do you think that's why the Tories are not making the advances that you must have hoped when you came into office eight years ago they would be making?

Thatcher: No but I think we have made the advances there is I think we have actually transformed Britain

8 Gives incomplete reply
Five different forms of incomplete reply are distinguished.:
(a) Starts to answer but doesn't finish (self-interruption), for example:

Frost: But why not then because of your principles?
Thatcher: Because the health service is run look Mr Frost you use the private health service as well you exercise your freedom of choice…

(b) Negative answer. The politician states what will not happen instead of what will happen, for example:

Day: Would you have no incomes policy?
Kinnock: …what I'm setting aside is the idea either the the guiding lights of Selwyn Lloyd or the legislated incomes policies of Mr Jenkins and Mr Wilson in the sixties or the incomes policies of fixed norms or Ted Heath's counter-inflation incomes policy those whilst having possibly an initial impact never managed to last and all they did was store up difficulties for the future much better to follow through…
Day: [interrupts] That is why I'm asking what you would do

(c) Partial reply
(d) Half answer
(e) Fractional reply

Examples for each of these three subcategories have already been given in the procedures for identifying questions, replies and non-replies above. Partial replies, half answers and fractional replies are regarded as intermediate replies in the procedure for identifying questions, replies and non-replies. However, because these responses supply only part of the information requested, they are regarded as forms of equivocation, and hence included in this typology.

9 Repeats answer to previous question, for example:

Kinnock: What I've said is that the US President whoever the US President was would only take a decision to commence or to respond to nuclear war according to United States priorities

Dimbleby, J.: Well supposing he decided to respond what would you do then?

Kinnock: ...even our strongest allies the United States of America would only take a decision to use their nuclear weapons either for themselves or on behalf of others according to their own priorities

10 States or implies that the question has already been answered, for example:

Kinnock: ...as far as secondary picketing is concerned er in pursuit er of a trade dispute in connection with that trade dispute the same kind of right that workers enjoyed for seventy years in this country is a right that should be enjoyed in order to be able to do that and the reason why it was awarded...

Dimbleby, J.: [interrupts] That means you do approve of secondary picketing being restored or not?

Kinnock: to well I think I made that pretty clear

11 Apologises, for example:

Dimbleby, D.: ...isn't one of the difficulties for the Tories that your way of governing and talking about government gets up the noses of a lot of voters?

Thatcher: Well I'm sorry if it does it's not intended to I'm very sorry if it does

12 Literalism
The literal aspect of a question which was not intended to be taken literally is answered, for example:

Lawley: So are you suggesting in fact that rooming houses in Brixton and Downing Street are not so far apart after all?

Major: Well they're about four miles as the crow flies

In using the equivocation typology, it is important to realise that one response to a question can be coded in terms of several categories. In the following example, Jonathan Dimbleby asked Margaret Thatcher a question about pensioners; the equivocation categories are given in square brackets:

Dimbleby, J.:   Would you accept they live in poverty Prime Minister?

Thatcher: Please there's just one other thing *[acknowledges the question without answering it]* when we get bad weather the Labour Party only gave 90 million pounds a year on heating allowances *[makes political point – external attack]* with us it's up over 400 million and that too is important and we've been able to do these things because under a Conservative govern-ment we've had strong growth and a strong economy without that we'd not be able to do them *[makes political point – talking up one's own side]* of course one would always like to do more but fortunately now most people are retiring with two pensions the basic and an occupational pension a large number have savings 71 per cent of pensioners who retire have savings a half of them have their own homes and of course more and more will have shares *[makes political point – offers political analysis]*

Overall comparison of forms of equivocation

A comparison was made of the equivocation profiles for Margaret Thatcher, Neil Kinnock and John Major, which is shown in Table 7.4. Making politi-cal points was by far the most frequent technique used by all three poli-ticians (76 per cent for Margaret Thatcher; 66.7 per cent for Neil Kinnock; 64.8 per cent for John Major). Attacking the question was the second most

Table 7.4 Equivocation profiles for John Major, Margaret Thatcher and Neil Kinnock

Equivocation category	Thatcher	Kinnock	Major
1 Ignores the question	5.5	5.3	2.1
2 Acknowledges the question	3.7	8.8	7.0
3 Questions the question	1.9	1.8	0.7
4 Attacks the question	25.9	36.8	33.1
5 Attacks the interviewer	13.0	–	–
6 Declines to answer	22.2	7.0	36.0
7 Makes political point	76.0	66.7	64.8
8 Gives incomplete reply	9.3	12.3	4.8
9 Repeats answer	5.5	3.5	2.1
10 States or implies has already answered question	–	7.0	1.4
11 Apologises	1.9	–	–
12 Literalism	–	–	1.4

Notes

All figures represent a percentage of the total number of equivocal responses for each speaker, e.g. 76 per cent of Margaret Thatcher's equivocations contain political points. Columns add to more than 100 per cent because categories are not mutually exclusive.

frequent form of equivocation for both Margaret Thatcher (25.9 per cent) and Neil Kinnock (36.8 per cent). For John Major, declining to answer was the second most frequent form of equivocation (36 per cent), the third was attacking the question (33.1 per cent).

Pairwise comparisons showed highly significant correlations between the three politicians on the superordinate equivocation categories. Margaret Thatcher/Neil Kinnock 0.93 (N [number of categories] = 11; $df = 9$; $p < 0.01$, two-tailed); Margaret Thatcher/John Major 0.94 (N [number of categories] = 12; $df = 10$; $p < 0.01$, two-tailed); Neil Kinnock/John Major 0.88 (N [number of categories] = 10; $df = 8$; $p < 0.01$, two-tailed). The mean correlation between the three pairwise comparisons was 0.92. Thus, in terms of the superordinate categories, the three politicians equivocated in highly similar ways.

Individual differences in communicative style

However, if both superordinate and subordinate categories are analysed, it is possible to discern distinctive forms of equivocation, unique to each of the three politicians.

Margaret Thatcher (Bull and Mayer, 1993)

A highly distinctive feature of Margaret Thatcher's style was to make personal attacks on the interviewer. So, for example, Sir Robin Day asked Margaret Thatcher which she regarded as a greater evil: a coalition between Thatcherism and the Alliance and other minority parties or letting in a Kinnock minority government committed to socialism and unilateral disarmament. In her reply, Margaret Thatcher said:

> nothing you say will trap me into answering what I do not believe will happen or trap me into saying er precisely how we would react to that circumstances you know I might indeed I would consult my cabinet colleagues *the very thing you've accused me of not doing.*

Sir Robin Day replied, 'I didn't accuse you of anything Prime Minister you keep on accusing me of accusing you of things.' This tactic of attacking the interviewer is entirely consistent with the aggressive strategies discussed in Chapter 6, in which Margaret Thatcher was found to wrong-foot interviewers and put them on the defensive by making frequent objections to interruptions, by personalising issues and by taking questions and criticisms as accusations.

There was also one occasion in which Margaret Thatcher used an apology as a form of equivocation. This was in a very challenging interview, in which David Dimbleby asked her: 'isn't one of the difficulties for the Tories that your way of governing and talking about government gets up the noses of a lot of voters?' Thatcher's response was to say: 'Well I'm sorry if it does it's not intended to I'm very sorry if it does.' It is interesting that in producing this apology, Thatcher neither acknowledged nor denied that one of the difficulties for the Tories was that her way of governing 'gets up the noses of a lot of voters', hence she did not actually reply to the question.

Neil Kinnock (Bull and Mayer, 1993)

The two forms of equivocation unique to Neil Kinnock in these interviews were *negative answers* and *reflecting the question*.

Reflecting the question is a subcategory of the superordinate category *questions the question*. It can be illustrated from the interview with Sir Robin Day, who asked Neil Kinnock if the Labour Party achieved an overall majority with about 350 MPs, what proportion of those would be on the hard left? Neil Kinnock's response was simply to say, 'You tell me', whereupon Robin Day simply reiterated the question. Reflecting the question in this way can be seen as a very ineffectual strategy, whereby Neil Kinnock failed to fulfil the role expected of an interviewee by not even attempting to answer questions put to him.

Negative answers are a subcategory of the superordinate category *gives incomplete reply*. They take the form of stating what will *not* happen instead of what *will* happen. A good example can be seen in Neil Kinnock's response to Sir Robin Day's question as to whether the Labour Party would have an incomes policy. Neil Kinnock replied:

> now all governments because they are governments have had incomes policy taxation itself is a policy for incomes what I'm setting aside is the idea either the the guiding lights of Selwyn Lloyd or the legislated incomes policies of Mr Jenkins and Mr Wilson in the sixties or the incomes policies of fixed norms or Ted Heath's counter inflation incomes policy.

Negative answers again can be seen as an ineffectual form of non-reply since they simply invite the interviewer to ask for a positive answer! This is precisely what Robin Day did: he replied, 'That is why I'm asking what you would do.'

The use of *negative answers* and *reflecting the question* contrasted sharply with the aggressive tactics of Margaret Thatcher. One way of assessing the effectiveness of these strategies is to look at the response of the interviewers. Following an attack on the interviewer by Margaret Thatcher, they typically asked a new question (in 83 per cent of cases) rather than reformulating the original question. However, Neil Kinnock's attempts to reflect the question on each occasion led to the interviewer simply reiterating the point. Most of his negative answers (75 per cent) also typically led to reformulations of the question by the interviewers. Thus, whereas Margaret Thatcher's aggressive tactics had the effect of inhibiting the interviewers from pursuing a particular line of enquiry, the defensive tactics of Neil Kinnock simply invited further questioning on the same topic.

John Major (Bull and Mayer, 1991)

There were three forms of equivocation distinctive to John Major. One of these was termed the *literalism*, in which a question is taken literally (and not in the sense in which it was clearly intended) as a means of not giving a reply. The other two forms of equivocation were subcategories of the superordinate category *declines to answer*. One of these was *pleading ignorance*, simply saying 'I don't know' in response to a question. The other was termed the *deferred reply*, in which the politician says he or she is unable to answer the question at the present time.

A good example of a *literalism* can be seen in John Major's response to the following question from Sue Lawley. Lawley's question was clearly intended to ask Major about the transition from his lowly origins in Brixton to his elevation to the position of Prime Minister. By taking the question literally and turning it into a joke, Major is able to avoid giving a reply, hence also to avoid talking about aspects of his early life, which perhaps he found potentially embarrassing:

Lawley: So are you suggesting in fact that rooming houses in Brixton and Downing Street are not so far apart after all?
Major: Well they're about four miles as the crow flies

A much more substantive example of a *literalism* comes from an interview with Brian Walden in the 1992 General Election (22 March). In this instance, Major used this device as a means of avoiding discussion of a serious policy issue. Walden cited a statement made by the then Chancellor of the Exchequer Norman Lamont in which he referred to unemployment and recession as 'the price we've had to pay to get inflation down . . . a price well worth paying'. Walden then said: 'I can't imagine a more uncaring statement than that and that's true isn't it?'

Being uncaring about unemployment was a charge often levelled at Conservative governments between 1979 and 1992. Major's defence against the charge is interesting. In an extended response, he referred to the condition of what were then called unemployment *offices*. 'Practically the first speech . . . that I made in the House of Commons was about actually improving the conditions in what were then called unemployment offices. They were such bare sparse nasty places to go into, it's no way to treat people and to deal with people when they're facing the very real difficulty they've changed dramatically across the country and they will change dramatically elsewhere. . .' Thus, rather than dealing with the substantive issue of employment, Major dealt with the question in a rather literal way by confining his response simply to the physical state of unemployment offices.

The other two forms of equivocation distinctive to John Major were both different ways of declining to answer a question. In a *deferred reply*, the politician says he or she is unable to answer the question for the present time. In John Major's case, this might be termed the 'wait and see' strategy, as can be seen from the following two extracts from an interview with Brian Walden (14 April, 1991). In these examples, Walden was questioning Major about a new local services tax intended to replace the disastrous poll tax in which a flat rate had been imposed upon each individual under Margaret Thatcher.

Walden: ...are you getting at when that document is published we shall find that this new local services tax is a twin tax, which has a property element and it has a personal element. And if one stretched all sorts of points and especially if one was a Tory and supported the poll tax one could regard the personal element as still being a bit like the poll tax is that what you're getting at?

Major: Brian I believe in the constitutional proprieties that when you're working out a proposal and you have to take it through cabinet you do take it through cabinet and then you discuss it and defend it and propound its virtue – that is what I'm going to do. I'm not going to leak to you piecemeal what is going to be in that document you will have to wait and see

Walden: All right...

Major: You won't have long to wait...

The second extract comes from later in the same interview:

Walden: ...is what you're telling me that and it's not unreasonable if this is what you want to say – well yeah I did wobble a bit on it as a matter of fact Brian I thought one thing and then I had all this technical advice which I rate so highly not to mention some very serious chats with the chief whip and other people and I changed my mind is that what you're telling me?

Major: Brian I'm telling you to wait for the consultation document which will be published very shortly

Walden: Will I will I then see that you have changed your mind or see that you haven't?

Major: Wait for the consultation document Brian and then you can make up your own mind

Walden: Well Prime Minister of course we shall have different judgements perhaps as to whether you've wholly dispelled the fears that you have in fact fudged and wobbled on the poll tax...

The problem with this strategy is that it does nothing to dispel Walden's formulation that Major has 'fudged and wobbled'. Major was widely criticised throughout his premiership as weak, ineffectual and indecisive, and this strategy of 'wait and see' could be seen as making him look ineffectual and unable to deal competently with the issues of the day.

This is even more true of his second means of declining to answer questions – through pleading ignorance. This was highly distinctive to John Major, and is probably the most surprising coming from a leading politician, especially one who was Prime Minister for seven years. While both Neil Kinnock and Margaret Thatcher would admit to an inability to answer some questions, this usually applied to subjects that everyone accepts are difficult to predict, such as inflation or unemployment. It was also usually stated categorically that these are difficult and complex subjects, for which no one can predict the outcome, as in the example below with Margaret Thatcher and Sir Robin Day.

Day: Can you tell us that if there is four or five more years of Thatcherism whether you can promise or at least hope to achieve any of the following things for instance will unemployment be brought down below two million?

Thatcher: I cannot promise you a specific figure I think you must have asked me that question this time last election possibly in this room in 1983 I could not forecast then that there would have been by now one million more jobs created over a million but there have in fact been er I wouldn't give a forecast then and now unemployment is falling it will depend upon many things it will depend upon world trade that is one reason why one is going to Venice it will depend upon the the world economy it will also depend upon how far thousands and thousands of companies whether in manufacturing extraction or service respond to the markets of the world our strength our economic strength our standard of living depends upon our companies producing goods that people will buy at the price at the quality. . .

However, the difference between this type of statement and John Major's is that he would specifically state that he does not know the answer. Claiming to be uninformed is a particularly ineffective way of presenting non-replies when applied to subjects that everyone assumes he does know. For example, it was common knowledge that Margaret Thatcher made extensive use of image makers. John Major's denial of this in the following extract from an interview with Sue Lawley simply stretched credulity.

Lawley: Er the whole business of bettering yourself bettering yourself in in your book obviously doesn't mean being taken over by the image

makers does it ... your predecessor thought there was wisdom in
it though I mean beyond clothes and hair I mean there was the
voice training and the teeth I mean don't you think there's anything in you that could be improved?

Major: Well I well I don't know that she did or not...

Pleading ignorance can thus be seen as a particularly ineffectual strategy. By
stating a lack of knowledge, one is exposed as either extremely naïve (which
a Prime Minister should not be) or as 'being economical with the truth'.
Either way, it is a 'Catch-22' situation – and the opinion of the viewing
audience is liable to be negative. Furthermore, the interviewer is less
likely to abandon the question but may repeat it on a number of occasions,
or alternatively, may dissent with the aired lack of knowledge. In the
following extract, the interviewer (Brian Walden) challenged John Major's
claim that he did not know the views of another leading Conservative
(Michael Heseltine) on the European Community. The interview was
broadcast on 25 November, 1990. This was during the period of the
Conservative leadership election following the fall of Margaret Thatcher,
when John Major was one of the three candidates alongside Michael
Heseltine and Douglas Hurd.

Major: ...at the moment the position is the substance of the question is
quite simple – could we accept an independent non-elected
central bank with external control over our domestic monetary
situation that is at its heart the question you are putting and my
answer to that is that the House Of Commons will not accept
that at the moment and I do not think we should concede that at
the moment and we will argue that case consistently in the European Community.

Walden: Let me put it to you Mr Major that at least one other candidate I
say at least because I don't want to bring Mr Hurd into this at
the moment but at least one other candidate in this election Mr
Heseltine would not accept that view would he?

Major: Well I don't know whether Michael would accept that view at all

Walden: *You've read his speeches*

Major: Well I've also – it's not for me to answer for Michael he is an
extremely competent and would do so himself

This tactic of pleading ignorance was even used by John Major on occasion
when he did reply to a question. The following example again relates to the
Conservative Party leadership election of 1990. John Major replied to a
question as to whether he consulted his family about becoming leader by
claiming that he was unaware that there would be an election or that he
would be a candidate. Given that the media were discussing little else that
week, this reply seems scarcely credible.

Lawley: The decision of course to run for prime minister when you're a family man is perhaps more difficult than if you're a man on his own how big a decision was it did you sit down with the family and discuss the pros and cons of it?

Major: No there was no time not really you see I wasn't expecting there to be an election for Prime Minister and I wasn't expecting to be a candidate

Since John Major was also in the habit of declining to answer questions through deferred replies (the 'wait and see' strategy), pleading ignorance simply reinforced the negative impression of him as a colourless person with no views of his own. This is where John Major appeared to differ in communicative style from both Margaret Thatcher and Neil Kinnock. Mrs Thatcher, when 'put on the spot', used the aggressive tactic of attacking the interviewer, thereby diverting attention away from the (unanswered) question. Neil Kinnock, whilst not as skilful at distracting attention from the question as Margaret Thatcher, gave long negative replies detailing what he would not do. John Major alone did not attempt to hide the fact that he was not replying to a question. Both in taking questions literally and in declining to answer, John Major showed open evasiveness.

Conclusions

Thus, at a fine level of detail, it is possible to discern interesting stylistic differences between the three politicians. However, at a gross level of analysis, what is also striking is the degree of similarity between them. They failed to reply to a similar proportion of questions and in a similar fashion, especially through making political points and attacking the question. In short, the analyses both highlight individual differences between the politicians but also show that their overall equivocation style was highly similar. Thus, not only do the results support the popular belief that politicians frequently do not answer questions in televised interviews, they also show in detail how that equivocation is achieved.

However, it is also important to know why equivocation is such a characteristic feature of political interviews. This is the focus of the study reported in the next chapter.

8   Face management

Introduction

The previous chapter comprised a detailed analysis of both *how* and *how much* politicians equivocate. The focus of this chapter is on *why* politicians equivocate. Politicians are frequently depicted as slippery and evasive, even as downright deceitful: they are the sort of people who will not give a straight answer to a straight question. According to this view, equivocation can be seen as an aspect of their personalities. An alternative view is that politicians equivocate not necessarily because of their intrinsic evasiveness, but also as a response to the kinds of questions which they are asked in political interviews. To test this hypothesis, two studies are reported in this chapter. The first is based on interviews from the 1992 General Election, and presents an analysis of the way in which questions in political interviews pose threats to face (Bull *et al.*, 1996). The second is based on the 2001 General Election. It compares questions posed to politicians by professional political interviewers with those posed by members of the general public (Bull and Wells, 2002b).

Face-threats in questions

Introduction

The analysis of face-threats in questions was based directly on the theory of equivocation devised by Bavelas *et al.* (1990). They argue that people typically equivocate when placed in what is termed an *avoidance–avoidance conflict*, where all of the possible replies to a question have potentially negative consequences, but nevertheless a reply is still expected. Thus, although it is individuals who equivocate, this has to be understood within the communicative context; equivocation does not occur without a situational precedent. In this sense, equivocation can be seen to occur in response to particular kinds of questions.

This theory, it should be noted, is a general theory of equivocation, not just a way of analysing political interviews. According to Bavelas *et al.*, many ordinary everyday situations are characterised by *avoidance–avoidance conflicts*. Perhaps the most common involves a choice between saying something false but kind and something true but hurtful. For example, a person who is asked to comment on an unsuitable gift from a well-liked friend has two negative choices: saying, falsely, that he or she likes the gift or saying, hurtfully, that he or she does not. According to equivocation theory, the person will, if possible, avoid both of these negative alternatives – especially when a hurtful truth serves no purpose. What they do instead is equivocate; for example, someone might say, 'I appreciate your thoughtfulness' with no mention of what they thought of the actual gift.

Nevertheless, *avoidance–avoidance conflicts* can be seen as particularly prevalent in the context of political interviews (Bavelas *et al.*, 1990). For example, there are many controversial issues on which the electorate is divided. Politicians often seek to avoid direct replies supporting or criticising either position, which would offend a substantial number of voters. Another set of conflicts is created by the pressure of time limits. If the politician is asked about a complex issue but is forced to answer briefly, he or she has to make a choice between two unattractive alternatives: reducing the issue to a simple, incomplete answer, or appearing long winded, circuitous and evasive. Again, if the candidate lacks sufficient knowledge of the issue being addressed, he or she has to make the unfortunate choice between acknowledging ignorance, or improvising, even fabricating an answer.

Why should *avoidance–avoidance conflicts* occur with a high degree of frequency in political interviews? According to one analyst (Jucker, 1986, p. 71), 'It is clear that what is primarily at issue in news interviews is the interviewee's positive face.' Jucker studied interviews not only with politicians, but also with 'experts' and news correspondents (hence, his use of the rather broader term 'news interviews' to refer to these encounters). However, Jucker's research is of direct relevance to developing an understanding of interviews with politicians. He presented a number of analyses, including a flow-chart representation of the structure of interviews, and a consideration of the interactive function of specific words such as 'well', 'now' and 'but'. He also discussed the role of face, and identified 13 different ways in which the face of a politician may be threatened during the course of an interview.

Jucker's face analysis was based on a theory of politeness developed by Brown and Levinson (1978, 1987). They argued that face is important in all cultures; it can be lost, maintained or enhanced. Face preservation is a primary constraint on the achievement of goals in social interaction. 'Some acts are intrinsically threatening to face and thus require "softening",' according to Brown and Levinson (1978, p. 24). Linguistic actions such as commands or complaints may be performed in such a way as to minimise the threat to what are termed 'positive' and 'negative' face, where positive face is the desire to be approved of by others, negative face the desire to have autonomy of action. So, for example, a request to do something may threaten someone's negative face (by restricting their freedom of action), whereas disagreements may threaten positive face (by showing a lack of approval).

According to Jucker (1986), it is upholding positive face which is of particular importance for democratically-elected politicians in the context of political interviews. This is because their political survival ultimately depends on the approval of a majority of people in their own constituency. Negative face, on the other hand, is of little importance, because the politician by consenting to be interviewed has already consented to his or her freedom of action being limited in this way (Jucker, 1986).

Politeness theory was itself based on a highly influential paper 'On Face-Work' by Goffman (1955). The intellectual roots of virtually all contemporary research on face can be traced to this 'seminal' essay, according to Tracy (1990). Goffman (1955, p. 5) characterised face as 'the positive social value a person effectively claims for himself by the line others assume he has taken during a particular contact'. He regarded face as salient in virtually all social encounters, calling 'facework' the means whereby threats to face could be minimised. He specified two kinds of 'face-work': an avoidance process (avoiding potentially face-threatening acts) and a corrective process (performing a variety of redressive acts).

Goffman's observations have a number of important implications for the analysis of political interviews. For example, Goffman points out that not only do people defend their own face in social interaction, there is also an obligation to defend the face of others. Thus, in the context of a political interview, politicians might seek to support the face of political colleagues and allies; at the same time, they would not wish to support the face of negatively valued others, such as their political opponents. Goffman further observed that in many relationships, members of a group come to share a collective face. In the presence of third parties, an improper act on the part of one member can become a source of acute embarrassment to other group members. This is especially true of the British party political system, where the party is paramount. Typically, the politician appears on television as the representative of that party to defend and promote its collective face.

Thus, there are a number of good reasons for arguing that face is of central importance in political interviews. On the basis of politeness theory, it can be argued that politicians must seek to uphold their positive face. On the basis of Goffman's analysis, it can be argued that politicians must concern themselves with three aspects of face: their own individual face, the face of significant others and the face of the party which they represent. Furthermore, the concept of face can also be used to provide an underlying rationale for the *avoidance–avoidance conflicts* identified by Bavelas *et al.* in political interviews, which were described above (p. 131). For example, in equivocating over controversial issues on which there is a divided electorate, politicians can be seen to protect their own face by not espousing opinions which a substantial body of voters may find offensive or unacceptable. Again, the danger of losing face may underlie conflicts created by the pressure of time limits. A politician under pressure to respond briefly to a complex question will neither wish to appear incompetent (by reducing the issue to a simple, incomplete answer) nor devious (by appearing long-winded, circuitous or evasive). Finally, in instances where the politician lacks sufficient knowledge of a particular issue, the risk to face is of either appearing incompetent (by admitting ignorance), or of putting face at risk in the future, if subsequently it can be shown that the answer was less than adequate.

In short, issues of face arguably underlie all the *avoidance–avoidance conflicts* identified by Bavelas *et al.* as responsible for equivocation in political interviews. Indeed, not only can the phenomenon of equivocation be explained in terms of face, it can also be used to explain when and why politicians *do* reply to questions. So, for example, if a politician is asked to justify a specific policy, failure to offer some kind of rationale may raise doubts about the politician's professional competence, or the validity of the policy, or both.

This emphasis on threats to face, it should be noted, is not presented as an alternative to the concept of the *avoidance–avoidance conflict*, rather as an explanation as to why politicians find particular responses aversive (Bull, 1998a). Nor is it being proposed that *avoidance–avoidance conflicts* in political interviews will *only* be created by threats to face. For example, when former President Clinton was questioned over the Monica Lewinsky affair, he was not only at risk of losing face by looking incompetent, treacherous and downright deceitful, he was also in real danger of criminal prosecution and impeachment. Nevertheless, the argument presented in this and the succeeding two chapters is that face management is of prime importance in political interviews, and that it is central to an understanding of the discourse which takes place in this social situation.

In this chapter, an analysis is presented of the extent to which responses to questions in political interviews can be understood in terms of their face-threatening structure. To test this empirically, a new typology of questions was devised, since none of the existing schemas were considered suitable for this purpose. Brown and Levinson's politeness theory is too general: it does not address (nor was it intended to address) the specific threats to face which occur in political interviews. Jucker's typology of face-threatening acts *was* based on the analysis of news interviews, but it focusses principally on the way in which politicians defend their own individual face without reference to the collective face of the political parties which they represent. Furthermore, Jucker's categories were rather too general for the detailed analysis of specific questions.

The typology presented here was derived from the analysis of 18 interviews with the leaders of the three main political parties in the 1992 British General Election. On the basis of this new typology, it was then possible to test the specific hypothesis that politicians, in responding to questions, will tend to opt for the least face-threatening response. As such, this study was intended as a logical counterpart and sequel to the analysis of non-replies described in Chapter 7. Whereas the purpose of that study was to analyse the different ways in which politicians equivocate, the purpose of this study was to investigate why politicians answer some questions and not others, and thereby to test the theory of question–response sequences in political interviews proposed above.

Method

Interviews

A set of 18 interviews from the 1992 British General Election with John Major, Neil Kinnock and Paddy Ashdown formed the basis of this study. Full details of these interviews have already been given in Chapter 7.

Procedure

Transcripts were made of each interview. Questions, replies and non-replies were identified according to the procedures described in Chapter 7. All interviews were coded by at least two raters, one of whom was always the author; disagreements were resolved by discussion.

Based on the complete set of 18 interviews, a coding system was then devised for the measurement of threats to face in political interviews; four raters collaborated in the development of this typology. To check the reliability of this system, one rater independently scored three interviews (one from each politician) which had been coded by the other three raters. The results, using Cohen's (1960) kappa, showed $k = 0.80$ on the face typology. Satisfactory reliability having been demonstrated for the coding system, all 18 interviews were then scored by two raters (one of whom was the author of this book), any disagreements being resolved by discussion. Full details of the coding system are presented in the following section.

The typology of face-threats in questions

The coding system is organised in terms of the three principal components of face which it was argued that politicians must defend: personal face, the face of the political party and the face of significant others. These three components are regarded as superordinate categories and further subdivided into a number of sub-categories. The full list of 19 sub-categories, together with examples of their use, is presented on the following pages; each code is designed to be prefaced with the phrase, 'To answer X would involve the threat of...'

It should be noted that in no sense is it being claimed that this list of 19 potential face-threats is exhaustive for all political interviews. Rather, these were the categories which could be coded reliably and provided the 'best fit' for the 18 interviews studied in this analysis. Nevertheless, given that the study was based on a large sample of questions (557), the typology should be widely applicable, forming a basic framework for the analysis of face-threats in political interviews.

Personal–political face

1   Creating/confirming a negative statement or impression about personal competence.

According to Jucker (1986), an interviewer may threaten a politician's face by accusations, criticisms or disagreements, but a politician may also threaten his or her face by excuses, apologies or by admissions of guilt or responsibility. The creating/confirming distinction in this code is intended to embrace both these possibilities.

For example, Jeremy Paxman asked John Major:

Isn't all this emphasis on personality a cover for the fact that you haven't got a big idea?

If John Major answered 'yes' to this question, it would represent an admission that he has no significant political ideas, and hence threaten his own personal competence.

2   Failing to present a positive image of self, if offered the opportunity.

Some questions do not directly challenge or criticise the politician, but rather present the politician with an opportunity for presenting a positive image of self. However, failure to take advantage of such an opportunity will reflect badly on the politician, and in that sense can be seen to create a threat to face.

For example, David Frost asked Neil Kinnock:

Can you just give me some specific things these are still frames of how your life will be different after twelve months of Neil Kinnock in Number 10?

If Neil Kinnock failed to reply to this question, it would obviously reflect badly on him, since he was being given the chance to say how things would be different if he became Prime Minister.

3   Losing credibility.

If a politician makes a statement which is clearly incredible, then this will threaten face by throwing into doubt the politician's personal judgement.

Credibility refers to all aspects of a statement's credibility – factual, logical or otherwise.

For example, Jeremy Paxman asked John Major:

> But on the nature of the campaign so far this whole pitch of you can't trust Labour, negative campaigning, it's no reason to assume we can trust you is it?

If John Major answered 'yes' to this question, it would ascribe properties to negative campaigning that logically it does not possess. Hence, it would raise doubts about John Major's judgement, and consequently about his credibility.

4   Contradicting past statements, policies, etc.

Although politicians can often be anything but consistent, there is an expectation that they should be consistent in their statements and policies. Hence, if inconsistency can be demonstrated, this is considered to threaten the face of the politician.

For example, Neil Kinnock, in an interview with David Frost, had already stated at the outset that he was not prepared to discuss specific details of the forthcoming shadow budget. David Frost then asked:

> And you're not going to increase Corporation Tax?

If Neil Kinnock either confirmed or denied this question, he would be contradicting his previous statement that he would not give details

5   Personal difficulties in the future.

Goffman suggests that there is a duty to protect one's face against even the possibility of threat: people avoid performing actions which, although acceptable in the present, may reflect badly upon them in the future. Hence, a politician will be careful to avoid making statements which may hamper or constrain his or her future freedom of action.

For example, Sir Robin Day asked Paddy Ashdown whether, if John Major lost the General Election:

> he should resign in those circumstances?

If Paddy Ashdown answered 'yes', John Major should resign, this could create future difficulties, since Paddy Ashdown might have had to work with John Major if, in the event of a hung Parliament, a coalition were formed with the Conservatives.

6   Creating/confirming a negative statement or impression about one's own public persona.

Politicians typically have a personal image which they need to support in public. For example, John Major presented himself as softer and more caring than Margaret Thatcher, while Paddy Ashdown cultivated an image associated with forthrightness and integrity, as occupying the moral high ground in contrast to the other two major political parties.

For example, Jeremy Paxman asked Paddy Ashdown:

> Are you embarrassed at all about the way in which this whole Liberal Democrat campaign has been hung on you?

If Paddy Ashdown answered 'no' to this question, it might imply he encourages a cult of personality, which would be inconsistent with his self-presentation as a committed democrat, hence undermining his claim to occupy the moral high ground.

7   Difficulty in producing/clarifying personal or party beliefs, statements, aims, principles, etc.

If a professional politician is asked to give a view or opinion on a particular issue, then he or she is expected to be able to do so. Failure to reply may result in a loss of face, in that it implies either that the politician has no relevant opinion, or that he or she has not thought through the situation adequately.

For example, David Dimbleby asked John Major:

> I wonder whether wavering voters aren't influenced by not quite knowing where you Prime Minister stand and in particular whether you stand for what Mrs Thatcher your predecessor stood for or whether you stand for something different from her?

If John Major failed to reply to this question, it would imply some uncertainty or reluctance to state what he stands for.

Party face

8   Creating/confirming a negative statement/impression about the party or its policies, actions, statements, aims, principles, etc.

This corresponds to category 1 of the personal–political face. The politician may threaten the face of the party either by confirming a negative statement or by creating a negative statement through, for example, excuses, apologies, admissions of guilt or responsibility.

For example, Brian Walden said to John Major:

> Mr Major things aren't looking all that good for your party are they? You've had to go into this election without that clear and sustained lead that you must have hoped for haven't you?

If John Major answered 'yes' to this question, he would be confirming both the negative characterisation of the Conservative Party, and the implication that the Conservatives will not win the election.

9   Failing to present a positive image of the party if offered the opportunity.

Again, this category corresponds to category 2 of the personal–political face. Some questions do not directly challenge or criticise the party, but rather present the politician with an opportunity for presenting it in a positive light. However, failure to take advantage of such an opportunity will reflect badly on the party, and in that sense can be seen to be face-threatening.

For example, David Frost asked Neil Kinnock:

> Can you just give me some specific things these are still frames of how your life will be different after twelve months of Neil Kinnock in Number 10?

If Neil Kinnock failed to reply to this question, it would obviously reflect badly on the Labour Party, since he was being given an opportunity to present a positive image of the party. (NB this extract is also scored under category 2, since it affects both his personal face and the face of the party.)

10   Future difficulties for the party.

This category corresponds to category 5 of the personal–political face. Just as a politician will be careful to avoid constraining his or her future freedom of action, so too will a politician be careful to avoid restricting the future freedom of action of the party which he or she represents.

For example, David Dimbleby asked John Major:

> It looks very likely that you're going to be short, at any rate, of an overall majority. If that happens, will you do what the Tories did last time they were short of an overall majority and try and do some deal with somebody to keep yourself in office?

If John Major either confirmed or denied this statement, he would be constraining the future freedom of action of the Conservative Party.

11 Contradictions between the party's policies, statements, actions, aims, principles, etc.

Even though political parties are often highly inconsistent in their policies, statements, actions and aims, nevertheless there is an expectation that they should be consistent; if inconsistencies or contradictions can be exposed, this is seen to reflect badly on the party.

For example, Brian Walden asked John Major:

> Are you now admitting that the tax cuts that you are planning for the future will not in fact have such a great impact on the improvement of the public services as if you gave them the money directly?

If John Major confirmed this question, he would be contradicting existing Conservative policies in relation to taxation and the funding of public services.

12 Creating/confirming a negative assessment of the 'state of the nation' (for the party in power only).

This category makes no direct reference to the party and concerns only the 'state of the nation'. However, since negative assessments of the nation may be seen to reflect badly on the party in power, then this is also included under party face.

For example, David Frost asked John Major:

> But this one the latest recession was made in England however it may have been prolonged by overseas factors but it started here didn't it?

If John Major confirmed this statement, that the recession started in England, there is a strong implication that this was somehow the fault of the government, and hence it would reflect badly on his own party.

Significant others

Not only do politicians seek to defend their own face and the face of the party which they represent, they are also under pressure to defend the face of others. This can be subdivided into both supporting positively valued others (such as the electorate, colleagues and members of one's own party) and not supporting negatively valued others, such as political opponents.

13 Not supporting the electorate.

In any democratic political system, a politician must be careful to avoid casting any aspersions on the electorate as a whole.

For example, David Frost asked Paddy Ashdown:

> But before proportional representation becomes as it were final there would be a referendum?

If Paddy Ashdown answered 'no' to this question, it would suggest that the Liberal Democrats did not want to give people any say in what changes would be made to the electoral system.

14 Not supporting a significant body of opinion in the electorate (where there is a division of opinion).

On major social and political issues, where it is possible to discern a substantive division of opinion in the electorate, the politician may also run the risk of offending substantial portions of the electorate.

For example, Brian Walden asked John Major:

> Are you saying that when these people tell the polls what I desperately care about are the public services I reject tax cuts I want the money spent on the public services they are actually lying?

Clearly John Major cannot answer 'yes' to this question, because then he would be casting the 'caring voters' as wilfully lying.

15 Not supporting a colleague.

The term 'colleague' is used to refer to members of the Government (for the party in power) or to members of the Shadow Cabinet/spokespeople (for those who are not in power).

For example, Brian Walden, in an interview with John Major, said:

> Listen to this wonderfully blithe statement that the Chancellor of the Exchequer Norman Lamont gave to the House of Commons during Treasury Questions last year he said rising unemployment and the recession have been the price we've had to pay to get inflation down this is a price well worth paying a lot of people say I can't imagine a more uncaring statement than that and that's true 'n it?

Clearly, if John Major replied 'yes' to this question, he would not be supporting the face of his then colleague Norman Lamont.

16 Not supporting a sub-group of one's own party.

In all the major parties, there are discernible sub-groups whom a politician may have to be careful not to offend.

For example, David Dimbleby asked John Major:

> But do you think the Conservative Party was wrong to have removed her [i.e. Margaret Thatcher]?

If John Major confirmed that it was wrong to have removed Margaret Thatcher, he risked offending those Conservatives who voted her out, whereas if he suggested that it was right to have removed her, then he ran the risk of offending the Thatcherites within the party.

17 Not supporting other positively valued people or institutions.

Outside the party which the politician represents, there will be people or institutions who are the natural allies of that party, whom the politician will be careful to avoid offending, e.g. the trade unions for the Labour Party, the Confederation of British Industry for the Conservative Party.

For example, Jeremy Paxman asked Neil Kinnock:

> Would sympathy actions be legal or illegal?

If Neil Kinnock said that they would be illegal, then he would certainly offend a positively valued institution in the Labour Party, namely, the trade unions.

18 Not supporting a friendly country.

Politicians will not wish to offend friendly countries with whom their own country has strong financial, commercial or military links.

For example, David Frost asked Neil Kinnock:

> If at some stage President Bush were to ring you up and ask the favour that he asked of Mrs Thatcher in 1986 to fly American bombers from British bases against Libya, would you be disposed to agree?

If Neil Kinnock answered 'no' to this question, then he would not be supporting a friendly country, namely the USA.

19 Supporting a negatively valued other.

Negatively valued others may be politicians of opposing political parties, or representatives of countries or organisations with which the country currently has poor relations, e.g. in Britain, the IRA. The politician will seek to avoid supporting the face of such negatively valued others, either by withholding praise or by actively criticising them.

For example, David Frost asked John Major:

Is there really a shift of opinion towards the Liberal Democrats or is it because they have run a better campaign than you have?

In this question, David Frost offered John Major two alternatives, confirming either of which would be offering praise to an opposition party.

Rules of application

Types of question

In Chapter 7, three types of questions were distinguished: yes–no, interrogative word and disjunctive. To each type of question, a number of principal modes of response can be identified. Thus, there are three principal ways of responding to a yes–no question: reply by confirming the proposition; reply by denying the proposition; equivocate. There are two principal ways of responding to an interrogative-word question: reply or equivocate. There are four principal ways of responding to a disjunctive question: reply by choosing the first alternative, reply by choosing the second alternative, reply by choosing a third alternative (not specified in the question) or equivocate. Each possible response option to each of the three types of question is coded in terms of its possible face-threats (the face-threatening structure of the question). If all the principal modes of response to a question are regarded as potentially face-threatening, then it is judged as creating an *avoidance–avoidance conflict*.

No necessary threat

It is important to note that with some questions it is possible to produce a response which does not necessarily involve a threat to face, i.e. a response which is convincing, relevant and can be adequately defended. *No necessary threat* is scored if it is possible to produce such a response, regardless of whether such a response actually occurs.

Furthermore, it is also important to note that a *no necessary threat* response can take the form of either a reply or a non-reply. Sometimes, replying to a question does not necessarily pose any threat to face. Some questions simply ask for a definition; giving a reply should pose *no necessary threat* to face. For example, Sir Robin Day asked John Major in respect of the term 'shroud waving':

I'm interested in that phrase I've not heard before I heard you make it earlier today what does it mean?

Other questions are so favourable that they give the politician an open invitation to make positive statements about him or herself and the party the politician represents. So, for example, Sir Robin Day asked John Major:

> Why do you deserve ... why does the Conservative Party deserve under your leadership what the British people have never given any political party in modern times – a fourth successive term of office?

Conversely, it is also possible for a non-reply to offer *no necessary threat* to the politician, if the question itself is either factually incorrect, or if its presuppositions are seriously open to dispute. In these circumstances, a non-reply can be used to demonstrate the inadequacy of the question without damaging the face of the politician, whereas a reply could imply that the politician had failed to discern either the factual inaccuracies or the contentious presuppositions in the question. For example, Sir Robin Day asked John Major:

> Why have you changed your mind on the desirability of proportional representation?

John Major could quite legitimately attack the question by pointing out that he had never supported proportional representation; were he to attempt to reply, he would be implicitly accepting the proposition that he had changed his mind.

Again, Jeremy Paxman asked John Major:

> If you've got it wrong and if you lose the party'll hang you out to dry won't they?

John Major's response was to say:

> I haven't got it wrong and I'm not going to lose

If John Major were to confirm this statement, he would threaten his own personal position, whereas any attempt at denial would clearly lack credibility. By not replying, he avoids these pitfalls while quite legitimately attacking the speculative and hypothetical nature of the question.

Default codings

Sometimes the very way in which a question is phrased projects a particular answer. So, for example, David Frost asked Neil Kinnock: 'You would in fact admit that they (i.e. taxes) will rise?' Anything less than an explicit refutation of this statement by Neil Kinnock would imply that it is correct, that is, that taxes would rise under a Labour Government. To deal with non-replies to such questions, a number of extra categories are employed, referred to as 'default codings'. These are each considered in turn.

CONFIRMS BY DEFAULT

This occurs where the politician fails to rebut a suggestion conveyed by the question, thereby implicitly confirming it. Typically, such a question involves some kind of negative characterisation of the politician or the party which the politician represents. In the example above, when David Frost asked Neil Kinnock, 'You would in fact admit that they (i.e. taxes) will rise?', a non-reply would be coded as 'confirms by default'.

DENIES BY DEFAULT

This typically occurs where a politician fails explicitly to confirm a suggestion implied by the question. So, for example, David Frost asked Neil Kinnock, 'You're definitely not going to pull more people into that bracket?' (the standard rate tax bracket). This question must be confirmed explicitly because anything less than an explicit confirmation would imply that the Labour Party are intending to increase the number of people paying the standard rate of tax.

NO CLEAR DEFAULT

Not every non-reply has a clear default meaning, in the sense that the politician's non-reply could be taken as meaning either 'yes' or 'no', or that there is no clear default at all. For example, David Dimbleby asked John Major, 'Do you think the Conservative Party was wrong to have removed her?' (i.e. Margaret Thatcher). If John Major confirmed this statement, then he ran the risk of offending those who voted against Margaret Thatcher; if he denied the statement, then he ran the risk of offending the Thatcherites. Since there were clear face-threats in both directions, the default remains unclear.

Use of multiple categories

It is important to note that the categories of face-threat (1–19) are not mutually exclusive. For example, it is possible for a question simultaneously to threaten more than one superordinate category of face (e.g. replying to a question might threaten both the politician's personal–political face and the face of the party which the politician represents). It is also possible for a question to threaten more than one sub-category of a particular type of face (e.g. replying to a question might create or confirm a negative statement both about the politician's personal competence and about the politician's persona).

The meaning of pronouns

In political interviews the problem often arises of reference for pronouns such as 'you'. For example, when David Dimbleby asked John Major, 'Did you expect to be ahead in the polls by now?', the 'you' could refer either to John Major personally or to the Conservative Party as a whole. Given the essentially ambiguous nature of these pronouns it is assumed that they refer to both politician and party unless there are clear contextual cues for deciding otherwise. One way of establishing whether the 'you' is ambiguous is by inserting the name of the individual politician and then the name of the party. If both versions of the sentence still make sense, then it is considered that the 'you' refers to both the individual politician and to the political party the politician represents.

Results

Of the 557 questions analysed in this study, 40.8 per cent were considered to create an *avoidance–avoidance conflict*, in the sense that all the principal modes of response posed some kind of threat to face. This provided strong support for Bavelas *et al.*'s contention that *avoidance–avoidance conflict* questions are particularly prevalent in political interviews. In the remaining 59.2 per cent of questions, it was considered possible to produce a *no necessary threat* response.

Overall, it was hypothesised that politicians will respond to questions in a way which incurs the least damage to face. In *no necessary threat* questions, a *no necessary threat* response was predicted, irrespective of whether this was a reply or a non-reply. In *avoidance–avoidance conflict* questions, an equivocal response was predicted, based on Bavelas *et al.*'s (1990) theory of equivocation. However, it should be noted that an equivocal response is regarded in the face-threat coding system as potentially face-damaging, because it may make the politician seem evasive (Category 7: Difficulty in producing/clarifying personal or party beliefs, statements, aims, principles, etc.). Nevertheless, equivocation is arguably less face-damaging than other threats to personal–political face specified in the coding system (Categories 1–6). It might also be seen as potentially less face-damaging than undermining either the face of the party (Categories 8–12) or significant others (Categories 13–18). Again, equivocation might be seen as preferable to supporting the face of negatively valued others (Category 19).

No necessary threat questions

In 81.5 per cent of *no necessary threat* questions, the politicians produced a *no necessary threat* response. In a further 5.3 per cent of questions, they either answered part of the question, or gave an answer by implication, in the appropriate direction for a *no necessary threat* response. Out of these

86.8 per cent of questions, 69.3 per cent of the responses were replies, 20.3 per cent non-replies and 10.3 per cent intermediate responses.

It is possible to calculate the proportion of *no necessary threat* responses which might be expected to occur by chance. This can be based on the number of possible responses for each type of question (see above, Rules of application, p. 142). For example, with yes–no questions, there are three principal modes of response (confirm, deny, non-reply); hence, the probability of each of these responses occurring by chance is, of course, 33 per cent. For questions beginning with an interrogative word, there are only two principal response options (50 per cent). With disjunctive questions, there are four possible response options (25 per cent).

On the basis of this analysis, Table 8.1 lists the probability for a *no necessary threat* response occurring by chance for each question type, together with the actual incidence of its occurrence. This table clearly shows that the actual proportion of *no necessary threat* responses for all types of question far exceeded that which might have been expected to occur by chance alone.

Avoidance–avoidance conflict questions

44.9 per cent of responses to *avoidance–avoidance conflict* questions were non-replies, a further 18.9 per cent were some kind of answer by implication or incomplete reply, which for these purposes can be regarded as a weaker form of equivocation. Thus, only a third of these questions received a direct reply.

Table 8.2 shows the amount of equivocation that might be expected to occur by chance alone for these *avoidance–avoidance conflict* questions. For yes–no questions, the amount of equivocation is twice what would be expected by chance alone. For the other three question types, equivocation only slightly exceeds what might have been expected by chance, but it

Table 8.1 Probability of *no necessary threat* (*NNT*) responses occurring by chance

Type of question	Probability of NNT by chance (%)	Total no. of responses	Proportion of NNT responses (percentage in parentheses)	Proportion of answers by implication and incomplete replies in appropriate direction (percentage in parentheses)	Total NNT responses (percentage in parentheses)
Yes–No	33	209	167 (80)	14 (7)	181 (87)
Interrogative word	50	103	86 (83)	3 (3)	89 (86)
Disjunctive	25	7	7 (100)	0	7 (100)

Table 8.2 Probability of equivocation occurring by chance in response to
avoidance–avoidance questions

Type of question	Probability of equivocation occurring by chance (%)	Total number of avoidance–avoidance questions	Proportion of non-replies (percentage in parentheses)	Proportion of answers by implication and incomplete replies (percentage in parentheses)	Total proportion of equivocal replies (percentage in parentheses)
Yes–No	33	198	89 (45)	41 (21)	130 (66)
Interrogative word	50	19	10 (53)	1 (5)	11 (58)
Disjunctive	25	10	3 (30)	0 (0)	3 (30)

should be noted that the number of such questions is relatively small. In fact, they constituted only 13 per cent of the total sample, the remaining 87 per cent were yes–no questions.

Discussion

Thus, the results provided strong support for the main hypothesis of the study – that politicians, in responding to questions, will tend to produce the least face-damaging response. Where a *no necessary threat* response was possible, this was the response the politician tended to produce, most typically in the form of a reply to the question. In *avoidance–avoidance conflict* questions, equivocation was the most frequent response, just as Bavelas *et al.*'s theory would predict. In short, whether or not a politician replies to a question seems to be largely determined by the face-threatening structure of the question: this is the main tenet of the face model presented here.

Audience participation in political interviews

Introduction

The second study reported in this chapter took advantage of a novel development in political interviewing in the 2001 General Election. In the traditional televised interview, one politician is typically interviewed by one professional political interviewer. Growing dissatisfaction with this arrangement led the ITN network in the 1997 General Election to experiment with a different format. This allowed members of the public the opportunity, alongside professional interviewers, to put questions directly to the leaders of the three main political parties. In the 2001 General Election, the BBC also adopted this procedure.

This novel format provided an excellent opportunity to further test the hypothesis that equivocation by politicians is associated with the kinds of questions posed in political interviews. This is because members of the general public may differ from political interviewers in the kinds of questions which they ask. In particular, members of the public might be expected to ask relatively fewer *avoidance–avoidance conflict* questions, given their more complex structure. Again, whereas interviewers may seek to highlight inconsistencies in policy through the use of *avoidance–avoidance conflict* questions, voters may be more concerned to establish simply where a party stands on a particular issue without creating such conflicts. Consequently, if members of the public ask a smaller proportion of *avoidance–avoidance conflict* questions, then politicians might be expected to give them significantly more replies.

To test these hypotheses, an analysis was conducted of six sessions in which questions were put to the party political leaders by both professional interviewers and members of the general public. Three of these were with Jonathan Dimbleby, the other three with David Dimbleby. The format employed by the two interviewers differed slightly. Jonathan Dimbleby began with a short interview with the party leader and then opened the session to questions from the audience. Conversely, David Dimbleby started immediately with questions from the audience. Both interviewers followed up questions from the audience with questions of their own, often developing points raised by audience members. It was announced that none of the politicians knew the questions in advance.

The specific hypotheses of the study were as follows:

1   Politicians will reply to significantly more questions from the general public.
2   Members of the general public will pose significantly fewer questions which create an *avoidance–avoidance conflict*.
3   There will be a significant correlation between *avoidance–avoidance conflict* questions and equivocation, and between *no necessary threat questions* and replies.

Method

Interviews

The politicians observed in this study were Tony Blair, William Hague and Charles Kennedy. The television interviewers were Jonathan Dimbleby and David Dimbleby. The Jonathan Dimbleby programmes were broadcast on ITV, and entitled *Ask Tony Blair*, *Ask William Hague* and *Ask Charles Kennedy*. The David Dimbleby programmes were broadcast on BBC1, all three were entitled *Challenge the Leader: Question Time Special*. Each session took place in front of an audience of members of the public, who were given the opportunity to pose questions directly to the political leaders.

The length of each of the six programmes (to the nearest minute) was as follows:

David Dimbleby
Tony Blair   55
William Hague   55
Charles Kennedy   56

Jonathan Dimbleby
Tony Blair   52
William Hague   53
Charles Kennedy   55

Procedure

Transcripts were made of each interview. Questions, replies and non-replies were identified according to the procedures described in Chapter 7. Questions were further analysed in terms of potential face-threats, according to the procedures described in this chapter. On this basis, questions were dichotomised according to whether or not they were considered to pose an *avoidance–avoidance conflict*. Responses to questions were dichotomised into replies or equivocations (which included incomplete replies and answers by implication).

Reliability for the procedures for identifying responses to questions and for identifying face-threats have already been reported in this and the preceding chapter. In this study, all the interview analyses were performed by the author.

Results

It was found that politicians replied to 73 per cent of questions from members of the public, and to 47 per cent of questions from political interviewers (see Table 8.3). This comparison was significant at the $p < 0.025$ level (one-tailed; $T = 0$, Wilcoxon Signed Ranks Test).

It was also found that political interviewers used a significantly higher proportion of *avoidance–avoidance conflict* questions than members of public ($p < 0.025$ one-tailed; $T = 0$, Wilcoxon Signed Ranks Test). 58 per cent of their questions were judged as creating an *avoidance–avoidance conflict*, in comparison to 19 per cent from members of the public (see Table 8.4).

Finally, Phi correlation coefficients were calculated between questions (*avoidance–avoidance conflict* or *no necessary threat*) and responses (replies or equivocations) for both political interviewers and members of the public. The correlation coefficients were 0.76 for political interviewers ($df = 4$, $p < 0.05$ one-tailed), 0.70 for members of the audience ($df = 4$, $p > 0.05$ one-tailed).

Table 8.3 Reply rates to questions posed by political interviewers and members of the
public

	Interviewers	Members of the public
David Dimbleby		
Tony Blair	47.8 (23)	73.9 (23)
William Hague	35.3 (34)	65.6 (32)
Charles Kennedy	54.3 (33)	65.0 (20)
Jonathan Dimbleby		
Tony Blair	30.3 (33)	75.0 (12)
William Hague	56.8 (44)	84.2 (19)
Charles Kennedy	60.0 (15)	75.0 (28)

Notes
Data represent the percentage of questions which received a reply. Figures in parentheses are the
total number of questions.

Table 8.4 Proportion of *avoidance–avoidance* questions posed by political interviewers
and members of the public

	Interviewers	Members of the public
David Dimbleby		
Tony Blair	43.5 (23)	21.7 (23)
William Hague	67.6 (34)	25.0 (32)
Charles Kennedy	33.3 (33)	30.0 (20)
Jonathan Dimbleby		
Tony Blair	70.0 (33)	16.7 (12)
William Hague	52.3 (44)	10.5 (19)
Charles Kennedy	33.0 (15)	7.1 (28)

Notes
Data represent the percentage of questions judged to create an *avoidance–avoidance* conflict.
Figures in parentheses are the total number of questions.

Discussion

The results clearly showed that politicians replied to significantly more
questions from members of the public than from professional interviewers,
and that members of the public asked significantly fewer *avoidance–
avoidance conflict* questions. *Avoidance–avoidance conflict* questions were
significantly correlated with equivocation when politicians were questioned
by political interviewers; the comparable correlation coefficient just missed
statistical significance when politicians were questioned by members of the
public.

The overall reply rate of politicians to questions from members of the
public in these six programmes was 73 per cent, in comparison to 47 per
cent for the two political interviewers. It was noteworthy that this latter

figure is almost identical to the 46 per cent reply rate for the set of 33 political interviews reported in Chapter 7. Furthermore, only 19 per cent of questions from members of the public were judged to create an *avoidance–avoidance conflict*, in comparison to 58 per cent of questions for the political interviewers in this study and 41 per cent of questions for political interviewers in the first study reported in this chapter.

Thus, the results of this second study provided further support for the view that equivocation by politicians occurs in response to the high proportion of *avoidance–avoidance conflict* questions posed by political interviewers. In contrast, members of the public were found to ask a much smaller proportion of such questions, and as a consequence the politicians' reply rate was much higher.

A good example of the different kinds of questions used by members of the public and professional interviewers can be seen in this extract from the BBC1 *Question Time* programme with Tony Blair and David Dimbleby:

Audience member:	Why is it that er after four years of office the railways are in a worse state than we've ever seen in this country given that the policy is to encourage us not to use our cars?
Blair:	Because the railways have been er because the railways have been under-invested for a very long period of time, and if we don't get the money into the railways, then we will carry on with a second or third class service.
Dimbleby:	Are you ashamed of British railways?
Blair:	I'm not proud of the state of British railways no I mean I think you'd be pretty odd if you said that . . .

The question from the audience member, although face-threatening, does not present Blair with an *avoidance–avoidance conflict*. This is because he can reply by drawing attention to the chronic long-term under-investment in the railways which preceded his own government, although in doing so he is tacitly accepting that 'the railways are in a worse state than we've ever seen in this country'. However, the question from Dimbleby does place Blair in an *avoidance–avoidance conflict*. If Blair says 'yes', that he is ashamed of British railways, it is damaging both to his own personal face and that of his party, given that New Labour had already been in power for four years. To say 'no', that he is not ashamed of British railways would simply stretch credibility, given that the problems of major train accidents, cancellations and frequent delays in the years immediately preceding the 2001 General Election. Blair resolved this problem by saying that he is not 'proud of the state of British railways'. This does not directly answer Dimbleby's question, but enables Blair to provide a credible response which is not too face-damaging to either himself or his own political party. In this way, it can be seen how Blair equivocates in response to the conflict created by David Dimbleby, but can give a reply to a similar question from the member of the public without incurring serious face-damage.

Conclusions

To observe that politicians fail to reply to questions in political interviews is no more than a commonplace; in lay explanations, it is typically ascribed to evasiveness, deviousness or downright dishonesty. The results of both the studies reported in this chapter show that equivocation by politicians is closely associated with the kinds of questions which they are asked. Thus, the higher the proportion of *avoidance–avoidance conflict* questions, the more likely politicians are to equivocate.

It was also argued that a prime cause of *avoidance–avoidance conflicts* could, in the context of political interviews, be attributed to the way in which questions create threats to face. Questions can be seen as having a face-threatening structure, from which it is possible to predict whether or not a politician is likely to give a reply. The novelty of this approach is not only that it provides a means of analysing questions in political interviews, it also demonstrates that the occurrence of both replies and non-replies can be understood within the same theoretical framework.

Furthermore, this novel conceptualisation has important implications for evaluating the interview performance of both interviewers and politicians. In the next chapter, attention will be given to evaluating the interview skills of political interviewers; in Chapter 10, this approach is extended to the evaluation of politicians.

9   Evaluating interviewers

Introduction

In the last chapter, an analysis was presented of political interviews in terms of threats to face. This has significant implications for evaluating the performance of interviewers, which are discussed in this chapter (Elliott and Bull, 1996; Bull and Elliott, 1998).

Despite a burgeoning research literature on the political interview, there have been comparatively few studies of political interviewers. One exception to this is the study of neutrality. Political interviewers are expected to be impartial. For example, publications by the BBC frequently mention the issue: 'The BBC's journalism is required constitutionally and by long practice, to be editorially independent, objective, impartial and fair' (May 1983 General Advisory Council BBC). The BBC's 'Producers' Guidelines' (1996) contains a special section on accuracy and impartiality, while in the BBC's second annual Statement of Promises (15 October, 1997), one of its five key promises was 'to maintain the highest standards of fairness, impartiality and taste and decency'.

How interviewers maintain a stance of neutrality has been the focus of a series of studies by Clayman (1988, 1992). In the first instance, neutrality needs to be understood in the context of the distinctive pattern of turn-taking in news interviews. Thus, the typical format is one whereby the interviewer asks questions to which the interviewee is expected to respond. By restricting themselves only to asking questions, interviewers can seek the opinions and perspectives of others, while refraining from overt comment. A stance of formal neutrality can be maintained as a consequence (Clayman, 1988).

However, the achievement of a neutral 'questioning' stance is more complex than might be apparent at first sight. Thus, interviewers often embed statements within questions. They frequently depart from asking questions alone and sometimes do so at considerable length. Furthermore, such departures may be used to introduce statements of opinion that disagree with, criticise or in some other way challenge an interviewee. However, these departures still occur in conjunction with asking questions and are designed to be continuous with them. Accordingly, such statements can still be seen as integral to the overall activity of asking questions.

This is important, because politicians may characterise interviewer utterances as 'accusatory', 'opinionated', 'leading' or ' argumentative' (e.g. Harris, 1986). Thus, such turns may be subjected to a variety of hostile criticisms. But interviewers still claim that such utterances are 'questions', and this can provide an important line of defence should such attacks arise (Clayman, 1988). For example, in an interview with Margaret Thatcher during the 1987 General Election, Robin Day posed the question: 'Prime Minister what do you say to those who say . . . that you're autocratic, domineering and intolerant of dissent?' In an extended reply, Margaret Thatcher characterised Day's question as an 'accusation', whereupon Day responded: 'No I'm not accusing you I'm inviting you to answer some criticisms that are frequently made of you Prime Minister.' It was later in the same interview after Thatcher had again characterised Day's question as an 'accusation' that he famously remarked: 'I didn't accuse you of anything Prime Minister, you keep on accusing me of accusing you of things.'

While interviewers primarily restrict themselves to asking questions, they may occasionally produce non-questioning utterances which challenge, counter or in some other way seek to undermine the stated position of the interviewee. Rather than merely requesting information, such challenges may constitute an overt commentary on what the interviewee has said. In these instances, there are still procedures whereby an interviewer can sustain a neutral stance with respect to such challenges. Such procedures may also be used when asking questions to sustain their neutral character (Clayman, 1988).

One such device is attributing statements to third parties. This device can be understood in the context of what Goffman (1981) called 'footing' (Clayman, 1992). Goffman introduced this concept in order to explore the nature of involvement and participation in interaction. He argued that participation is not a simple either/or affair in which one party speaks, while the other party listens. There are varying degrees of participation: speakers may take up different footings in relation to their own remarks, variously described as 'animator', 'author' and 'principal'. Thus, whereas the animator is the person who actually utters the words, the author is the one who originated the beliefs and sentiments, and perhaps also composed the words through which they are expressed. The principal is the person whose viewpoint or position is currently being expressed through the utterance. Although the speaker may be animator, author and principal all at the same time, this is not necessarily the case. Through various shifts in footing, speakers can deflect responsibility as author and/or principal, and thereby distance themselves from what they are saying.

Footing shifts are particularly useful for political interviewers (Clayman, 1988). By attributing statements to third parties, they are able to indicate that the viewpoints they present originated elsewhere. In Goffman's terms, the interviewer as 'animator' can thus deflect responsibility for 'authorship'. Furthermore, interviewers can thereby also systematically refrain from either endorsing or rejecting those views, so that the third party is also presented as the sole 'principal' throughout the turn (Clayman, 1988). In this way, the interviewer's personal position is not stated, not officially 'on record' in the discussion. Consequently, it is not something for which either the interviewer or the news organisation can be held responsible (Clayman, 1988). Footing shifts through third party attributions can thus be seen as an important means of sustaining interviewer neutrality.

Another device is referred to as 'doing delicacy' (Clayman, 1988). When producing a statement of opinion, the interviewer may treat it is a departure from the 'ordinary' or routine course of events. Unlike footing shifts or questioning, this procedure does allow interviewers to express their own opinions. However, this can at the same time be treated as a temporary departure from what should be occurring, and therefore not significantly interfering with the overall intent to remain neutral. The very nature of this device may explain why it is comparatively uncommon; its more frequent use would undermine its basic claim to be a departure from the norm.

Embedding statements within questions, attributing statements to third parties and 'doing delicacy' are three means whereby interviewers seek to sustain a stance of neutrality (Clayman, 1988). Neutrality can thus be seen not simply as a trait of individual interviewers, it is something which can be achieved through talk. Maintaining such a stance is extremely important. Unless political interviewers constitute their talk as neutral, politicians may accuse them of bias – a useful tactic for the politician who does not wish to reply to a difficult question (Clayman, 1992). Thus, the position of neutrality enables interviewers to 'fulfil the complex journalistic requirement . . . of being interactionally "adversarial" while remaining officially "neutral"' (Clayman, 1992, p. 196).

How effective interviewers are in sustaining a stance of neutrality is another issue. Interviewers claim that because they are only asking questions, they cannot be criticised for taking a particular standpoint, or expressing a particular opinion. This is a specious argument, according to Harris (1986), because questions do more than simply request information: in an important sense, they encode points of view, opinions and attitudes. They may also convey information through the presuppositions on which they are based, some of which may be seriously open to dispute, although deliberately contentious in order to obtain an interesting and challenging interview.

Apart from these studies of neutrality, there has been no other systematic research concerned with political interviewers. However, the analysis of face reported in the previous chapter has significant implications not only for evaluating interviewer neutrality, but also for other aspects of interviewer performance. Of particular importance is the distinction between *avoidance–avoidance* and *no necessary threat* questions (Elliott and Bull, 1996).

Avoidance–avoidance questions are arguably tougher than those which allow a *no necessary threat* response. Hence, the relative proportion of *avoidance–avoidance* questions in an interview can be used as a measure of interviewer toughness: the higher the proportion of *avoidance–avoidance* questions, the tougher the interview. This proportion is referred to as *level of threat* (Bull and Elliott, 1998) and forms the theoretical basis for the analyses of interviewer performance to be presented in this chapter.

This concept of *level of threat* is based on the evidence that politicians find *avoidance–avoidance* questions problematic. For example, in the study of interviews from the 1992 General Election reported in the previous chapter, 63.8 per cent of *avoidance–avoidance* questions were responded to with some form of equivocation (either a non-reply, answer by implication or incomplete reply). This supported Bavelas *et al.*'s (1990) theory, according to which the typical response to such questions is to equivocate. Most of the *avoidance–avoidance* questions in this data set (87 per cent) were couched in a yes–no format (Quirk *et al.*, 1985). Given that there are three principal modes of responding to such questions (confirm, deny, equivocate), the probability of an equivocal response occurring by chance is 33 per cent; in fact, the total proportion of equivocal responses to yes–no questions was 66 per cent. The fact that equivocation occurs at twice the rate expected by chance alone would suggest that politicians found difficulty with this kind of question and were unsure how to tackle them. A high proportion of *avoidance–avoidance* questions would therefore constitute a tough form of interview, and would tend to make a politician appear evasive.

In the analyses to be reported in this chapter, *level of threat* is used as a means of assessing interviewer performance. Interviewer toughness is evaluated in terms of the relative proportion of *avoidance–avoidance* questions posed by an interviewer. *Level of threat* is also used as a means of assessing interviewer neutrality. If it can be shown that an interviewer consistently asks a higher proportion of *avoidance–avoidance* questions to members of one political party rather than another, then it can be argued that this is indicative of interviewer bias. Thus, whereas Clayman's studies were concerned with the kinds of devices which interviewers use to maintain a stance of neutrality, face analysis provides a means of assessing interviewer bias.

Level of threat can be further elaborated through analyses of interviewer style. The face-threat typology itself distinguishes between 19 types of face-threat, and hence can be effectively applied to different types of face-threats posed by different political interviewers (Elliott and Bull, 1996). To further elaborate the concept of interviewer toughness, an analysis is presented here of stylistic differences between the interviewers with regard to face-threats they posed in *avoidance–avoidance* questions.

Finally, it is important to investigate whether behavioural measures of *level of threat* correspond to how political interviewers are perceived. To this end, a questionnaire was devised to investigate how interviewers were perceived in terms of toughness and impartiality, and whether those perceptions were consistent with the behavioural analyses already outlined.

Method

Interviews

The set of 18 interviews from the 1992 British General Election analysed in the previous chapter also formed the basis of this study. Full details of the interviews were given in Chapter 7.

A questionnaire intended to measure perceptions of the six interviewers was also completed by 30 undergraduates (15 men, 15 women, aged between 18 and 21). There were 10 Conservative voters, 10 Labour voters and 10 Liberal Democrat voters (five men and five women in each group).

Procedure

The participants who responded to the questionnaire were all pre-selected on the basis that they reported watching televised political interviews at least once a month. Thus, they were not actually asked to watch all 18 interviews from the 1992 General Election, rather to make assessments on the basis of their knowledge of the interviewers acquired by regular viewing. The questionnaire itself comprised two sets of six 7-point scales, one in which the participants rated the six interviewers in terms of toughness (very tough ... not very tough), the other in terms of impartiality (very impartial ... not impartial). The six interviewers were listed in the order shown on p. 101. In addition, participants were asked, if they considered any of the interviewers to favour any one political party, to indicate that party against the interviewer's name.

Transcripts were made of each interview. Questions, replies and non-replies were identified according to the procedures described in Chapter 7. All questions were also analysed in terms of their face-threatening structure, according to the procedures described in Chapter 8. All interviews were coded by at least two raters, one of whom was always the author; disagreements were resolved by discussion.

Results

The results are presented with regard to toughness, neutrality and interviewer style.

Toughness

The relative proportion of avoidance–avoidance to no necessary threat questions

The six interviewers were compared in terms of the relative proportion of *avoidance–avoidance* to *no necessary threat* questions. Table 9.1 shows the results for each of the six interviewers from their three interviews with each of the party leaders. The questions are graded into three levels of threat: *avoidance–avoidance* questions, questions affording a single *no necessary threat* option and questions where more than one *no necessary threat* response was possible (multiple *no necessary threat* questions).

It should be noted that the data for Jonathan Dimbleby were treated with some caution, because he adopted an interview style which involved asking relatively few direct questions (only 24 in total). Since the data were analysed in terms of percentages, small differences can thus become artificially exaggerated. Hence, Jonathan Dimbleby was omitted from all the subsequent quantitative analyses reported in this chapter. Of the remaining five interviewers, Brian Walden was the toughest, with almost half (49.4 per cent) of his questions carrying a threat in every direction. This was almost twice as many as those for David Frost, who was the softest interviewer, with only 28.9 per cent of *avoidance–avoidance* questions.

Ratings of toughness

Observer ratings of toughness were subjected to a three-way (political affiliation $\times$ gender $\times$ interviewer) split-plot analysis of variance, which showed a highly significant ($p < 0.001$) main effect for interviewers (see Table 9.2). Mean toughness ratings for the six interviewers were: Jeremy Paxman 6.57; Brian Walden 5.27; David Dimbleby 5.00; Sir Robin Day 4.93; Jonathan Dimbleby 4.70; David Frost 4.27 (7 is the highest rating for toughness, 1 the lowest). Pairwise comparisons using Tukey's HSD test showed that Jeremy Paxman was perceived as significantly tougher than all the other five interviewers, also that Brian Walden was perceived as significantly tougher than David Frost ($p < 0.05$).

Style

An analysis (shown in Table 9.3) was conducted of all the *avoidance–avoidance* questions for the five interviewers (excluding Jonathan Dimbleby) using the 19 categories of the face-threat coding system. It should be noted that not replying to an *avoidance–avoidance* question was considered in every case to create the face-threat for the politician of being seen as evasive. This is described in the face-threat category system as

Table 9.1 Level of *threat* in the questions posed by each interviewer

Level of threat	Robin Day	David Dimbleby	Jonathan Dimbleby	David Frost	Jeremy Paxman	Brian Walden
Avoidance–avoidance	50 (43.1)	37 (34.3)	19 (79.2)	37 (28.9)	43 (43.0)	41 (49.4)
No necessary threat	64 (64.2)	70 (64.8)	5 (20.8)	88 (68.8)	52 (52.0)	40 (48.2)
Multiple 'no threat' avenues	2 (1.7)	1 (0.9)	0 (0)	3 (2.3)	4 (4.0)	1 (1.2)
Uncoded	0 (0)	0 (0)	0 (0)	0 (0)	1 (1.0)	1(1.2)
Total	116 questions	108 questions	24 questions	128 questions	100 questions	83 questions

Note:
Values enclosed in parentheses are percentages.

Table 9.2 Analysis of variance for rating of interviewers in terms of toughness

Source	df	F
	Between participants	
Party affiliation (PA)	2	1.77
Gender (G)	1	0.01
PA × G	2	0.73
P within-group error	24	(1.64)
	Within participants	
Interviewer (I)	5	18.75*
PA × I	10	0.62
G × I	5	1.04
PA × G × I	10	1.49
I × *P* within-group error	120	(0.98)

Note
Values enclosed in parentheses represent mean square errors; P = participants; $*p < 0.001$.

difficulty in producing/clarifying personal or party beliefs, statements, policies, actions, aims, principles, etc. Because the figure for all three politicians for this category is 100 per cent, it is not discussed any further in this section on style.

Overall, the data obtained from this analysis of *avoidance–avoidance* questions were similar in pattern to the analysis of the total corpus of questions (i.e. *avoidance–avoidance + no necessary threat*). Correlations (Pearson's *r*) between the face-threat categories for *avoidance–avoidance* questions and the total corpus of questions for the five interviewers were: Robin Day 0.89, David Dimbleby 0.92, David Frost 0.86, Jeremy Paxman 0.81, Brian Walden 0.97. Thus, if an interviewer had a high proportion of questions associated with a particular type of face-threat, this tended to be the case not only for his *avoidance–avoidance* questions, but for his sample of questions as a whole.

The way in which these face-threats were used in *avoidance–avoidance* questions is illustrated for each of the five interviewers below, and related to the toughness of their questioning. Thus of the five interviewers, Brian Walden came out highest on the face-threats of creating/confirming a negative statement about the party (78 per cent) and loses credibility (68 per cent). In almost half of his *avoidance–avoidance* questions (49 per cent), these face-threats occurred in combination, when he posed highly critical questions which cannot easily be rebutted because they contain some obvious truth, but cannot be confirmed because they put the politician's party in a negative light.

For example, Brian Walden asked John Major, in connection with the Poll Tax (a flat rate charge for local services which aroused widespread popular hostility):

Table 9.3 Types of face-threat in *avoidance–avoidance* questions posed by interviewers

Types of face-threat	RD	DD	DF	JP	BW
Personal competence	34 (17)	30 (11)	22 (8)	14 (6)	10 (4)
Failure to present positive image	0 (0)	3 (1)	0 (0)	0 (0)	0 (0)
Loses credibility	38 (19)	59 (22)	35 (13)	33 (14)	68 (28)
Personal contradictions	16 (8)	16 (6)	35 (13)	14 (6)	17 (7)
Future difficulties (personal)	12 (6)	14 (5)	8 (3)	28 (12)	0 (0)
Difficulty in clarifying	100 (50)	100 (37)	100 (37)	100 (43)	100 (41)
Negative persona	22 (11)	0 (0)	0 (0)	12 (5)	10 (4)
Negative party	44 (22)	70 (26)	51 (19)	28 (12)	78 (32)
Failure to present positive party image	0 (0)	0 (0)	0 (0)	0 (0)	0 (0)
Future difficulties (party)	8 (4)	16 (6)	11 (4)	30 (13)	0 (0)
Party contradictions	14 (7)	5 (2)	22 (8)	21 (9)	24 (10)
Negatively assesses 'state of nation'	0 (0)	3 (1)	3 (1)	5 (2)	0 (0)
Not supporting electorate	0 (0)	0 (0)	0 (0)	7 (3)	0 (0)
Not supporting significant opinion in the electorate	34 (17)	19 (7)	41 (15)	70 (30)	44 (18)
Not supporting colleague	16 (8)	16 (6)	5 (2)	2 (1)	7 (3)
Not supporting sub-group of party	24 (12)	11 (4)	11 (4)	14 (6)	0 (0)
Not supporting positively valued others	8 (4)	3 (1)	3 (1)	12 (5)	2 (1)
Not supporting friendly country	0 (0)	0 (0)	5 (2)	12 (5)	0 (0)
Supports negatively valued other	20 (10)	14 (5)	11 (4)	16 (7)	0 (0)
Total number of *avoidance–avoidance* questions	50	37	37	43	41

Note
Figures are in percentages, raw scores in parentheses. RD Robin Day; DD David Dimbleby; DF David Frost; JP Jeremy Paxman; BW Brian Walden. Raw scores in parentheses represent the total number of times each face-threat occurred; the percentages represent the proportionate number of times each face-threat occurred as a function of the total number of *avoidance–avoidance* questions.

What did you choose to do? You chose to have a tax where everybody except the very poor had to pay at exactly the same level – the dustman and the duke alike and moreover of course you were wildly out in your estimates of what the bills would be. Even your own reckoning showed that they'd be comfortably over £200 er you sold [told] the House of Commons that it was going to be £224 per person. Now people say that is a monstrously uncaring thing to do isn't it?

If John Major had confirmed this statement, he would be making a negative statement about his party, but it was hard to deny it without losing credibility. This type of question poses real problems, since the politician neither wishes to make damaging statements about his or her own party, nor lose credibility in the eyes of the electorate; as such, this style of questioning confirms the impression from Table 9.1 of Brian Walden's toughness as an interviewer.

Robin Day came out highest on questions which posed the threat of creating/confirming a negative statement or impression about the politician's personal competence (34 per cent), creating/confirming a negative statement or impression about the politician's public persona (22 per cent), supporting a negatively valued other (20 per cent), and of not supporting a subgroup of one's own party (24 per cent). A good example of how a number of these face-threats operate in combination can be seen when Robin Day asked John Major whether he would be prepared to debate the Health Service on television with Neil Kinnock. This puts John Major in a classic *avoidance–avoidance conflict*. In the United Kingdom, there is no tradition of such debates, and it is generally acknowledged that such an encounter is to the advantage of the Opposition Leader, because it makes him (or her) appear to be of comparable status to the sitting Prime Minister. Hence, if John Major agreed to this proposal, he would be supporting a negatively valued other. On the other hand, if John Major declined to participate, he might simply be seen as frightened, thereby damaging both his perceived professional competence and his public persona. If he failed to reply, he might still be seen as frightened, as well as evasive. In the event, while John Major did not actually give a direct reply to the question, he made quite a skilful response, by claiming that he was already debating with Neil Kinnock on television: 'I'm happy to debate it at any time and we debate I debate it with Mr Kinnock in the House of Commons twice a week...' (referring to his twice weekly televised confrontations with Neil Kinnock at Prime Minister's Question Time).

Jeremy Paxman came out highest on questions which pose the face-threat of not supporting a significant body of opinion in the electorate (70 per cent), and of future difficulties at both the party (30 per cent) and the personal (28 per cent) level. The threat of not supporting a significant body of opinion in the electorate can be illustrated by this question to John Major concerning the Anglo-Irish agreement:

Are you prepared to give a guarantee that under no circumstances will that [i.e. the Anglo-Irish agreement] be abandoned, re-draughted, re-negotiated, that it stands for the entirety of a fourth Conservative term?

If John Major gave this absolute guarantee, then he ran the risk of offending the Protestants, but if he failed to do so, then he ran the risk of offending the Catholics. If he failed to reply, he might simply be seen as evasive, and Paxman could respond by insisting that the public has a right to know where he stands on this particular issue. In his response, Major offered reassurance to Protestants by not giving the absolute guarantee requested by Paxman, while at the same time reassuring Catholics by stating that 'we are not in the business of ditching the Anglo-Irish agreement'.

David Dimbleby came out highest on none of the face-threat categories, but the most frequent face-threat posed in his *avoidance–avoidance* questions was that of creating/confirming a negative statement/impression about the party (70 per cent). This was typically combined with the face-threat of loses credibility (51 per cent of cases), which was also David Dimbleby's second most frequent type of face-threat (59 per cent). So, for example, David Dimbleby asked John Major:

Well you'd have lost it [i.e. the Election] lost it by a wide margin if you hadn't abolished the Poll Tax wouldn't you?

If John Major had confirmed this statement, he would be making a negative statement about his own party (in relation to its policy concerning the Poll Tax). If he denied the statement, he would simply lose credibility, because the Poll Tax was extremely unpopular. If he failed to reply, he might simply appear evasive. In this way, David Dimbleby posed the same kind of problems as Brian Walden, although his overall proportion of *avoidance–avoidance* questions was much lower (34 per cent as opposed to 49 per cent).

David Frost came out highest on the face-threat of contradicting past statements at the personal level (35 per cent). This seemed to be due at least in part to his tendency to check on the politician's response by asking the same question in a slightly different way. This does not necessarily pose any serious problems for the politician, provided the original assertion can be justified (Elliott and Bull, 1996). However, there are some occasions on which David Frost creates more serious problems through this type of face-threat. This is particularly true of his interview with Neil Kinnock, where he challenged the Labour Party leader with reference to statements he has made not earlier on in the interview, but earlier in his political career.

For example, at one time Neil Kinnock was opposed to Britain's membership of the European Community, whereas by the time of the 1992 General Election the Labour Party advocated continued membership. With reference to this change of policy, David Frost asked:

Do you admit that you were wrong then, or were you right? Do you still say you were absolutely right then?

This puts Neil Kinnock in a classic *avoidance–avoidance conflict*. He cannot possibly support withdrawal from the European Community now, since that would be counter to his party's current policy. However, if he acknowledged that he was wrong in the past, then he would suffer the face-threats of contradicting past statements, as well as creating/confirming a negative statement about his own personal competence (through showing faulty judgement). If he failed to reply, then he might be seen as evasive, with the added implication that he thought his earlier judgement was wrong, but is not prepared to say so.

Clearly, this kind of face-threat is extremely serious, since it threatened Neil Kinnock's personal competence, and so his fitness to be Prime Minister. In fact, Kinnock to some extent tacitly acknowledged that his earlier anti-European stance was at fault by stating 'I frankly wish that in the late '70s . . . I'd used my own judgement', and that '. . . if I'd thought about it as deeply as I think I should have, then I would have been much more assertive about the need to remain in the European Community'. Thus, although in general Frost does use a softer approach than the other interviewers, he can be just as threatening when using the *avoidance–avoidance* question to full effect.

Neutrality

The distinction between *avoidance–avoidance* and *no necessary threat* questions was used as a means of analysing interviewer neutrality in four principal ways:

1   by comparing the relative proportion of question types posed overall to each of the three party leaders.
2   by comparing the relative proportion of question types posed by each individual interviewer to each of the three party leaders.
3   by comparing the three party leaders with respect to the types of face-threats posed in *avoidance–avoidance* questions.
4   through observer ratings of impartiality.

The relative proportion of question types posed to each of the three party leaders

An analysis was conducted of the *level of threat* in the questions received overall by the three party leaders. From Table 9.4, it can be seen that John Major received the toughest interviews. In terms of the relative proportion of *avoidance–avoidance* and *no necessary threat* questions, nearly half of the questions he received created an *avoidance–avoidance conflict* (48.6 per

Table 9.4 Level of threat in questions received by each politician

Threat level of questions	Major	Kinnock	Ashdown
Avoidance–avoidance	90 (48.6)	72 (41.6)	65 (32.3)
No necessary threat	94 (50.8)	100 (57.8)	125 (62.2)
Multiple 'no threat' avenues	0 (0)	1 (0.6)	10 (5.0)
Uncoded	1 (0.5)	0 (0)	1 (0.5)
Total	185 questions	173 questions	201 questions

Note
Percentages are in parentheses

cent). Paddy Ashdown received the easiest interviews, with only 32.3 per cent of *avoidance–avoidance* questions; Neil Kinnock received 41.6 per cent of *avoidance–avoidance* questions.

In all 18 interviews, 557 questions were analysed, of which only 11 afforded multiple 'no threat' options; that is to say, there was more than one direction in which the politician could reply without loss of face. The majority of these (10) were posed to Paddy Ashdown, only one to Neil Kinnock and none to John Major. Again, there were also six instances in which the questions appeared to have no face-threats at all – in every case, these questions were directed to Paddy Ashdown. An example of this kind of innocuous question comes from David Frost:

> The polls today are encouraging for you because you've hit 20 in two of the polls and how do you chart them now?

This sort of anodyne question could be responded to in any way Paddy Ashdown chose. He could reply by saying that the polls are very encouraging and show the Liberal Democrats are doing well. Or he could not reply by saying of course it's always difficult to predict which direction the polls will go in the future.

Thus, from a variety of perspectives, it would appear that Paddy Ashdown was given the softest interviews.

The relative proportion of question types posed by each individual interviewer to each of the three party leaders

Table 9.5 shows the results of a second analysis carried out to compare the *level of threat* in the questions directed to the three party leaders by the five interviewers (excluding Jonathan Dimbleby).

Of these five interviewers, four conformed to the trend of giving Paddy Ashdown the easiest interview, John Major the toughest. The one exception to this trend was David Frost, who gave only 16.7 per cent of *avoidance–avoidance* questions to John Major, but 38.3 per cent to Paddy Ashdown. The standard deviations show that the spread of scores for each

Table 9.5 Proportion of *no necessary threat* questions posed by each interviewer to the three party leaders

Interviewer	Major	Kinnock	Ashdown	Standard deviation
Robin Day	18 (43.9)	18 (51.4)	28 (70.0)	13.44
David Dimbleby	17 (48.6)	27 (73.0)	27 (75.0)	14.50
David Frost	30 (83.3)	32 (71.1)	29 (61.7)	10.83
Jeremy Paxman	19 (54.3)	9 (39.1)	28 (66.6)	14.17
Brian Walden	9 (36.0)	13 (52.0)	19 (57.6)	12.83

Note
Percentages are in parentheses

of the five interviewers was relatively constant across the three politicians. There was therefore a similar degree of bias shown by each interviewer, though in the case of David Frost, the bias was in favour of John Major, rather than Paddy Ashdown.

Comparison of the three party leaders with respect to the types of face-threats posed in avoidance–avoidance questions

An analysis was also conducted of *avoidance–avoidance* questions using the 19 categories of the face coding system; the results are shown in Table 9.6. Correlations between the types of face-threats posed to each of the three politicians were statistically highly significant (John Major/Neil Kinnock 0.82; Neil Kinnock/Paddy Ashdown 0.83; John Major/Paddy Ashdown 0.80 (all correlations Pearson's r, $p < 0.01$, two-tailed). This analysis suggested that the interviewers were remarkably even-handed in the kinds of face-threats they posed to the three politicians in *avoidance–avoidance* questions.

(NB Since not replying to an *avoidance–avoidance* question was considered in every case to create the face-threat for the politician of being seen as evasive, the data for the category of 'difficulty in producing/clarifying personal or party beliefs, statements, policies, actions, aims, principles, etc.' were not included in these analyses, to avoid artificially inflating the size of the correlations.)

Observer ratings of neutrality

Table 9.7 presents the results of a three-way (political affiliation × gender × interviewer) split-plot analysis of variance on observer ratings of neutrality. This showed no significant effects whatsoever; in fact, remarkably little variation was perceived between the interviewers. Mean ratings were: Robin Day 4.37, David Dimbleby 4.43, Jonathan Dimbleby 4.33, David Frost 4.80, Jeremy Paxman 4.67, Brian Walden 4.37 (where 7 is a high rating for impartiality, 1 a low rating).

Table 9.6 Types of face-threat posed to politicians in *avoidance–avoidance* questions

Type of face-threat	Major	Kinnock	Ashdown
Personal competence	32 (29)	17 (12)	14 (9)
Failure to present positive image	1 (1)	0 (0)	0 (0)
Loses credibility	41 (37)	41 (29)	53 (34)
Personal contradictions	19 (17)	25 (18)	19 (12)
Future difficulties (personal)	10 (9)	17 (12)	9 (6)
Difficulty in clarifying	100 (90)	100 (70)	100 (64)
Negative persona	27 (24)	4 (3)	2 (1)
Negative party	58 (52)	52 (37)	61 (39)
Failure to present positive party image	0 (0)	0 (0)	0 (0)
Future difficulties (party)	8 (7)	23 (16)	11 (7)
Party contradictions	9 (8)	10 (7)	33 (21)
Negatively assesses 'state of nation'	4 (4)	0 (0)	0 (0)
Not supporting electorate	0 (0)	0 (0)	2 (1)
Not supporting significant body of opinion in electorate	39 (35)	58 (41)	31 (20)
Not supporting colleague	18 (16)	3 (2)	2 (1)
Not supporting sub-group of party	7 (6)	17 (12)	14 (9)
Not supporting positively valued others	8 (7)	15 (11)	2 (1)
Not supporting friendly country	4 (4)	3 (2)	2 (1)
Supports negatively valued other	12 (11)	10 (7)	2 (1)
Total number of *avoidance–avoidance* questions	90	70	64

Note
Figures in percentages, raw scores in parentheses

Table 9.7 Analysis of variance for rating of interviewers in terms of neutrality

Source	df	F
Between participants		
Party affiliation (PA)	2	2.65
Gender (G)	1	0.33
PA × G	2	0.22
P within-group error	24	(5.47)
Within participants		
Interviewer (I)	5	1.07
PA × I	10	0.55
G × I	5	0.12
PA × G × I	10	1.11
I × *P* within-group error	120	(1.27)

Note
Values enclosed in parentheses represent mean square errors; *P* = participants.

Participants were also asked to identify whether they considered the interviewers favoured any political party. Most did not do so, but where they did, those identifications were consistent with the behavioural analyses reported above (pp. 165–166). That is to say, David Dimbleby, Jeremy Paxman and Brian Walden all gave Neil Kinnock a softer interview than John Major and were all identified as favouring Labour (Dimbleby, $N = 3$; Paxman, $N = 3$; Walden, $N = 4$); David Frost gave his softest interview to John Major, and was identified by two participants as favouring the Conservatives.

Summary

Overall, the results for neutrality showed that, in terms of the relative proportion of *avoidance–avoidance* questions, John Major received the toughest interviews, Paddy Ashdown the softest; Neil Kinnock was intermediate between the two. The one interviewer who bucked this trend was David Frost, who gave his softest interview to John Major. These findings were entirely consistent with observer ratings of neutrality. When observers identified an interviewer as favouring a particular political party, most interviewers were seen as favouring Labour, with the exception only of David Frost, who was seen as favouring the Conservatives. However, it should be noted that detailed analysis of the specific types of face-threat posed in *avoidance–avoidance* questions showed that, in this respect, all three politicians were treated in a highly similar fashion.

Discussion

Previous research on interviewers has been principally focussed on devices used to sustain neutrality. In this chapter, data has been presented which shows how interviewer toughness, style and neutrality can be evaluated on the basis of the distinction between *avoidance–avoidance* and *no necessary threat* questions.

With regard to interviewer toughness, the closest relationship between behavioural analysis and observer ratings was found for David Frost. He emerged as the softest interviewer, in terms both of his low proportion of *avoidance–avoidance* questions and in terms of the type of face-threat which he posed to the politicians (one characteristic being frequent checking). Observer ratings also showed that David Frost was perceived as the least tough of the six interviewers – significantly so when compared to both Brian Walden and Jeremy Paxman.

Nevertheless, a word of caution is still required. Precisely because of this gentler style of interviewing, when David Frost does ask a tougher question, it may have greater impact because the politician is not expecting it. This was explicitly commented on by John Prescott (Deputy Leader of the Labour Party since 21 July, 1994) in an interview with the *Guardian*, 6 February, 1995:

> I find [David] Frost one of the most deadly [interviewers] myself, because he talks to you in such an easy manner but then slips in the difficult question – the one which gets you into trouble if you're not watching out for it.

Observer ratings also showed that Jeremy Paxman was perceived as significantly tougher than all the other five interviewers, whereas in the behavioural analysis, he was only one of the three toughest interviewers. However, question difficulty in terms of potential loss of face is likely to be only one feature which affects perceptions of toughness; for example, other features might be interruption rate, aggressive intonation or hostile nonverbal style. Thus, perhaps too close a relationship should not be expected between behavioural measures and observer ratings of toughness.

The results on neutrality can be interpreted in a variety of ways. The overall trend of giving the leader of the minority party (Paddy Ashdown) the easiest interviews could be interpreted as more sympathetic treatment for the underdog, or might simply indicate that the interviewers did not take the Liberal Democrats very seriously. Conversely, John Major might get the toughest interviews because he could be attacked on the government's record. Alternatively, Conservatives could argue that these findings supported their view that there was an anti-government bias amongst television interviewers, whilst Opposition politicians could argue that the atypicality of the David Frost interviews reflected a pro-Tory bias by this particular interviewer.

It is in this context that the questionnaire responses are of interest. Although only a minority of observers identified individual interviewers as favouring a particular political party, where they did so those identifications were consistent with the analysis of neutrality in terms of *level of threat*. That is to say, David Dimbleby, Jeremy Paxman and Brian Walden were all identified as favouring Labour, and all these interviewers gave Neil Kinnock a softer interview than John Major with respect to the relative proportion of *avoidance–avoidance* questions. David Frost was identified as favouring the Conservatives, and gave his softest interview to John Major. However, there were no significant differences between interviewers in overall ratings of neutrality. Furthermore, the detailed analysis of the different types of face-threat showed that, in this respect, each of the three politicians were treated in a highly similar way.

The research reported in this chapter shows how the analysis of political interviews in terms of face management has significant implications for the evaluation of interviewer performance. Thus, the concept of *level of threat* can be used to assess interviewers in terms both of toughness and neutrality. Behavioural analyses conducted on this basis do broadly correspond to how the interviewers were perceived in terms of observer ratings. Furthermore, the 19 categories of the face-threat coding system can also be used to delineate differences in interviewer style, and to show in detail how they exert pressure on politicians through various forms of 'tough' questioning.

But the significance of face management is not just confined to assessing the interview performance of interviewers. It also has important implications for evaluating the interview performance of politicians, and this forms the focus of the next chapter.

10 Evaluating politicians

Introduction

The interview performance of politicians is, of course, regularly evaluated by journalists, political commentators and other politicians. Up to now this is not an issue which has been addressed by academic research. Nevertheless, it can be evaluated in terms of the face model of political interviews, just as can the performance of interviewers. Indeed, the concept of face management has the particular advantage that a politician's communicative skill can be appraised irrespective of a politician's political stance. Instead, analysis can be focussed on how well each politician succeeds in presenting that stance, in terms both of personal face and the face of the party which he or she represents.

It is important to note that the concept of presenting the best possible face should in no sense be regarded as some sort of euphemism for deceit. In avoiding unnecessary damage to face, the politician is merely opting for the most strategic response, without necessarily being deceptive. Indeed, in terms of face analysis, deception can present serious risks. A politician who is demonstrably deceitful may do serious damage to his or her standing in the eyes of the electorate, in short, may suffer a serious loss of face. The politician may also, as a consequence, damage the face of the party which he or she represents, and indeed the collective face of politicians as a whole, by fostering the belief that as a group they are dishonest and not to be trusted.

By the same token, face management should not be regarded as synonymous with equivocation. Equivocation can, in fact, present a substantive threat to face, in the sense that, if a professional politician is asked to give a view or opinion on a particular issue, then he or she is expected to be able to do so. Failure to reply may result in a loss of face; it may imply that the politician either has no relevant opinion, or has not thought through the situation adequately, or is even engaging in some sort of deception. Failure to reply is only regarded as not face-threatening when the politician can legitimately point out that there is something wrong with the question, e.g. that it is factually incorrect, or that it is based on misleading or highly contentious presuppositions.

In this chapter, two studies are presented of politicians' interview performance, based on their skills in face management. Both were conducted in terms of the distinction between *no necessary threat* and *avoidance–avoidance conflict* questions. The first was focussed on how best to handle *no necessary threat* questions (Bull and Elliott, 1995), the second on how best to handle *avoidance–avoidance conflict* questions (Bull, 2000b).

No necessary threat questions

Introduction

In Chapter 8, it was shown that when politicians are posed a *no necessary threat* question, they typically produce a *no necessary threat* response. That is to say, if it is possible for politicians to respond without damage to face, then they will do so. But politicians do not invariably take advantage of such opportunities. On some occasions, they will make gaffes, producing what might be termed *avoidable face-damaging responses* (Bull, 1998b). Such responses may be regarded as unskilled, given the adversarial nature of British politics in which politicians need to present the best possible face. From this perspective, a *no necessary threat* response is not only the modal way of responding to *no necessary threat* questions, it may also be regarded as the optimal one.

Thus, one way of evaluating the interview skills of politicians is in terms of *avoidable face-damaging responses*. This was the approach adopted in the first study reported in this chapter. It was based on an analysis of the 18 interviews from the 1992 General Election, which have already been examined in the preceding three chapters. Specifically, the interview performance of John Major, Neil Kinnock and Paddy Ashdown was compared in terms of the relative proportion of *avoidable face-damaging responses* which they produced.

Another way of evaluating politicians' interview performance is in terms of the extent to which they reply to questions. If one politician replies to significantly more questions than another, his supporters may cite this as evidence of his candour, his detractors may simply say he was asked easier questions. However, it is possible to test the 'toughness' of interview questions in terms of the concept of *level of threat*, as outlined in the previous chapter. Thus, the reply rates of politicians can be evaluated in the context of the relative proportion of *avoidance–avoidance conflict* and *no necessary threat* questions which they received. In the study reported here, this approach was used to provide a second measure of the interview performance of John Major, Neil Kinnock and Paddy Ashdown.

Method

The study was based on 18 interviews from the 1992 General Election with John Major, Neil Kinnock and Paddy Ashdown. Full details of these interviews, as well as how they were transcribed and analysed, have already been given in Chapters 7 and 8

Results

Avoidable face-damaging responses

To illustrate what were considered to be *avoidable face-damaging responses*, an example is presented below for each of the three politicians, all from interviews with Sir Robin Day. In each of these examples, Day threatened the personal competence of the politician. The detailed study of interviewer style reported in the previous chapter showed that this particular type of face-threat was a characteristic feature of Day's interview technique.

Thus, Kinnock found himself in serious trouble when Day tackled him about his views on defence. As a former member of the Campaign for Nuclear Disarmament, Kinnock was at one time committed to unilateral disarmament, a policy subsequently abandoned by the Labour Party following its disastrous performance in the 1983 General Election. Kinnock's about-turn on this issue was forcefully challenged by Day in the following question: 'Why is it that you wanted to scrap our nuclear weapons when the Soviet Union er was our potential enemy and had and had them of their own yet you now want to keep them when the Soviet Union doesn't exist and isn't a danger to us?' Day then went on to ask Kinnock: 'Was it an error of judgement?' Kinnock replied: 'I think that the way in which there was a complete adherence to the idea of unilateral . . . that the only way to promote the change er . . . may have been an error of judgement.' Rather than admit to this 'error of judgement', Kinnock could have justified his previous adherence to unilateralism in the era before Gorbachev came to power in the Soviet Union as one way of trying to break the logjam in disarmament negotiations, which subsequently became inappropriate with the change in the international situation. This would also have been consistent with his line of argument at other points in this interview. However, by acknowledging his adherence to unilateral disarmament as an error, Kinnock not only lost face personally, but also gave Day an opportunity to ask the even more face-threatening question: 'By you?' Kinnock's response was to produce a stumbling apology: 'Um yes as by as an individual.' In failing adequately to deal with this line of questioning, Kinnock undermined his own personal competence, which the Conservatives were in any case seeking to make a central issue in the election campaign.

Day created problems for Major when he asked him about the

contentious issue of Britain's membership of the European Exchange Rate Mechanism (ERM). Day appeared to finesse Major into a face-damaging response by asking him if he agreed with the assertion of Nigel Lawson (the former Chancellor of the Exchequer) that 'had we joined the ERM the Exchange Rate Mechanism in 1985 that's several years earlier than we did the boom in the late eighties would not have been so great nor the recession so prolonged as it has been wasn't that another mistake?' Major's response was to say: 'I think er . . . it would have been desirable in retrospect if we'd joined the Exchange Rate Mechanism earlier.' Day then asked Major: 'You shared in that mistake?' Major replied: 'But I no I was not in the Treasury in 1985. . .' Unlike Kinnock, Major did not take any personal responsibility for this decision, but by seeking to exonerate himself he still fell into Day's trap, tacitly acknowledging that a mistake had been made, thereby damaging the face of his own party. A *no necessary threat* response in this instance could have been a non-reply, attacking the presupposition of the question that a mistake had been made. Major could have said that the Government acted in what seemed the most appropriate manner at that time, and only with the benefit of hindsight was it possible to say that it would have been better to have joined the ERM at an earlier date. In responding in this way, he would not have been contradicting himself, since his previous statement was only an admission that 'it would have been *desirable* in retrospect if they had joined the ERM earlier'.

To Ashdown, Day asked about the proposal in the Liberal Democrats' manifesto proposal to levy a hypothecated tax, a penny in the pound specifically earmarked for education: 'You promised to put an extra penny on the standard rate of tax for education and training. Can you call this courageous and honest when very few people think you're ever going to be in a position to do that?' Ashdown did not reply to this question, instead he attacked it; in fact, he could have given a reply in the affirmative. He could have argued for the possibility of a hung Parliament, and maintained that in such circumstances the Liberal Democrats would use all their influence to try to get this measure through the House of Commons. By not replying to the question, Ashdown gave the impression that he didn't really believe that he could substantiate the stance that this policy was courageous and honest, thereby undermining the face of his party.

The three politicians were compared on those questions where a *no necessary threat* response was considered possible; the results are shown in Table 10.1. Major nearly always selected this option (90.4 per cent of questions), whereas Kinnock appeared to miss some of the possible escape routes, and had the lowest proportion of 'no threat' responses (83.0 per cent of questions); Ashdown fell in the middle, with 87.2 per cent of questions. However, these differences are not statistically significant ($H = 2.105$, Kruskal–Wallis one-way analysis of variance).

(It should be noted that, just as in the previous chapter, the data from the three interviews conducted by Jonathan Dimbleby were omitted from these

Table 10.1 Proportion of *no necessary threat* responses selected by each politician

Interviewers	Politicians		
	John Major	*Neil Kinnock*	*Paddy Ashdown*
Robin Day	83 (15/18)	78 (14/18)	80 (24/30)
David Dimbleby	88 (15/17)	86 (24/28)	92 (24/26)
Jonathan Dimbleby	100 (1/1)	100 (2/2)	100 (2/2)
David Frost	97 (29/30)	80 (24/30)	86 (25/29)
Jeremy Paxman	84 (16/19)	100 (9/9)	93 (26/28)
Brian Walden	100 (9/9)	77 (10/13)	83 (15/18)
Totals	90.4 (85/94)	83.0 (83/100)	87.2 (116/133)

Note
Figures are in percentages, raw scores are in parentheses.

and all other statistical tests reported in this Results section because he posed comparatively few questions relative to the other five interviewers.)

Non-reply rates to questions

Another way of comparing the three politicians is to look at that their reply rates. Major gave a direct reply to only 39.5 per cent of questions, Kinnock 51.4 per cent, Ashdown 63.2 per cent ($H = 6.125$, $p < 0.049$, Kruskal–Wallis one-way analysis of variance). Pairwise comparisons (*t*-tests, independent samples, $df = 8$) showed that Ashdown replied to significantly more questions than Major ($t = 2.867$, $p < 0.05$); the other two comparisons were non-significant (Major/Kinnock, $t = 1.582$; Kinnock/Ashdown, $t = 2.227$). Supporters of the Liberal Democrats could claim that this higher reply rate reflected well on Ashdown, although it is also possible that he was not asked such difficult questions.

It is possible to test this latter explanation in terms of the distinction between *avoidance–avoidance conflict* and *no necessary threat* questions. A comparison of the three politicians in these terms showed that, in 67.2 per cent of the questions Ashdown received, at least one *no necessary threat* response was possible, in comparison to 58.4 per cent for Kinnock and 50.8 per cent for Major. However, these differences were not statistically significant ($H = 2.48$, Kruskal–Wallis one-way analysis of variance). Furthermore, even in *avoidance–avoidance conflict* questions alone, Ashdown's reply rate was still much higher: 56.7 per cent in contrast to 25.7 per cent for Kinnock, and 17.6 per cent for Major. Thus, it does not appear that Ashdown's higher reply rate was simply a consequence of being asked easier questions

Discussion

The one significant result in this study showed that Paddy Ashdown's rate of replying to questions was higher than that of John Major's. Ashdown's reply rate (67.2 per cent) is noticeably higher than that found amongst politicians both in this and other studies reported in Chapter 7. It does not seem to be the result of softer questioning, as measured by the relative proportion of *avoidance–avoidance* questions. This is interesting, in that the Liberal Democrats often claimed to be practising a different form of politics, more open and less adversarial than the two major parties, and these data could be used to support this claim. However, their political opponents could still argue that it was much easier for Paddy Ashdown to reply to questions, because the Liberal Democrats had no realistic chance of forming the next government.

There was no significant difference between the politicians in the relative proportion of *avoidable face-damaging responses*. However, it is possible that this represented something of a ceiling effect, given that politicians for the most part typically produce a *no necessary threat* response whenever possible. Nevertheless, it is interesting that John Major produced the lowest proportion of *avoidable face-damaging responses* – given the extent to which his communicative style was criticised in the media. Even his Conservative biographer, Bruce Anderson, who was a member of John Major's leadership campaign team in 1990, was less than impressed by his communicative style: 'John Major did give one combative interview to Charles Moore of the *Daily Telegraph* ... not surprisingly the published interview is flat and uninteresting' (Anderson, 1991, p. 189). Again:

> John Major became Prime Minister with no public persona. He has therefore found the greatest difficulty in projecting himself to a larger audience... On such occasions, his voice seems to lose its resonance and his command of language goes. He tends to repeat phrases, and dissipate any forcefulness in his text by interpolating qualifying phrases and unnecessary adjectives or adverbs.
>
> (Anderson, pp. 303–304)

However, whereas John Major's detractors – and even his supporters – have criticised his style of communication, the analysis presented here would suggest that they might have underestimated his communicative skills in terms of the actual content of what he says.

Of course, it could always be argued that if a politician's responses are perceived as too obviously concerned with saving face, there is a danger that they may be less than effective as a consequence. However, there is an interesting parallel here with what Edwards and Potter in their Discursive Action Model (1993) call the problem of stake or interest (see Chapter 1, pp. 8–9). An interested or motivated account runs the risk of being discounted on precisely that basis (for example, with the remark, 'Well, he would say that, wouldn't he?'). Thus, according to Edwards and Potter, speakers endeavour to construct their account in such a way that it will be understood as factual, and not dismissed as partisan or simply biased. In exactly the same way, it can be argued that an optimal strategy for a politician replying to questions is to construct responses which are neither face-damaging nor readily construed as merely face-saving.

Avoidance–avoidance conflict questions

Introduction

The second study was concerned with how best to handle *avoidance–avoidance conflict* questions, based on interviews with Tony Blair during the 1997 British General Election (Bull, 2000b). The study was set in the context of the enormous changes which had taken place in the Labour Party during its long period in opposition. It was argued the scale of these changes was such that, in seeking to justify them, Blair was presented with a classic *avoidance–avoidance conflict*. This has to be understood within the relevant political context, which is summarised briefly in the following paragraph.

In the General Election of 1983, the Labour Party suffered its greatest electoral defeat since 1918. Labour secured just 209 MPs (the lowest since 1935) from only 27.6 per cent of the vote, the smallest share ever won by a principal opposition party; its 8.4 million votes was only just ahead of the 7.8 million cast for the Liberal–SDP Alliance. During the 1980s, Labour was widely seen as 'extremist, irresponsible and disunited' (King, 1992). Even following its fourth successive electoral defeat in 1992, the *Sunday Times* editorial (12 April, 1992), entitled 'Socialism, RIP', stated bluntly: 'The most significant lesson of the general election of 1992 is that, in its present form, Labour is unelectable.' But in 1997, it achieved the greatest electoral victory in its entire history, winning 418 seats with 43.2 per cent of the vote.

Between 1983 and 1997, the policies of the Labour Party had been transformed. The 1983 Manifesto was memorably dubbed by Gerald Kaufman (a leading member of Labour's Front Bench at that time) as 'the longest suicide note in history'. It called for unilateral nuclear disarmament, withdrawal from the Common Market, massive nationalisation and re-nationalisation with much greater planning of the economy, exchange controls and trade barriers. Following the election debacle of 1983, Neil Kinnock replaced Michael Foot as leader and, over the next decade, these proposals were progressively dropped. By 1992, none of these proposals appeared in the Party's Manifesto for the General Election of that year. Neil Kinnock quickly resigned three days after the 1992 election defeat; his successor, John Smith, died of a heart attack in 1994 to be replaced by Tony Blair. By 1997, the Manifesto had an explicit commitment to retaining the Trident nuclear deterrent, to the rapid completion of the European Union single market, to the retention of the Conservative trade union legislation of the 1980s and a five-year pledge to no increases in income tax: in short, a complete reversal of what the Labour Party stood for in 1983.

These remarkable changes within the Labour Party presented an ideal opportunity to test predictions derived from Bavelas *et al.*'s (1990) theory of equivocation. Dramatic changes in policy typically pose political parties with a major problem of presentation. A complete about-turn inevitably reflects badly on what has gone before: there is a clear implication that the previous policies were ill-judged and inappropriate. Presenting the new policies also creates a problem; they may be depicted as cynical, opportunist and unprincipled, simply a means of currying support with the electorate. Nowhere is this problem of presentation more pronounced than in the context of a political interview, where interviewers can ask repeated questions, challenge equivocal responses and draw attention to contradictions in policy.

It was hypothesised that when questioned about the changes in the Labour Party, Blair would be confronted with exactly the kind of *avoidance–avoidance conflict* analysed by Bavelas *et al.* It should be noted that the General Election of 1983 marked the start of Blair's parliamentary career, when he was returned to the House of Commons for what has come to be known as 'old Labour'. Thus, if he condemned the old Labour Party, he would at the very least be open to the charge of inconsistency; if he were to admit to any lack of belief in the Manifesto of 1983, then he would be open to the charge of hypocrisy. Furthermore, if he was too critical of old Labour, it might also make his party look bad and he might well alienate support within his own party. Conversely, as the man pre-eminently associated with the modernisation of the Labour Party, if he failed to acknowledge criticisms of old Labour, then it would naturally invite the question – why had all the changes to New Labour taken place?

This communicative problem can be aptly illustrated from the attacks of his Conservative political opponents. Soon after Blair's election as Leader of the Labour Party, he was lampooned on the BBC Radio 4 *Today* programme by the then Deputy Prime Minister Michael Heseltine, who posed the question: 'Why should you believe a man who has got all the major judgements wrong in the first half of his life, when he tells you he is going to get them all right in the second half of his life?' Blair was similarly mocked by John Major, in his last speech to the Conservative Party's annual conference as Prime Minister (11 October, 1996): 'But it simply won't do for Mr Blair to say, "Look I'm not a socialist any more, now can I be Prime Minister please?"'

Thus, the modernisation of the Labour Party created a potentially enormous communication problem for Tony Blair, which forms the focus of this study. Specifically, it was hypothesised that questions about modernisation would create an *avoidance–avoidance conflict*, and that Blair would equivocate in response to such questions. It should be noted that, in the analysis of face-threats presented in Chapter 8, equivocation itself is regarded as potentially face-threatening, especially given that politicians are widely criticised for being evasive. But in this context, replies which might have reflected badly either on the Labour Party and/or on Blair's own competence or integrity were arguably much more face-threatening than the risk of simply being seen as evasive. Hence, it was hypothesised that Blair would avoid or mitigate these face-threats through equivocation. Consideration was also given to the form taken by Blair's equivocation in order to evaluate its interactional significance.

Method

Interviews

Five televised interviews from the 1997 British General Election with Tony Blair formed the basis of this study. Interviewers and interview durations (to the nearest minute) were:

David Dimbleby   28
Jonathan Dimbleby   24
Sir David Frost   33
Jeremy Paxman   25
Peter Sissons   8

Procedure

Questions concerning the modernisation of the Labour Party were identified from transcripts of each interview. Each of these questions was analysed in terms of potential face-threats, according to the procedures described in Chapter 8. On this basis, questions were then dichotomised according to whether or not they were considered to pose an *avoidance–avoidance conflict*. Responses to questions were analysed according to the procedures described in Chapter 7. From this analysis, responses were dichotomised into replies or equivocations.

Reliability for the procedures for identifying responses to questions and for identifying face-threats have already been reported in Chapters 7 and 8. In the study reported in this chapter, all the interview analyses were performed by the author. An independent rater also coded responses to questions in four of the interviews (David Dimbleby, David Frost, Jeremy Paxman and Peter Sissons) according to whether they were replies or equivocations. A correlation of 0.83 (Phi coefficient) was found with the author's ratings. All the categorisations for each of the questions on modernisation are presented in full in the Results section below.

Results

Preliminary analysis of all five interviews showed that not every interviewer challenged Tony Blair on the issue of modernisation, nor was every question on this issue regarded as putting him in an *avoidance–avoidance conflict*. In the interview by Jonathan Dimbleby, there were no questions about the changes to the Labour Party under Tony Blair's leadership; rather, the questions were all addressed to specific policy issues. However, the other four interviewers all posed at least one question about modernisation, giving a total of 17 such questions. Questions were dichotomised into those regarded as creating an *avoidance–avoidance conflict*, and those where a *no necessary threat* response was judged possible. Responses were dichotomised into replies and equivocations. Thus, it was possible to correlate the two variables using a Phi coefficient. The analysis showed a highly significant correlation of 0.87 ($p < 0.001$). This confirmed that Blair typically equivocated in response to questions about modernisation judged as creating an *avoidance–avoidance conflict*, and replied to those judged as not creating such a conflict. A detailed analysis of the 17 question–response sequences is presented in the following section, divided into *avoidance–avoidance conflict* and *no necessary threat* questions.

Avoidance–avoidance conflict questions about modernisation

Twelve questions on modernisation were considered to create an *avoidance–avoidance conflict*. Only one of these questions received a reply; Blair's response to a second question was interrupted before he had finished speaking, so it was not possible to say whether it was an equivocation or a reply. Responses to the other ten questions were judged to be equivocal.

DAVID DIMBLEBY (DD)

Towards the beginning of his interview with Tony Blair, David Dimbleby poses the following three questions about modernisation:

DD: But did you believe in old Labour? *(Question 1)*
TB: I believed in the values of the Labour Party yes
DD: No did you believe in what they stood for? Did you believe in CND? Did you believe in union power not being curtailed? Did you believe in nationalisation no privatisation? *(Question 2)*
TB: There were a whole series of policy positions that I adopted with along with the rest of the Labour Party but the very process of modernisation has been the very process that I have undertaken in the Labour Party for example yes
      [interrupts]
DD: I know that but did you have you abandoned have you did you believe what you said you believed in the eighties? *(Question 3)*
TB: Look of course we always believed in the idea of a more just a more fair society and the Labour Party believed for a long period of time that the way to do that was for example greater nationalisation err

was for example simply more increased state spending. The whole process of modernisation David has been to take the Labour Party away from that to keep true to its principles but put those principles properly in a modern setting

Questions 1, 2 and 3 can all be seen to pose the same kind of *avoidance–avoidance conflict*. If Blair affirmed that he did believe in old Labour, he would show himself as inconsistent, since it invites the question why has he made so many changes. If he denied that he believed in old Labour, he could still be seen as inconsistent, as well as laying himself open to the charge of hypocrisy – given that he was first elected to Parliament in 1983. An equivocal response would pose the face-threat of being seen as evasive. Blair's response to Question 1 was considered equivocal because his use of the word 'values' (which he also stresses) suggests only qualified support for old Labour, i.e. there were some aspects of old Labour which he did not support. Dimbleby did not treat this response as a full reply, because in Question 2 he posed it again in a slightly different way; he then interrupted Blair's response, so it is not possible to say whether Blair replied or equivocated. His response to Question 3 was regarded as equivocal because he did not say whether or not he believed in what he said in the 1980s.

   Of course, equivocation can be followed up by the interviewer, although at the risk of appearing verbally aggressive. Here, Dimbleby pursued the point by saying 'most of it was wrong?' (i.e. most of what old Labour stood for was wrong) *(Question 4)*. An affirmative response to this question would clearly be damaging to the face of the Labour Party. A negative response would threaten Blair's credibility, given that, if most of what old Labour stood for was not wrong, then it invites the question of why the Labour Party had made such dramatic changes. An equivocal response posed the threat of being seen as evasive. Blair's response was regarded as equivocal, because he did not say whether or not he considered most of what old Labour stood for was wrong:

> er I simply say what is important is to apply those principles to the modern world. Look for example John Major stood in the 1970s on a platform of Scottish devolution. Margaret Thatcher was the person that closed more grammar schools than anyone else, she was a member of Ted Heath's government you know times move on

Dimbleby returned to this same issue later on in the interview when he posed the question:

DD: What Britain should have elected should have elected a Labour government a Labour government under Michael Foot in '83 unilateral disarmament? *(Question 5)*

TB:	of course I wanted them to elect
	[interrupts]
DD:	unilateral disarmament
TB:	David please of course I wanted the Labour Party to be elected

If Blair confirmed this proposition *(Question 5)* he would make himself appear extremely inconsistent (given that the 1997 manifesto had completely reversed many of the principal policies of the 1983 manifesto). If he denied that Labour should have been elected in 1983, he would be making a very negative statement about the Labour Party, as well as exposing himself to the charge of hypocrisy. If he equivocated, he would appear evasive. In his response, Blair subtly changes the wording of the question from 'Britain *should* have elected a Labour government' to 'of course I *wanted* the Labour Party to be elected...'. Given that *wanted* is not the same as *should*, Blair's response is regarded as equivocal.

Dimbleby also posed a number of questions about Blair's stance in relation to the trade unions. The Labour Party has traditionally been closely aligned with the trade union movement, as well as being dependent on it for financial support. Labour has also been widely perceived as in the 'pocket of the unions', and presumably to counter this perception, New Labour sought to distance itself from the unions. If Blair gave an affirmative response to the following question *(Question 6)*, he might be seen as lending credence to this perception. If he gave a negative response, he would run the risk of alienating the support of important political allies, as well as damaging his own personal face through contradicting his previous statements on the unions. An equivocal response would pose the face-threat of being seen as evasive. Blair's response was regarded as equivocal, because he did not make it clear whether he still stood by his earlier statement.

DD:	Was your instinct right for instance when you talked about er ho the Tories as people with hob-nailed boots ready to trample over the rights of trade unionists I mean is that something you defend saying now did you mean to say it? *(Question 6)*
TB:	Er look at that time people thought for perfectly understandable reasons that the best way to have an industrial relations framework was to get the law out of it that changed indeed I was one of those people that changed that position of the Labour Party

Later in the interview, Dimbleby asked two questions concerning the conflict between the print unions at Wapping and the newspaper magnate, Rupert Murdoch, in the 1980s. This exceedingly acrimonious dispute stemmed from Murdoch's decision to re-site the printing of his newspapers from Bouverie Street to Wapping. In 1992, the hostility of Murdoch's newspaper, the *Sun*, was widely believed to have contributed significantly to the defeat of the Labour Party in the General Election of that year. Subsequently, under Blair's leadership, some kind of deal was allegedly struck with Murdoch, in which Blair agreed not to oppose the newspaper magnate's monopolistic media ambitions in return for electoral support. Hence, in the following sequence, Dimbleby referred to Murdoch as 'your new ally':

DD: ...your new ally Rupert Murdoch was he right to take on at Wapping the print unions and was Labour wrong to support the unions against him? *(Question 7)*

TB: Look these days are passed they are gone...
 [interrupts]
DD: I know they are passed
TB: they are passed and gone and there's no point in going back in the past
DD: But were you you supported all that were you were you right in doing so? *(Question 8)*
TB: We believed that these changes could have been done in a different way. But there is no point in going back over the past. There is a different world today. Let us address this world today and let us see how we can make improvements to it. Let us see how we can make Britain a better place

If Blair responded to these two questions by coming out in favour of Murdoch against the print unions, he would run the risk of offending not only the trade unions, but also that body of opinion both in his own party and in the electorate, who supported the print unions and were opposed to Murdoch. If he came out in favour of the print unions, he would run the risk of alienating Rupert Murdoch, whose support Blair went to considerable lengths to secure. Furthermore, if he admitted he was wrong in supporting the unions at that time, it would threaten his personal competence, as well as making him appear inconsistent. Equivocal responses simply posed the face-threat of being seen as evasive. These are both classic *avoidance–avoidance conflict* questions. Blair declined to answer both by simply saying these things were all in the past, and there's no point in going over them again.

JEREMY PAXMAN (JP)

Paxman tackled the issue of modernisation by suggesting – perhaps disarmingly – that people actually admired Blair for acknowledging that he had changed his mind on issues such as privatisation and council house sales. Blair did not explicitly acknowledge that he had changed his mind, responding rather that he had always been a 'moderniser'. Paxman then posed the question directly:

JP: Well you haven't changed your mind on those things? *(Question 9)*
TB: No sure of course I've changed my mind on issues

For Blair to confirm that he had not changed his mind would be hard to believe, given the enormous changes to New Labour, for which he has been one of the prime instigators. To acknowledge that he had changed his mind poses the face-threat of personal contradictions. Not to reply would make him seem evasive. Blair's response is regarded as equivocal, because he only acknowledged he has changed his mind 'on issues'. Paxman's question referred specifically to 'those things' (i.e. privatisation and council house sales), which Blair neither confirmed nor denied.

Paxman appeared not to regard Blair's response as a reply, because he then asked specifically:

JP: But when exactly did you stop er thinking that council house sales were wrong for example? *(Question 10).*
TB: Well it was actually under the last Labour government the idea of selling council houses first came out and you know I think there are lots of people in the Labour Party I myself erm along with many others who tried to change the Labour Party round from some of these attitudes

If Blair replied by giving a specific time or date when he changed his mind on selling council houses, he would have to acknowledge the inconsistencies in his position. If he failed to reply, he would appear evasive. Given that the question specifically asked when he stopped thinking that the sale of council houses was wrong, his response is regarded as equivocal, because he did not provide the requested information.

PETER SISSONS (PS)

Sissons tackled Blair on the issue of modernisation with regard to the oft-made criticism that New Labour were indistinguishable from the Conservative Party:

PS: But privatisation, monetarism, union law, choice in education, obeisance to the middle classes she (i.e. Margaret Thatcher) was reported as saying there's nothing to fear from a Labour government under Tony Blair. Is that a compliment to you you will cherish *(Question 11)*
TB: Well I certainly hope there is nothing to fear and I know there's nothing to fear from a Labour government...

If Blair confirmed this statement (i.e. yes, it is a compliment which he will cherish), he would align himself with a political opponent (Margaret

Thatcher), who was regarded as anathema by many Labour Party supporters during her period as Prime Minister. Hence, Blair might also cause offence both to members of his own party and to Labour Party supporters in the country. Conversely, if he denied the statement (no, it is not a compliment he will cherish), it might suggest that there is something to fear about a Labour government, hence damaging the face of his own party. It might also damage his own persona, by possibly making him seem churlish. If he failed to reply, it would simply make him seem evasive. His response is regarded as a non-reply, because he gave no indication as to whether or not he would cherish this compliment.

DAVID FROST

Frost asked a specific question about the trade unions: 'But when you said about trades union law that it was scandalous and undemocratic I mean at the moment you said it did you mean it?' *(Question 12)*.

Conservative Party trade union law was vigorously opposed by Blair when he was Shadow Employment Secretary (1989–1992), but the Labour Party Manifesto for 1997 gave an explicit commitment not to reverse that legislation. If Blair confirmed this proposition, then he had to acknowledge the inconsistency in his position. If he denied it, he would make himself look hypocritical, as well as putting himself in an extremely bad light with both the trade unions and the Labour Party. Failure to reply would not only seem evasive, but might be understood as meaning that he did not mean what he said, but was unwilling to admit this publicly. In fact, Blair replied to the question, thereby explicitly acknowledging the inconsistency in his position: 'Yes because at the time we were arguing that you could do this in a different way you know, and the argument was that you got the law out of industrial relations. Now I think the whole of the argument has changed...' Although there are many qualifications in Blair's response, it is regarded as a reply, because he confirmed that he meant what he said at the time (which was what Frost specifically asked him). This was the one *avoidance–avoidance conflict* question to which Blair gives a reply.

No necessary threat questions about modernisation

DAVID DIMBLEBY

Dimbleby began his interview by asking: 'Isn't there a problem that there is an old Blair who believed quite different things which makes it rather difficult for people to trust the new one?' *(Question 13)*. If Blair were to agree to this proposition – that there is a problem – it would clearly be face-damaging to him individually (i.e. that he is not to be trusted), as well as damaging to the Labour Party, as its elected leader. An equivocal response would also pose similar face-threats by failing to rebut the negative implication in the question. Blair in fact could reply to this question without necessarily incurring threats to face by emphasising that the process of change is one of modernisation. He said: 'No I don't agree at all I mean we have been through a big process of change and modernisation in the Labour Party...' Blair's response was regarded as a reply because Dimbleby's question specifically asked him '...isn't there a problem...', and Blair explicitly disagreed that there was a problem.

Later on in the interview, Dimbleby asked Blair: 'So was so was Britain right not to vote in a Labour Government in 1983 in 1987 and in 1992 in your opinion?' *(Question 14)*. If Blair were to agree with this proposition, he would clearly be making a highly damaging statement about his own party, as well as damaging his own individual face by failing to show party loyalty. Even if he equivocated, thereby failing to explicitly rebut the negative characterisation of the Labour Party, he might be taken as implicitly confirming David Dimbleby's proposition, as well as making himself look evasive. Blair replied: 'No no of course not I have I've supported the Labour Party I stood as a Labour candidate.' In denying this proposition, he could reply without necessarily incurring any threats to face: to argue for the modernisation of the Labour Party is one thing, to advocate that they deserved to lose all three General Elections is quite another.

JEREMY PAXMAN

When Paxman asked Blair: 'Do you still consider yourself a socialist?' *(Question 15)*, he could be seen to be posing a question about the modernisation of the Labour Party. If Blair were to state that he was no longer a socialist, he could undoubtedly seriously damage his face in the light both of the Labour Party and a significant proportion of the electorate as a whole, as well as making himself appear inconsistent and hypocritical. Similarly, if he equivocated, he might be understood as no longer regarding himself as a socialist, but unable to acknowledge it publicly. But the question was not considered to pose an *avoidance–avoidance conflict*, because Blair could reply by confirming that he did still consider himself a socialist, defining the term in such a way as to emphasise continuity with his earlier values. Thus, Blair responded: 'I do in the sense of the values I don't share the idea that socialism's about some fixed economic prescription...' Although this response was heavily qualified, it was regarded as a reply because it could be understood to convey the information requested, that yes, he did still regard himself as a socialist.

PETER SISSONS

Sissons began his interview with Blair by asking: 'If Labour wins on Thursday it's a fourth victory for Margaret Thatcher she said she'd bury socialism you've completed that for her you left all the principal landmarks she created in place' *(Question 16)*. If Blair were to agree with this proposition, he would clearly be confirming a highly negative statement about both himself and his own party, as well as aligning himself with a prominent member of the political opposition. If he equivocated, thereby failing to rebut this negative characterisation, he might be seen as tacitly acknowledging it, as well as being seen as evasive. But because this characterisation was so extreme, it was possible for Blair to reply by disagreeing with it without necessarily incurring any threats to face. In doing so, it can be seen that he was careful to distance himself from the Conservatives by making criticisms of their performance both on the National Health Service and on education. He stated:

> No I I wouldn't agree with that at all. What I think is sensible however is that the Labour Party wants to take the country forward and it is New Labour and we don't want battles over public versus private sector, bosses versus workers, those are things of the past. But on the National Health Service for example the Conservatives have gone badly wrong we will rebuild it. On our education system we are failing large numbers of our children we will extend educational opportunity.

DAVID FROST

With regard to the modernisation issue, David Frost asked Blair: 'Did you personally believe those things then and you've changed your mind or did you not believe those things then and you went along with it for the sake of party loyalty?' *(Question 17)*.

This might at first sight be seen as an *avoidance–avoidance conflict* question. If Blair chose the first alternative (i.e. he did believe what he stood for in 1983, but subsequently changed his mind), he would threaten his own personal face by appearing inconsistent and lacking in judgement (threat to personal competence). But if he chose the second alternative (i.e. he did not believe in the 1983 Manifesto, but simply went along with it out of party loyalty), he would show a lack of integrity (he supported things in which he did not believe). If he failed to reply, then he would appear evasive. However, because the question is disjunctive in form (it posed a choice between two alternatives), it was possible to reply by rejecting the two alternatives and offering a third without necessarily incurring threats to face. This was what Blair seems to do by indicating that 'yes I believe things could have been done in a different way' (thereby acknowledging that change has taken place), but also that he said so at the time: 'the very first interviews I gave straight after the '83 election were about how the Labour Party had to reach out to new support and the principles that I believe in will never change...' (thereby stressing continuity and consistency).

The form of equivocation

To evaluate the potential consequences of Blair's equivocation, consideration also needs to be given to the form that equivocation took. The content of his responses can be summarised in a series of propositions, which are presented below, together with a consideration of their significance in terms of face management:

1   The term 'modernisation' allowed Blair to emphasise both continuity and change.

With old Labour, he stated 'I believed in the values of the Labour Party' *(Question 1)*, whereas the process of modernisation has been 'to keep [the Labour Party] true to its principles but put those principles properly in a modern setting...' *(Question 3)*.

This allowed Blair not only to explicitly acknowledge the changes which have taken place, but also to present them as principled – as representing an adaptation of the traditional values of the Labour Party to the contemporary political situation. In this way, he could claim a positive face for his party – it is both principled but also moving with the times.

2   The Conservative Party has also changed.

'John Major stood in the 1970s on a platform of Scottish devolution. Margaret Thatcher was the person that closed more grammar schools than anyone else, she was a member of Ted Heath's government you know...' *(Question 4)*. (John Major vigorously campaigned *against* Scottish devolution in the 1997 General Election; Margaret Thatcher was Secretary of State for Education in Ted Heath's government (1970–1974) but vigorously *defended* grammar schools during her subsequent Premiership.)

By drawing attention to these changes in the Conservative Party, Blair sought to present change as a more general process of political life, not as something peculiar just to the Labour Party.

3   In response to an extremely difficult question about the serious trade union dispute in the 1980s between the media magnate Rupert Murdoch and the print unions *(Question 8)*, Blair simply declined to reply.

'There is no point in going back over the past. There is a different world today. Let us address this world today and let us see how we can make improvements to it. Let us see how we can make Britain a better place.'

All these points, it is proposed, add up to what might be termed a 'rhetoric of modernisation': a means of equivocating in response to awkward questions about the dramatic changes in Labour Party policy between 1983 and 1997, whereby Blair could avoid making highly face-damaging remarks both about himself and the Labour Party as a whole.

Discussion

The results of this study strongly supported predictions derived from Bavelas *et al.*'s (1990) theory of equivocation. As hypothesised, the majority of questions about modernisation created an *avoidance–avoidance conflict* (71 per cent), and with only one exception, Blair's response was to equivocate; to questions about modernisation not judged as creating such a conflict, he consistently gave a reply.

The results also strongly support the modifications to equivocation theory in terms of face management proposed in Chapter 8. According to that analysis, threats to face are a prime cause of *avoidance–avoidance conflicts* in political interviews. Threats to face could be readily identified for each of the principal potential responses to questions about modernisation judged to create such conflicts. Furthermore, Blair always produced a *no necessary threat* response to those questions where this was judged possible, just as predicted in the study reported in Chapter 8 (in each instance, this response also happened to be a reply).

In fact there was only one *avoidance–avoidance conflict* question to which Blair did not equivocate. This was when Frost asked: 'But when you said about trades union law that it was scandalous and undemocratic I mean at the moment you said it did you mean it?' *(Question 12)*. Blair replied to the question by confirming that he did mean what he said at the time. However, in this instance, equivocation might have made him seem hypocritical: anything less than an explicit confirmation that his previous criticisms of trade union law were genuine could be understood as a tacit admission that he had been less than sincere. Given the crucial importance of personal integrity to Blair's electoral stance, this could have been extremely face-threatening. Although he explicitly acknowledged the inconsistency in his position, his reply could still be seen as the least face-threatening response because thereby he avoided any threat to his personal integrity.

Thus, even this apparent exception to the predictions of equivocation theory could be understood within the concept of face management. It is important to note here that the concept of face is not so elastic that any response a politician produces can be seen as presenting the best possible face. In particular, in the case of questions where it is possible to produce a *no necessary threat* response, this may not be the one which the politician produces. In the first study reported in this chapter, it was argued that because face-damaging responses to *no necessary threat* questions are avoidable, they can, as a consequence, be regarded as unskilled. The study also showed that the interview performance of former Labour Leader Neil

Kinnock was quite poor: he produced the highest proportion of *avoidable face-damaging responses* of the three main party leaders in the 1992 General Election. In contrast, in the 1997 General Election, Tony Blair produced no such *avoidable face-damaging responses* to questions about modernisation.

In short, Blair could be seen as highly attentive to presenting the best possible face both for himself and for his party in his responses to all 17 questions about the modernisation of the Labour Party. In this sense, Blair's interview performance was highly skilled. The concept of social interaction as a form of skill dates back to Argyle and Kendon's (1967) social skills model and has been enormously influential in research on interpersonal communication (see Chapter 1, pp. 11–13). However, one of its major problems has always been to specify what are the most important skills in different situations and how best they can be evaluated. In this respect, the analysis of face management presented here provides one set of criteria whereby the communicative skills of a politician in an interview may be more readily appraised.

In fact, Blair's 'rhetoric of modernisation' could be seen to do much more than simply enable him to avoid answering difficult questions; it also had other important and significant political advantages:

1   for those members of the electorate who would never have voted for the old Labour Party, modernisation emphasised that the party had changed.
2   furthermore, the changes could be presented as principled, a process of applying the traditional values of the Labour Party to the modern world, just as the Conservative Party also had to change.
3   at the same time, change could be acknowledged without condemning or criticising the old Labour Party, in order to minimise the risk of alienating traditional Labour support. Although Blair was often invited to criticise or condemn old Labour, it is notable that he never did this *(Questions 1–5, 7, 10, 14)*.

Thus, Tony Blair's 'rhetoric of modernisation' could be seen as promoting an identity for New Labour characterised by a high degree of social inclusiveness: one which would both attract people who might never have voted for the old Labour Party but also avoid the risk of alienating Labour's traditional support. Indeed, the very name 'New Labour' could be seen to project this inclusive identity, emphasising change while still preserving the link with the Labour Party of old. In these terms, Blair's 'rhetoric of modernisation' can be regarded as a highly skilled form of political communication. Arguably, such inclusive social identities may play an important role in successful political movements. A comparable example from an entirely different political culture is that of South Africa, where Nelson Mandela, in his political autobiography, stressed the importance for the struggle against apartheid of developing a distinctive and more inclusive

African identity to counter the divisiveness of traditional tribalism (Mandela, 1995).

Thus, Blair's equivocal 'rhetoric of modernisation' enabled him not only to avoid the risks of making face-damaging remarks, but through the highly inclusive social identity of New Labour to present a positive image both for himself and for the party which he represented. This new rhetoric of New Labour arguably played a crucial role in the Labour Party's stunning land-slide victory in the British General Election of 1997 (Bull, 2000c).

Postscript: the 2001 General Election (Bull, 2001)

By May 2001, all this had changed. The policy *volte-face* between 1983 and 1997 was no longer at issue, New Labour went to the polls as the party of government with an apparently unassailable lead in the opinion polls. The modernisation of the Labour Party no longer required the elaborate rhetorical justification it had needed in 1997. However, Blair could still be seen to be in an *avoidance–avoidance conflict*, albeit a different one. There was the problem of complacency: if Labour voters thought the election was a foregone conclusion and stayed at home in sufficient numbers, this could have seriously damaged Labour's performance. There was the problem of disappointment from people who had expected more of New Labour on public services and public transport. To counteract these tendencies, Blair needed to run a sufficiently positive campaign to mobilise his supporters and persuade voters to give Labour a second term. On the other hand, there was the danger of making mistakes. Any serious face-damaging pratfalls might have significantly undermined Labour's standing in the opinion polls. The petrol crisis in the autumn of 2000 had already shown how rapidly even a commanding lead in the polls could evaporate. In the election campaign, Liberal Democrat leader Charles Kennedy repeatedly criticised Labour for the timidity of its electoral stance, which might well be seen as a reflection of these underlying *avoidance–avoidance conflicts*.

Labour's equivocal language on tax and public spending provided a good example of this. On the one hand, they did not wish to alienate support through being seen as a party of high taxation; on the other hand, they did not wish to disappoint their natural supporters who expect improved public services. In 1997, Labour promised not to increase income tax and, at the 2001 election, it renewed this pledge. Despite this unequivocal commitment, Labour's overall tax policy could still be seen as highly equivocal, given the lack of any comparable commitment on indirect taxation. This had allowed the Chancellor ample room for fiscal manoeuvring in the last Parliament and would continue to do so if Labour were re-elected to office. Labour's equivocation on this issue was denigrated by Conservative leader William Hague, who referred to the introduction of what he called 'stealth taxes'.

In the event, Labour won another massive election victory. But only 59 per cent of the electorate bothered to vote, perhaps because the result seemed a foregone conclusion. This poor turnout (the lowest since 1918) was down a full 13 per cent on 1997; New Labour's success was characterised by the media as an 'apathetic landslide'. However, if Blair's electoral campaign failed to inspire the voters, he was still successful in not driving them into the hands of the opposition parties. In this sense, his equivocal language could be justified through continued electoral success, his mastery of the arts of equivocation is arguably an important element of his political skill.

This point was not lost on Blair's long-standing political opponent, William Hague. Writing in the *Guardian* (26 April, 2002) five years on from Blair's landslide victory in the 1997 General Election, Hague singled out what he called Blair's 'skill for ambiguity' as one of his key political strengths, as one of the features which both helped him into power and helped keep him there. Blair's leadership skills, Hague wrote, lie in 'broad direction, ambiguity and the use of language' (the *Guardian G2*, p. 5).

Hague concluded (the *Guardian G2*, p. 5):

> Very often, it is the greatest strength of a political leader and the attributes that brought them to office that prove to be the cause of their downfall years later. Margaret Thatcher was elected because she was strong. Years later people objected to that and called it obstinacy. John Major was applauded because he was fair and generous. Years later people said that meant he was weak. Tony Blair was elected because he claimed to believe in almost everything. Before long people may decide that is the same as believing in nothing, with delivery to match.

It remains to be seen whether Tony Blair's talent for equivocation may eventually be the source of his political downfall.

Summary and conclusions

The research presented in this book has been focussed on two main settings for political communication: speeches and televised interviews. In this final chapter, a summary of the main findings is presented, together with a consideration of their theoretical and practical significance.

Summary of findings

Political speeches

The first study was concerned with the use of hand gesture, based on three speeches delivered at a Labour Party rally in the General Election of 1983. An analysis of two of these speeches focussed on the relationship between hand gesture and vocal stress. It was found that the majority of hand movements of both speakers were related directly or indirectly to vocal stress. Hand gestures were closely synchronised with speech both to highlight important words and to demarcate the extent of tone groups through the use of repeated movements. Hand movements not related to vocal stress typically took the form of contact movements, where the speaker adjusted the position of his hand on the rostrum.

In the third speech, the use of hand gesture in relation to audience applause was analysed. It was shown how hand gestures both articulate the structure of applause invitations (such as three-part lists and contrasts) and were used to refuse applause when it occurred at inappropriate points during a speech. This analysis was conducted in the context of a theory of rhetoric developed by the sociologist, Max Atkinson (1983, 1984a, 1984b), according to whom collective applause is highly synchronised with speech, invited through rhetorical devices employed by the speaker for this purpose.

Chapters 3, 4 and 5 presented a series of studies intended to test the validity of Atkinson's theory of rhetoric. Chapter 3 was concerned with collective applause which occurs in the absence of rhetorical devices. Such applause was found to be typically asynchronous with speech. A content analysis also showed that each applauded statement was a statement of political policy, hence applause seemed to be a direct response to the content of the speech itself. On this basis, it was proposed there are two principal forms of applause in political speeches. There is invited applause, which occurs in response to rhetorical devices embedded in the structure of speech specifically for this purpose. There is also uninvited applause, which occurs in the absence of rhetorical devices; unlike invited applause, this is typically asynchronous with speech and constitutes a direct response to speech content.

The study reported in Chapter 4 was concerned with the mistiming of applause. A typology of 'mismatches' was devised, which distinguished four different ways in which applause can be asynchronous: it can be delayed, isolated, the audience can interrupt, the speaker can interrupt. It was found that only a mean 61 per cent of applause events across six speeches were fully synchronised with speech. A detailed qualitative analysis also showed how each of these four principal types of mismatch could occur either in the presence or absence of rhetorical devices.

In the light of the two studies reported in Chapters 3 and 4, it was decided to conduct a formal analysis of invited and uninvited applause (Chapter 5). All incidences of applause in 15 speeches were coded in terms of whether they were invited or uninvited, synchronous or asynchronous, and whether or not they occurred in response to rhetorical devices. By far the most frequently occurring applause type was invited, rhetorical and synchronous (64.7 per cent of all applause incidents). But a substantial proportion of invited applause was also asynchronous (19.5 per cent of all applause observations). The remaining 13.8 per cent of all applause incidents were uninvited and almost exclusively asynchronous with speech (97.7 per cent of all incidents of uninvited applause). Uninvited applause occurred most frequently in conjunction with rhetorical devices (76.7 per cent of all incidents of uninvited applause) rather than in their absence.

The study presented in Chapter 5 is the first to make a comprehensive analysis of all incidents of invited and uninvited applause in political speeches. Overall, the results provided strong support for this distinction: invited applause is typically synchronous with speech, uninvited applause almost invariably asynchronous. The model needs to be extended by more systematic investigation of other factors which may affect audience applause, in particular the role of delivery.

Political interviews

The second major strand of the author's research on political communication has been concerned with the analysis of televised interviews. Chapters 6 and 7 were focussed on two distinctive features of interview discourse; namely, interruptions and equivocation. In Chapter 8, a theoretical framework was proposed for understanding equivocation, couched in terms of the demands of face management. In Chapters 9 and 10, the implications of this theoretical framework were considered for evaluating the interview performance of interviewers and politicians.

In Chapter 6, the development of the Interruption Coding System (ICS) was described. An analysis was then conducted with the ICS of eight interviews with Margaret Thatcher and Neil Kinnock from the 1987 General Election. According to an earlier study by Beattie (1982), Margaret Thatcher was frequently interrupted in interviews because of her use of what were termed misleading turn-yielding cues. In the study reported in Chapter 6, no evidence was found for this. Thatcher's interruptive style was unusual only in that she voiced frequent objections to being interrupted, although the objective evidence showed a striking degree of similarity in the way in which the politicians interrupted and were interrupted by the interviewers. The impression that she was badly treated was compounded by her tendency to personalise issues, to take questions and criticisms as accusations, and frequently to address the interviewers formally by title and surname, as if they needed to be called to account for misdemeanours. In fact, far from lacking basic conversational skills, as the misleading turn-yielding cue hypothesis seems to imply, Margaret Thatcher showed a striking mastery of the arts of political one-upmanship. She continually wrong-footed her interviewers and put them on the defensive, such that they felt obliged to justify and even apologise for their role as interviewers.

An analysis was also conducted of the reasons for interruptions in political interviews. Interviewer interruptions occurred most frequently in order to re-formulate questions. One possible reason for this is that politicians are notoriously evasive, hence interviewers may need to interrupt in order to get the politician to address a particular question. To investigate this further, the next set of studies were concerned with political equivocation.

The studies reported in Chapter 7 were focussed on a number of issues. In the first instance, criteria were established for identifying what constitute questions, replies and non-replies. These criteria were then used to conduct an assessment of the extent to which politicians fail to reply to questions. Politicians are notoriously evasive, but this could be just a stereotype; hence, the need for some basic facts on equivocation. Results showed a mean reply rate of 46 per cent across all 33 political interviews. Thus, the politicians were replying to only slightly more than two out of five questions. In comparison, an analysis of three televised non-political interviews showed a significantly higher reply rate of 79 per cent.

The next stage was to investigate the different ways in which politicians equivocate. A typology of equivocation was developed. This was organised in terms of both superordinate and subordinate categories, identifying in total 35 different ways in which politicians fail to reply to questions. The typology was used to analyse the communicative style of three political leaders: Margaret Thatcher, Neil Kinnock and John Major. In terms of the superordinate categories, there was a high degree of similarity between the three politicians. They failed to reply to a similar proportion of questions and in a similar fashion, especially through making political points and attacking the question.

However, if both superordinate and subordinate categories were analysed, it was possible to discern distinctive forms of equivocation, unique to each of the three politicians. Thus, Mrs Thatcher, when 'put on the spot', used the aggressive tactic of attacking the interviewer, thereby diverting attention away from an unanswered question. Neil Kinnock's approach was more defensive: he gave long negative replies detailing what he would not do, or simply reflected the question back to the interviewer. John Major alone did not attempt to hide the fact that he was not replying to a question. Both in taking questions literally and in declining to answer, John Major showed open evasiveness. Thus, at a fine level of detail it was possible to discern interesting stylistic differences between the three politicians.

The analyses reported in Chapter 7 not only supported the popular belief that politicians frequently do not answer questions in televised interviews, they also showed in detail how that equivocation is achieved. However, it is also of interest to know why equivocation is such a characteristic feature of political interviews. This was the focus of two studies reported in Chapter 8, which were based on the equivocation theory devised by Bavelas *et al.* (1990). It was argued that a prime cause of *avoidance–avoidance conflicts* in the context of political interviews could be attributed to the way in which questions pose threats to face. That is to say, politicians will tend to avoid certain kind of responses which may make them look bad. When all the principal ways of responding to a question may make them look bad, they tend to favour equivocation as the least face-threatening option.

To test hypotheses derived from this overall theoretical framework, an analysis was conducted of 18 interviews from the 1992 General Election. A typology was devised which distinguishes between 19 different ways in which questions in political interviews may pose threats to face, grouped into three superordinate categories (personal–political face, party face, face of significant others). An important distinction was made between *avoidance–avoidance conflict* questions and those where it was considered possible to produce a response which was not threatening to face (*no necessary threat* questions). In the case of the former, equivocation was predicted as the least face-threatening and therefore the most likely response. In the case of the latter, a *no necessary threat* response was predicted as the most likely. Both these predictions were confirmed.

A second study was conducted of six interviews from the 2001 General Election. This took advantage of a novel development in political interviewing, in which members of the general public were given the opportunity by both the BBC and ITV to put questions directly to the leaders of the three main political parties alongside professional interviewers. It was hypothesised that members of the public would ask relatively fewer *avoidance–avoidance conflict* questions, given their more complex structure. Accordingly, politicians might be expected to give significantly more replies than to those questions posed by professional political interviewers. Both these predictions were confirmed.

Thus, the results of both the studies reported in Chapter 8 showed that equivocation by politicians is closely associated with the kinds of questions which they are asked: the higher the proportion of *avoidance–avoidance conflict* questions, the more likely politicians are to equivocate. It was further argued that questions can be seen as having a face-threatening structure, from which it is possible to predict whether or not a politician is likely to give a reply. The novelty of this approach is not only that it provides a means of analysing questions in political interviews, it also demonstrates that the occurrence of both replies and non-replies can be understood within the same theoretical framework.

This analysis in terms of face management has important implications for evaluating the interview performance of both interviewers and politicians. In Chapter 9, a study was presented of six interviewers during the 1992 General Election. Interviewer toughness, style and neutrality were evaluated on the basis of the distinction between *avoidance–avoidance* and *no necessary threat* questions. Brian Walden emerged as the toughest interviewer with 49.4 per cent of his questions carrying a face-threat in every direction, David Frost as the softest (28.9 per cent of questions). An analysis in terms of neutrality showed that most of the interviewers gave John Major the toughest interviews, Paddy Ashdown the easiest interviews, except for David Frost, whose interviews showed the opposite trend. Observers were also asked to rate the interviewers in terms of their perceived toughness and neutrality. Results showed these ratings were broadly consistent with the analysis in terms of *level of threat* described above (pp. 157–170). In addition, distinctive features of interviewer style were examined through the 19 categories of the face-threat coding system.

The analysis of face management also has important implications for evaluating the interview performance of politicians, and this forms the basis of Chapter 10. Two studies were presented, the first focussed on how politicians handle *no necessary threat* questions, the second on how they handle *avoidance–avoidance conflict* questions. In the case of *no necessary threat* questions, it was argued that a politician's interview performance may be regarded as unskilled to the extent that they produce what were termed *avoidable face-damaging responses*. On this basis, an evaluation was conducted of interviews from the 1992 British General Election. This showed that John Major produced the lowest proportion of *avoidable face-damaging responses*, Neil Kinnock the highest.

An analysis was also conducted of questions which create an *avoidance–avoidance conflict*, based on five televised interviews with Tony Blair in the 1997 General Election. All the questions examined were concerned with the dramatic policy changes in the British Labour Party between 1983 and 1997, widely referred to as 'modernisation'. It was hypothesised that questions about modernisation would create an *avoidance–avoidance conflict* for Blair. In the majority of cases, this was found to be the case: Blair typically equivocated to questions about modernisation which created an *avoidance–avoidance conflict* and replied to those which did not create such a conflict. However, Blair's equivocation was not confined just to avoiding the risks of making face-damaging remarks. Through what was termed a 'rhetoric of modernisation', he was also highly attentive to presenting the best face both for himself and his party, in particular through promoting a highly inclusive social identity for New Labour. In this sense, Blair's performance in these 1997 interviews could be seen as highly skilled.

Blair's mastery of the arts of equivocation is arguably an important element of his political skill, a point not lost on his political opponents. William Hague, writing in the *Guardian* (26 April, 2002) five years on from Blair's landslide victory in the 1997 General Election, singled out what he called Blair's 'skill for ambiguity' as one of his key political strengths, as one of the features which both helped him into power and helped to keep him there. The analysis of Blair's 'rhetoric of modernisation' presented here shows in detail how this mastery of ambiguity is deployed.

Theoretical significance

Atkinson's theory of rhetoric

All the studies of political speeches reported in the first section of the book (pp. 25–77) were conducted with reference to Atkinson's theory of rhetoric. The case study reported in Chapter 2 showed its value in helping to understand the role of hand gesture both in articulating the structure of applause invitations, as well as in refusing applause when it occurs at inappropriate points during a speech. In Chapter 5, the comprehensive study of all the applause incidents occurring in 15 political speeches also provided strong support for Atkinson's observations. Of the eight different types of applause analysed, applause which was invited, rhetorical and synchronous (the type identified by Atkinson), occurred with by far the greatest frequency (64.7 per cent of all applause incidents). Overall, Atkinson's achievement has been to show how rhetorical devices embedded in the structure of speech are used as a means of inviting applause. These original insights have been of enormous value in understanding the use of rhetoric in political speeches.

However, this is by no means the whole story. If approximately two-thirds of applause in political speeches is invited, rhetorical and synchronous, this still leaves one-third unexplained, which any comprehensive theory of applause in political speeches also needs to be able to take into account. Indeed, one of the biggest problems with Atkinson's research is its failure to account for negative findings which may be inconsistent with the theory. Thus, applause is not always invited, rhetorical and synchronous; it may also occur in the absence of rhetorical devices, it may be uninvited, it may be asynchronous with speech. Thus, further investigation was required. To test the validity of Atkinson's theory of rhetoric, a series of studies were conducted, reported in Chapters 3, 4 and 5. Their significance is summarised in the following section with regard to a number of specific issues of importance in Atkinson's theory: synchrony, delivery, rhetorical devices, speech content, spontaneous applause and uninvited applause.

1 *Synchrony.* The studies presented in Chapters 4 and 5 show that Atkinson overestimated the degree to which speech and applause are synchronised. In the analysis of 15 speeches reported in Chapter 5, only 66.1 per cent of applause incidents were fully synchronised with speech. Furthermore, virtually all incidents of uninvited applause were asynchronous with speech (97.7 per cent).

2 *Delivery.* Whereas Atkinson proposed that delivery increases the chance of a rhetorical device receiving applause, the analysis reported in Chapter 5 suggests that delivery is important with regard to whether or not a rhetorical device is taken as an applause invitation. Furthermore, delivery appears to be particularly important in the synchronisation of speech and applause. Whereas Atkinson claimed that applause in political speeches is typically synchronous with speech, synchrony was only found in this study when rhetorical devices were accompanied by delivery appropriate for inviting applause (98.0 per cent of incidents of synchronous applause). The clear implication is that the importance of delivery was underestimated by Atkinson.

3 *Rhetorical devices.* The analysis in Chapter 5 clearly shows that applause is typically associated with rhetorical devices (94.8 per cent of applause incidents). However, it has been argued that rhetorical devices do not in themselves constitute an invitation to applaud; they also have to be accompanied by appropriate delivery. The finding that synchronous applause occurs almost exclusively in response to rhetorical devices accompanied by appropriate delivery would seem to support this view. Furthermore, applause can also occur in the absence of rhetorical devices, as was shown in detail in Chapter 3. Thus, although rhetorical devices have been shown to be extremely important in inviting applause, Atkinson has arguably overestimated their importance in relation to other factors such as delivery and speech content.

4 *Speech content.* The study in Chapter 3 showed how collective applause can occur uninvited in the absence of rhetorical devices, directly in response to the content of speech. Although the study in Chapter 5 shows such uninvited applause to be comparatively rare (only 3.2 per cent of all applause incidents), where it does occur it may concern issues of particular emotive importance to the audience. This would suggest that there is some justification to the criticism that Atkinson underestimates the importance of speech content.

5 *Spontaneous applause.* Atkinson is highly dismissive of the notion that applause at political rallies can be spontaneous (Atkinson, 1984a, pp. 45–46). Undoubtedly, a high proportion of applause at political rallies

is stage managed through applause invitations by the speaker, but not exclusively so. The analysis in Chapter 3 suggests that there may be occasions when applause is spontaneous, particularly in relation to emotive issues of especial significance to the audience. The concept of mutual monitoring also provides a mechanism to show how this may occur. Applause may be initiated by a few people, others joining in as they see the applause gaining momentum. This would suggest that Atkinson is arguably too dismissive of the concept of spontaneous applause.

6 *Uninvited applause.* In Chapter 3, the concept of uninvited applause was introduced. Although in the study in Chapter 5, only 13.7 per cent of applause incidents were judged to be uninvited, this is a phenomenon which Atkinson does not discuss at all. From the evidence presented in Chapters 3 and 5, it clearly needs to be considered in any comprehensive theory of how applause occurs in political speeches

The above analysis suggests that Atkinson's analysis of invited applause underestimates the importance of other features such as asynchrony, delivery, speech content and uninvited applause. It is the relative importance of these features in relation to rhetorical devices which will now need to be the focus of future research on applause in political speeches.

Equivocation theory

An important influence on the studies of political interviews reported in the second section of this book (pp. 79–192) was equivocation theory (Bavelas *et al.*, 1990). Bavelas *et al.*'s pioneering research has provided a number of valuable insights into how and why equivocation occurs, both through the concept of the *avoidance–avoidance conflict*, and through their proposal that equivocation can be understood in terms of four dimensions (sender, clarity, receiver and context). The sender dimension refers to the extent to which the response is the speaker's own opinion; a statement is considered more equivocal if the speaker fails to acknowledge it as his own opinion, or attributes it to another person. Clarity refers to comprehensibility, an unclear statement being considered more equivocal. The receiver dimension refers to the extent to which the message is addressed to the other person in the situation; the less this is so, the more equivocal the message. Context refers to the extent to which the response is a direct answer to the question – the less the relevance, the more equivocal the message. Bavelas *et al.* (1990, p. 34) state that 'All messages that would (intuitively or otherwise) be called equivocal are ambiguous in at least one of these four elements.'

The evidence for equivocation theory is derived essentially from experimental studies in which observers rate responses on these four dimensions. In contrast, all the studies reported in this book were based on the analysis of natural language and focussed exclusively on what Bavelas *et al.* call the 'context dimension'. Nevertheless, the results do suggest a number of ways in which equivocation theory can be modified and extended, which will be outlined now.

Thus, for example, the studies reported in Chapter 8 on why politicians equivocate were based directly on the concept of the *avoidance–avoidance conflict*. In the context of political interviews, it was argued that these conflicts are typically (although not solely) created by threats to face. This concept was not intended as an alternative to that of the *avoidance–avoidance conflict*, rather as a theoretical explanation for why these conflicts are so prevalent in political interviews. Furthermore, by linking the concept of face to that of the *avoidance–avoidance conflict*, it was possible to provide an explanation within the same theoretical framework, not only of why politicians equivocate but also of why there are some questions to which they do provide replies. Thus, from what is termed the *face-threatening structure* of questions, it is possible to predict the most likely direction of a politician's response.

The study reported in Chapter 9 showed how equivocation theory can be extended to evaluate the interview performance of political interviewers. Because *avoidance–avoidance conflict* questions create pressures towards equivocation, they can arguably be seen as a tough form of questioning. Hence, someone who asks a high proportion of such questions can be seen as a tough interviewer. Furthermore, if the interviewer asks a significantly higher proportion of such questions to members of one political party rather than another, he or she can also be seen as biased. Thus, the concept of the *avoidance–avoidance conflict* was used to develop the concept of *level of threat*, through which the interview performance of interviewers can be assessed.

In Chapters 7 and 10, studies were reported which showed how the analysis of equivocation can be used to evaluate the interview performance skills of politicians. In particular, it was argued that equivocation needs to be understood not only in terms of its *causes* but also of its *consequences*. In equivocation theory, the *avoidance–avoidance conflict* is regarded as the underlying communicative context in which equivocation occurs, but little attention is paid to the interactional *consequences* of equivocation. For this reason, it is important to be able to distinguish between different forms of equivocation: they can vary between the highly skilled and the totally inept. In Chapter 7, an equivocation typology was presented which identified 35 different ways in which politicians do not give a direct answer to the question. This typology was then used to evaluate the equivocation style and interview effectiveness of three leading British politicians: Margaret Thatcher, Neil Kinnock and John Major.

In Chapter 10, a study was reported of interviews with Tony Blair, which was directly concerned with how best to handle questions which create *avoidance–avoidance conflicts*. In this context, it was argued that Blair's 'rhetoric of modernisation' could be seen as a highly skilled form of equivocation. It enabled him not only to avoid awkward face-threats in questions about modernisation, but also to project a highly inclusive social identity of New Labour, thereby presenting a positive image both for himself and for the party which he represented. It is not obvious how these positive strategic advantages could be represented in Bavelas *et al.*'s existing theory, which focusses on equivocation essentially as a negative phenomenon, a means of not giving replies to awkward questions. In contrast, the analysis of equivocation in terms of face management can be applied both to the *causes* and *consequences* of Blair's rhetoric of modernisation.

Thus, the research presented here shows not only how different forms of equivocation can be identified, but also through the concept of face offers a way of representing the various strategic advantages of different forms of imprecise and ambiguous language. These represent significant modifications to equivocation theory.

Practical significance

One distinguishing feature of the microanalytic approach is that if communication is regarded as a skill, then it can be improved through appropriate forms of training (see Chapter 1, p. 13). Elsewhere, the author (Bull, 2002) has argued that the practical significance of microanalysis is not confined to formal training in communication skills, even the very act of carrying out such research may be influential. By highlighting the fine details of social interaction, it becomes much easier for people to change their behaviour, if they so desire. Changes may also occur in the way in which people actually think about communication. Although none of the studies reported in this book were directly concerned with training in political communication skills, nevertheless they may be of considerable practical significance.

For example, microanalytic research can help to make members of the electorate more perceptive. Through the microanalysis of political communication, it is possible to recognise more quickly whether or not a politician is inviting applause in a speech, or whether a politician is equivocating in response to an awkward question. At the same time, it is also possible through microanalysis for politicians or interviewers to change their behaviour, if they so desire. A politician can improve the delivery of a speech, an interviewer can hone his or her skills at asking penetrating questions.

Thus, the practical significance of microanalytic research on political communication can be approached from a variety of perspectives – from that of the electorate, the politicians and also the political interviewers (Bull, 2002).

The politicians

From the politicians' viewpoint, it is not difficult to see how microanalysis might be turned to their advantage. In the United Kingdom, politicians in recent decades have become far more sensitive to issues of presentation and media management. According to a recent analysis of political campaigning in the United Kingdom, 'Media work has increased in importance more than any other aspect of party political campaigning over the past fifty years' (Rosenbaum, 1997, p. 120).

The presentation of the annual party conferences, for example, has changed out of all recognition. Speeches by the party leaders are now broadcast in full on national television, thus reaching a far wider audience than ever before. The microanalysis of such speeches has provided politicians with easy tips on how to improve their oratory. The analysis of rhetorical devices in Atkinson's (1984a) book, *Our Masters' Voices*, virtually provides a manual on how to script applause points into a political speech. The analyses reported in this book can also be used to suggest some useful tips. For example, in Chapter 5, it was argued that the importance of delivery has been underestimated. Delivery – in terms, for example, of gaze, posture, gesture, tone of voice – can indicate not only when a rhetorical device is intended to invite applause, but also when it is *not* intended to invite applause. Delivery is important if applause is to be synchronous with speech: synchrony only occurred when the delivery clearly indicated that a rhetorical device was intended as an applause invitation. Hence, a mastery of appropriate and effective delivery is an essential skill for a politician if rhetorical devices are to work to full effect.

The quality of audience applause can also be a useful source of information for the political orator. Incidences of uninvited applause can be extremely significant. If the audience interrupts the speaker with uninvited but enthusiastic applause, this can be a useful barometer of popular feeling, indicating a high (and possibly unexpected) level of support on a particular issue. Again, the timing of applause may be important. Audience members may oblige the speaker by clapping at the appropriate completion point, but are perfectly capable of starting before or after it is reached. Interruptive applause may indicate audience enthusiasm, delayed applause quite the reverse.

The analysis of interviews can be instructive. In this setting, a politician may be posed with any number of tough and challenging questions. In Chapter 10, it was argued that face management is an essential skill for any elected politician, given the adversarial nature of United Kingdom politics. If the analysis of face management can be used to evaluate the interview performance of politicians, it can also be used to make practical recommendations as to what might be considered the optimal response. This will certainly not always be to equivocate. Equivocation in response to certain questions may be potentially more face-threatening than giving a reply, as was argued in Chapter 8. But when presented with an *avoidance–avoidance conflict*, equivocation is typically the least face-threatening option. However, not all forms of equivocation are necessarily equivalent. In Chapter 7, a number of examples of ineffectual forms of equivocation were discussed, such as pleading ignorance and giving negative replies. Conversely, analysis of televised interviews with Tony Blair in the 1997 General Election reported in Chapter 10 showed not only how he used a 'rhetoric of modernisation' to equivocate skilfully in response to questions about the *volte-face* in Labour Party policy between 1983 and 1997, but also to present a more positive, socially inclusive face for New Labour.

The interviewers

Microanalytic studies have practical implications for those who conduct interviews. Excessive equivocation by politicians can present a serious threat to the viability of the interview, if politicians make no real attempt to address questions or engage in any substantive dialogue with the interviewer. This was the view taken by the celebrated political interviewer Sir Robin Day in his memoirs (Day, 1989), who cited communication research by Bull and Mayer (1988) in support of his argument. 'What deeply concerns me,' he wrote, 'is that the very principle of the television interview – the ancient Socratic method of imparting or gathering information by the process of question and answer – has been deliberately devalued' (Day, 1989, p. 292).

However, there are ways in which interviewers can counter this. If the interviewer asks a high proportion of *avoidance–avoidance conflict* questions, this may make for a tough and challenging interview, but will also increase the tendency of politicians to equivocate. Softer questions may, in fact, encourage a politician to talk more freely, especially if couched in such a way that *not* to reply is the most face-threatening option. In the study of interviewers in the 1992 British General Election (Chapter 9), it was found that Sir David Frost asked the lowest proportion of *avoidance–avoidance conflict* questions (29 per cent; cf. Brian Walden 49 per cent). But precisely because of this gentler style of interviewing, a tough question from David Frost may have a greater impact because the politician is not expecting it. Thus, equivocation by politicians can sometimes be countered through the use of skilled questioning by interviewers.

The electorate

The microanalysis of political communication has implications for the electorate, as well as for politicians and interviewers. From the perspective of the electorate, such analyses can give greater awareness of the political process. The identification of rhetorical devices used by politicians to invite applause can give a much greater understanding of how political speeches can be stage managed. The 35 different forms of equivocation identified by Bull and Mayer (1993) can make it easier to identify how politicians evade questions. At the same time, an awareness of *avoidance–avoidance conflicts* and the face-threatening structure of questions can lead to a deeper insight into how and why equivocation occurs. It can also provide a means of evaluating the performance of interviewers. An ability to recognise *avoidance–avoidance conflict* questions can give a greater understanding of the relative toughness of interviewers, as well as of their fairness. An interviewer who consistently asked a much greater proportion of *avoidance–avoidance conflict* questions to members of one political party rather than another might be seen as open to accusations of bias.

Conclusions

In *Communication under the Microscope: The Theory and Practice of Micro-analysis* (Bull, 2002), the author set out to delineate the key features of the microanalytic approach, and to illustrate its application to different aspects of interpersonal communication. In this book, a series of original studies have been presented, concerned specifically with the analysis of political speeches and interviews. The aim of this research has been to show the value of microanalysis in evaluating political discourse. As a result, we now have a better understanding of how and why politicians equivocate, handle interruptions and seek to present themselves in the best possible light. We can evaluate more effectively the interview skills of both politicians and political interviewers. We now have a better understanding of how applause can occur, both invited and uninvited, in political speeches. It is often the case that political speeches are dismissed as just 'claptrap', while politicians are castigated for their evasiveness in interviews. But the detailed microanalytic research presented here brings fresh insights into the role played by this apparent 'claptrap and ambiguity' in the underlying political process.

References

Anderson, B. (1991) *John Major: The Making of the Prime Minister.* London: Fourth Estate Limited.

Anderson, K.J. and Leaper, C. (1998) Meta-analyses of gender effects on conversational interruption: who, what, when, where, and how. *Sex Roles*, 39, 225–252.

Argyle, M. (1969) *Social Interaction.* London: Methuen.

Argyle, M. (1978) *The Psychology of Interpersonal Behaviour.* Harmondsworth: Penguin (3rd edn).

Argyle, M. and Kendon A. (1967) The experimental analysis of social performance. *Advances in Experimental Social Psychology*, 3, 55–97.

Aries, E. (1996) *Men and Women in Interaction: Reconsidering the Differences.* New York: Oxford University Press.

Atkinson, J.M. (1983) Two devices for generating audience approval: a comparative study of public discourse and text. In K. Ehlich and H. van Riemsdijk (eds), *Connectedness in Sentence, Text and Discourse.* Tilburg, the Netherlands: Tilburg papers in Linguistics, pp. 199–236.

Atkinson, J.M. (1984a) *Our Masters' Voices.* London and New York: Methuen.

Atkinson, J.M. (1984b) Public speaking and audience responses: some techniques for inviting applause. In J.M. Atkinson and J.C. Heritage (eds), *Structures of Social Action: Studies in Conversation Analysis.* Cambridge and New York: Cambridge University Press, pp. 370–409.

Atkinson, J.M. (1985) Refusing invited applause: preliminary observations from a case study of charismatic oratory. In T. van Dijk (ed.), *Handbook of Discourse Analysis*, vol. 3. London: Academic Press, pp. 161–181.

Austin, J. (1962) *How To Do Things With Words.* Cambridge, MA: Harvard University Press.

Bavelas, J.B., Black, A., Chovil, N. and Mullett, J. (1990) *Equivocal Communication.* Newbury Park: Sage.

Bavelas, J.B. and Chovil, N. (2000) Visible acts of meaning: an integrated message model of language in face-to-face dialogue. *Journal of Language and Social Psychology*, 19, 163–194.

Beattie, G.W. (1982) Turn-taking and interruption in political interviews – Margaret Thatcher and Jim Callaghan compared and contrasted. *Semiotica*, 39, 93–114.

Beattie, G.W. (1989a) Interruptions in political interviews: a reply to Bull and Mayer. *Journal of Language of Social Psychology*, 8, 327–339.

Beattie, G.W. (1989b) Interruptions in political interviews: the debate ends? *Journal of Language of Social Psychology*, 8, 345–348.

Beattie, G.W., Cutler, A. and Pearson, M. (1982) Why is Mrs Thatcher interrupted so often? *Nature*, 300 (23/30 December), 744–747.

Birdwhistell, R.L. (1971) *Kinesics and Context*. London: Allen Lane, The Penguin Press.

Bolinger, D. (1978) Yes–no questions are not alternative questions. In H. Hiz (ed.), *Questions*. Dordrecht, the Netherlands: D. Reidel, pp. 87–105.

Brooks, R. (1987) BBC clamp on 'rude' interviewers. *The Observer*, 12 July, 1.

Brown, P. and Levinson, S.C. (1978) Universals in language usage: politeness phenomena. In E. Goody (ed.), *Questions and Politeness*. Cambridge: Cambridge University Press, pp. 56–310.

Brown, P. and Levinson, S.C. (1987) *Politeness: Some Universals in Language Use*. Cambridge: Cambridge University Press.

Bull, P.E. (1986) The use of hand gesture in political speeches: some case studies. *Journal of Language and Social Psychology*, 5, 103–118.

Bull, P.E. (1987) *Posture and Gesture*. Oxford: Pergamon Press.

Bull, P.E. (1994) On identifying questions, replies and non-replies in political interviews. *Journal of Language and Social Psychology*, 13, 115–131.

Bull, P.E. (1997) Queen of Hearts or Queen of the Arts of Implication? Implicit criticisms and their implications for equivocation theory in the interview between Martin Bashir and Diana, Princess of Wales. *Social Psychological Review*, 1, 27–36.

Bull, P.E. (1998a) Equivocation theory and news interviews. *Journal of Language and Social Psychology*, 17, 36–51.

Bull, P.E. (1998b) Political interviews: television interviews in Great Britain. In O. Feldman and C. De Landtsheer (eds), *Politically Speaking: A Worldwide Examination of Language Used in the Public Sphere*. Westport, CT: Greenwood Publishing Group, pp. 149–160.

Bull, P.E. (2000a) Do audiences only applaud 'claptrap' in political speeches? An analysis of invited and uninvited applause. *Social Psychological Review*, 2, 32–41.

Bull, P.E. (2000b) Equivocation and the rhetoric of modernisation: an analysis of televised interviews with Tony Blair in the 1997 British General Election. *Journal of Language and Social Psychology*, 19, 222–247.

Bull, P.E. (2000c) New Labour, New Rhetoric? An analysis of the rhetoric of Tony Blair. In C. De Landtsheer and O. Feldman (eds), *Public Speech and Symbols: Exploration in the Rhetoric of Politicians and the Media*. Westport, CT: Praeger, pp. 3–16.

Bull, P.E. (2001) Massaging the message: political discourse used in the recent election campaigns. *The Psychologist*, 14(7), 142–143.

Bull, P.E. (2002) *Communication under the Microscope: The Theory and Practice of Microanalysis*. London: Psychology Press.

Bull, P.E. and Connelly, G. (1985) Body movement and emphasis in speech. *Journal of Nonverbal Behaviour*, 9, 169–187.

Bull, P.E. and Elliott, J. (1995) Is John Major a major face-saver? An assessment of televised interviews with the party leaders during the 1992 British General Election. *Proceedings of the British Psychological Society*, 3, 65.

Bull, P.E. and Elliott, J. (1998) Level of threat: means of assessing interviewer toughness and neutrality. *Journal of Language and Social Psychology*, 17, 220–244.

Bull, P.E., Elliott, J., Palmer, D. and Walker, L. (1996) Why politicians are three-faced: the face model of political interviews. *British Journal of Social Psychology*, 35, 267–284.

Bull, P.E. and Mayer, K. (1988) Interruptions in political interviews: a study of

Margaret Thatcher and Neil Kinnock. *Journal of Language and Social Psychology*, 7, 35–45.

Bull, P.E. and Mayer, K. (1989) Interruptions in political interviews: a reply to Beattie. *Journal of Language of Social Psychology*, 8, 341–344.

Bull, P.E. and Mayer, K. (1991) 'Is John Major as unremarkable as he seems? A comparison of three political leaders.' Paper presented at the London Conference of the British Psychological Society, December.

Bull, P.E. and Mayer, K. (1993) How not to answer questions in political interviews. *Political Psychology*, 14, 651–666.

Bull, P.E. and Noordhuizen, M. (2000) The mistiming of applause in political speeches. *Journal of Language and Social Psychology*, 19, 275–294.

Bull, P.E. and Roger, D.B. (1989) The social psychological approach to interpersonal communication. In D.B. Roger and P.E. Bull (eds), *Conversation: An Interdisciplinary Approach*. Bristol: Multilingual Matters, pp. 9–20.

Bull, P.E. and Wells, P. (2002a) By invitation only? An analysis of invited and uninvited applause. *Journal of Language and Social Psychology*, 21, 230–244.

Bull, P.E. and Wells, P. (2002b). 'Audience participation in televised political interviews from the 2001 General Election.' Paper presented at the Annual Conference of the Social Psychology Section of the British Psychological Society, September.

Burns, T. (1992) *Erving Goffman*. London: Routledge.

Chance, M.R.A. (1967) Attention structure as the basis of primate rank orders. *Man* (New Series), 2, 503–518.

Clayman, S.E. (1988) Displaying neutrality in television news interviews. *Social Problems*, 35, 474–492.

Clayman, S.E. (1989) The production of punctuality: social interaction, temporal organization and social structure. *American Journal of Sociology*, 95, 659–691.

Clayman, S.E. (1991) News interview openings: aspects of sequential organization. In P. Scannell (ed.), *Broadcast Talk*. London: Sage, pp. 48–75.

Clayman, S.E. (1992) Footing in the achievement of neutrality: the case of news interview discourse. In P. Drew and J. Heritage (eds), *Talk at Work*. Cambridge: Cambridge University Press, pp. 163–198.

Clayman, S.E. (1993) Booing: the anatomy of a disaffiliative response. *American Sociological Review*, 58, 110–130.

Cohen, J. (1960) A coefficient of agreement for nominal scales. *Educational and Psychological Measurement*, 20, 37–46.

Cohen, J. (1969) *Statistical Power Analysis for the Behavioural Sciences*. New York: Academic Press.

Condon, W.S. and Ogston, W.D. (1966) Sound film analysis of normal and pathological behaviour patterns. *Journal of Nervous and Mental Disease*, 143, 338–347.

Cowley, S.J. (1998) Of timing, turn-taking and conversations. *Journal of Psycholinguistic Research*, 27, 541–571.

Day, Sir R. (1989) *Grand Inquisitor*. London: George Weidenfeld & Nicolson Ltd.

Duncan, S. (1969) Nonverbal communication. *Psychological Bulletin*, 72, 118–137.

Duncan, S. (1972) Some signals and rules for taking speaking turns in conversations. *Journal of Personality and Social Psychology*, 23, 283–292.

Duncan, S. and Fiske, D.W. (1977) *Face-to-face Interaction: Research, Methods and Theory*. Hillsdale, NJ: Lawrence Erlbaum.

Edwards, D. and Potter, J. (1992) *Discursive Psychology*. London: Sage.

Edwards, D. and Potter, J. (1993) Language and causation: a discursive action model of description and attribution. *Psychological Review*, 100, 23–41.

Eibl-Eibesfeldt, I. (1972) Similarities and differences between cultures in expressive movements. In R.A. Hinde (ed.), *Nonverbal Communication*. Cambridge: Cambridge University Press, pp. 297–314.

Eibl-Eibesfeldt, I. (1973) The expressive behaviour of the deaf-and-blind born. In M. von Cranach and I. Vine (eds), *Social Communication and Movement*. London: Academic Press, pp. 163–194.

Ekman, P. and Friesen, W.V. (1974) Nonverbal behaviour and psychopathology. In R.J. Friedman and M.M. Katz (eds), *The Psychology of Depression: Contemporary Theory and Research*. New York: John Wiley & Sons Ltd, pp. 203–232.

Ekman, P. and Friesen, W.V. (1978) Measuring facial movement. *Environmental Psychology and Nonverbal Behaviour*, 1, 56–75.

Ekman, P. and Rosenberg, E.L. (eds) (1997) *What the Face Reveals: Basic and Applied Studies of Spontaneous Expression Using the Facial Action Coding System (FACS)*. New York: Oxford University Press.

Elliott, J. and Bull, P.E. (1996) A question of threat: face threats in questions posed during televised political interviews. *Journal of Community and Applied Social Psychology*, 6, 49–72.

Ferguson, N. (1977) Simultaneous speech, interruptions and dominance. *British Journal of Social and Clinical Psychology*, 16, 295–302.

Freedman, N. and Hoffman, S.P. (1967) Kinetic behaviour in altered clinical states: approach to objective analysis of motor behaviour during clinical interviews. *Perceptual and Motor Skills*, 244, 527–539.

Fridlund, A.J. (1994) *Human Facial Expression: An Evolutionary View*. San Diego, CA: Academic Press.

Goffman, E. (1955) On face-work: an analysis of ritual elements in social interaction. *Psychiatry*, 18, 213–231. Reprinted in E. Goffman (1967) *Interaction Ritual: Essays on Face to Face Behaviour*. Garden City, New York: Anchor, pp. 5–45.

Goffman, E. (1959) *The Presentation of Self in Everyday Life*. Harmondsworth: Penguin.

Goffman, E. (1961) *Encounters: Two Studies in the Sociology of Interaction*. Indianapolis, IN: Bobbs-Merrill.

Goffman, E. (1971) *Relations in Public: Microstudies of the Public Order*. London: Penguin Press.

Goffman, E. (1981) Footing. In E. Goffman, *Forms of Talk*. Oxford: Basil Blackwell.

Graham, J.A. and Argyle, M. (1975) A cross-cultural study of the communication of extra-verbal meaning by gestures. *International Journal of Psychology*, 10, 57–69.

Greatbatch, D. (1988) A turn-taking system for British news interviews. *Language in Society*, 17, 401–430.

Hague, W. (2002) What I learned about Tony – the hard way. *The Guardian, G2*, 26 April, 2–5.

Halliday, M.A.K. (1970) *A Course in Spoken English: Intonation*. London: Oxford University Press.

Hargie, O.D.W. (1997) Interpersonal communication: a theoretical framework. In O.D.W. Hargie (ed.) (2nd edn), *The Handbook of Communication Skills*. London: Routledge, pp. 29–63.

Hargie, O.D.W. and Marshall, P. (1986) Interpersonal communication: a theoretical framework. In O.D.W. Hargie (ed.), *The Handbook of Communication Skills*. London: Croom Helm, pp. 22–56.

Harris, S. (1986) Interviewers' questions in broadcast interviews. *Belfast Working Papers in Language and Linguistics*, 8, 50–85.

Harris, S. (1991) Evasive action: how politicians respond to questions in political interviews. In P. Scannell (ed.), *Broadcast Talk*. London: Sage, pp. 76–99.

Heath, C. (1986) *Body Movement and Speech in Medical Interaction*. Cambridge: Cambridge University Press.

Heritage, J.C. (1989) Current developments in conversation analysis. In D. Roger and P. Bull (eds), *Conversation: An Interdisciplinary Perspective*. Clevedon: Multilingual Matters, pp. 21–47.

Heritage, J.C., Clayman, S.E. and Zimmerman, D. (1988) Discourse and message analysis: the micro-structure of mass media messages. In R. Hawkins, S. Pingree and J. Weimann (eds), *Advancing Communication Science: Merging Mass and Interpersonal Processes*. Newbury Park: Sage, pp. 77–109.

Heritage, J.C. and Greatbatch, D.L. (1986) Generating applause: a study of rhetoric and response at party political conferences. *American Journal of Sociology*, 92, 110–157.

Heritage, J.C. and Greatbatch, D.L. (1991) On the institutional character of institutional talk: the case of news interviews. In D. Boden and D. Zimmerman (eds), *Talk and Social Structure*. Cambridge: Polity Press, pp. 93–137.

Holmes, J. (1995) *Women, Men and Politeness*. New York: Longman.

Huxley, J.S. (1914) The courtship habits of the great crested grebe (*Podiceps cristatus*); with an addition to the theory of natural selection. *Proceedings of the Zoological Society of London*, 35, 491–562.

Huxley, J.S. (1963) *Evolution: The Modern Synthesis* (2nd edn). Northampton: John Dickens & Co.

James, D. and Clarke, S. (1993) Women, men and interruptions: a critical review. In D. Tannen (ed.), *Gender and Conversational Interaction*. New York: Oxford University Press, pp. 231–280.

Jefferson, G. (1984) On the organisation of laughter in talk about troubles. In J.M. Atkinson and J.C. Heritage (eds), *Structures of Social Action: Studies in Conversation Analysis*. Cambridge: Cambridge University Press, pp. 347–369.

Jefferson, G. (1990) List-construction as a task and resource. In G. Psathas (ed.), *Interaction Competence*. Lanham, MD: University Press of America, Inc., pp. 63–92.

Jucker, J. (1986) *News Interviews: a Pragmalinguistic Analysis*. Amsterdam: Gieben.

Kelly, S.D., Barr, D.J., Church, R.B. and Lynch, K. (1999) Offering a hand to pragmatic understanding: the role of speech and gesture in comprehension and memory. *Journal of Memory and Language*, 40, 577–592.

Kendon, A. (1982) Organization of behaviour in face-to-face interaction. In K.R. Scherer and P. Ekman (eds), *Handbook of Methods in Nonverbal Behaviour Research*. Cambridge: Cambridge University Press, pp. 440–505.

Kendon, A. (1985) Some uses of gesture. In O. Tannen and M. Saville-Troike (eds), *Perspectives on Silence*. Norwood, NJ: Ablex, pp. 215–234.

Kendon, A. (1988) Goffman's approach to face-to-face interaction. In P. Drew and A. Wootton (eds), *Erving Goffman: Exploring the Interaction Order*. Cambridge: Polity Press, pp. 14–40.

Kendon, A. and Ferber, A. (1973) A description of some human greetings. In R.P. Michael and J.H. Crook (eds), *Comparative Ecology and Behaviour of Primates*. London and New York: Academic Press, pp. 591–668.

King, A. (1992) *Britain at the Polls 1992*. New York: Chatham House.

Kiritz, S.A. (1971) 'Hand movements and clinical ratings at admission and discharge for hospitalised psychiatric patients.' Unpublished doctoral dissertation, University of California, San Francisco, CA.

Lalljee, M. and Widdicombe, S. (1989) Discourse analysis. In A.M. Colman and G. Beaumont (eds), *Psychology Survey 7*. Leicester: The British Psychological Society, pp. 76–97.

Lindenfeld, J. (1971) Verbal and nonverbal elements in discourse. *Semiotica*, 33, 223–233.

McClave, E.Z. (2000) Linguistic functions of head movements in the context of speech. *Journal of Pragmatics*, 32, 855–878.

McNeill, D. (1985) So you think gestures are nonverbal? *Psychological Review*, 92, 350–371.

Mandela, N. (1995) *Long Walk to Freedom: The Autobiography of Nelson Mandela*. London: Abacus.

Marey, É.J. (1895) *Movement*. New York: D. Appleton.

Mehrabian, A. and Williams, N. (1969) Nonverbal concomitants of perceived and intended persuasiveness. *Journal of Personality and Social Psychology*, 13, 37–58.

Mishler, E.G. and Waxler, N.E. (1968) *Interaction in Families: An Experimental Study of Family Processes and Schizophrenia*. New York: John Wiley & Sons Ltd.

Murray, S.O. and Covelli, L.H. (1988) Women and men speaking at the same time. *Journal of Pragmatics*, 12, 103–111.

Muybridge, E. (1899) *Animals in Motion*. Reprinted by Dover Publications, New York, 1957.

Muybridge, E. (1901) *The Human Figure in Motion*. Reprinted by Dover Publications, New York, 1957.

Parker, I. (1992) *Discourse Dynamics: Critical Analysis for Social and Individual Psychology*. London: Routledge.

Parkinson, B. (1995) *Ideas and Realities of Emotion*. London: Routledge.

Pittenger, R.E., Hockett, C.F. and Danehy, J.J. (1960) *The First Five Minutes: A Sample of Microscopic Interview Analysis*. Ithaca, New York: Martineau.

Potter, J. and Wetherell, M. (1987) *Discourse and Social Psychology: Beyond Attitudes and Behaviour*. London: Sage.

Power, R.D.J. and dal Martello, M.F. (1986) Some criticisms of Sacks, Schegloff and Jefferson on turn-taking. *Semiotica*, 58, 29–40.

Psathas, G. (1995) *Conversation Analysis: The Study of Talk-in-Interaction*. Thousand Oaks, CA: Sage.

Quirk, R., Greenbaum, S., Leech, G. and Svartvik, J. (1985) *A Comprehensive Grammar of the English Language*. London: Longman.

Roger, D.B., Bull, P.E. and Smith, S. (1988) The development of a comprehensive system for classifying interruptions. *Journal of Language and Social Psychology*, 7, 27–34.

Roger, D.B. and Nesshoever, W. (1987) Individual differences in dyadic conversational strategies: a further study. *British Journal of Social Psychology*, 26, 247–255.

Roger, D.B. and Schumacher, A. (1983) Effects of individual differences on dyadic conversational strategies. *Journal of Personality and Social Psychology*, 45, 700–705.

Rosenbaum, M. (1997) *From Soapbox to Soundbite: Party Political Campaigning in Britain since 1945*. London: Macmillan Press.

Sacks, H. (1992) (ed. G. Jefferson) *Lectures on Conversation*. Cambridge, MA: Blackwell.

Sacks, H., Schegloff, E.A. and Jefferson, G. (1974) A simplest systematics for the organisation of turn-taking for conversation. *Language*, 50, 696–735.

Scheflen, A.E. (1964) The significance of posture in communication systems. *Psychiatry*, 27, 316–331.

Scheflen, A.E. (1966) Natural history method in psychotherapy: communicational research. In L.A. Gottschalk and A.H. Auerbach (eds), *Methods of Research in Psychotherapy*. New York: Appleton-Century Crofts, pp. 263–289.

Scheflen, A.E. (1973) *Communicational Structure: Analysis of a Psychotherapy Transaction*. Bloomington, IN: Indiana University Press.

Schegloff, E.A. (1989) Harvey Sacks – lectures 1964–1965. An introduction/memoir. *Human Studies*, 12, 187–209.

Smith, W.J. (1969) Messages of vertebrate communication. *Science*, 165, 145–150.

Smith, W.J. (1977) *The Behaviour of Communicating*. Cambridge, MA: Harvard University Press.

Thomas, A.P., Bull, P.E. and Roger, D.B. (1982) Conversational Exchange Analysis. *Journal of Language and Social Psychology*, 1, 141–155.

Thorpe, W.H. (1979) *The Origins and Rise of Ethology*. London: Heinemann Educational Books.

Tinbergen, N. (1953) *Social Behaviour in Animals, with Special Reference to Vertebrates*. London: Methuen.

Tracy, K. (1990) The many faces of facework. In H. Giles and W.P. Robinson (eds), *Handbook of Language and Social Psychology*. Chichester: John Wiley & Sons Ltd, pp. 209–222.

Trager, G.L. and Smith, H.L. Jr (1951) *An Outline of English Structure* (Studies in Linguistics: Occasional Papers, 3). Norman OK: Battenberg Press. Republished: New York: American Council of Learned Societies, 1965.

Van Dijk, T.A. (1997) *Discourse as Structure and Process. Discourse Studies: A Multidisciplinary Introduction*, vol. 1. London: Sage.

Wood, L.A. and Kroger, R.O. (2000) *Doing Discourse Analysis: Methods for Studying Action in Talk and Text*. Thousand Oaks, CA: Sage.

Zimmerman, D.H. and West, C. (1975) Sex roles, interruptions and silences in conversation. In B. Thorne and N. Henley (eds), *Language and Sex: Difference and Dominance*. Rowley, MA: Newbury House, pp. 105–129.

Author index

Subject index